Sixteen honest-to-goodness reasons why
You Want Me to Do <u>What?</u> is a "must read"!

"Nan DeMars has tackled the thorny subject of business ethics with great aplomb. My copy rests next to my dictionary, with a paper-clip on the Ethical Compass page!"

> *Elva G. Murphy*
> *Secretary to Cyrus R. Vance*
> *(Former US Secretary of State)*

"Nan DeMars has written a very important book — it's a must read for all business professionals in hospitals, clinics and doctors' offices."

> *Dr. Robert F. Premer*
> *Clinical Professor of Orthopedics*
> *University of Minnesota*
> *and Emeritus Chief of Orthopedics*
> *Minneapolis V. A. Medical Center*

"Nan DeMars's unique book addresses office ethics in an open and common sense manner. She puts in perspective the extraordinary benefit office assistants can add to their organizations by not only observing office ethics but managing them as well."

> *Nancy Joy Corless, CPS*
> *Executive Assistant*
> *Amoco Corporation*

"Nan DeMars has been the foremost 'champion' for the office assistant profession for many years and the leading spokesperson on the topic of office ethics. *You Want Me to Do <u>What?</u>* brings to the forefront serious issues facing the office professional of today, with excellent steps for dealing with ethical situations. All office personnel should have a copy of this book in their libraries."

> *Cecilia B. Walker, CAM, CPS*
> *Customer Service Supervisor*
> *Pacificorp*
> *1991 International President of PSI*

"This book is a delightful capture of what really goes on in offices today. It is a practical, easy-to-use reference that provides the reader with a thought-provoking perspective of some of the ethical office dilemmas which continue to be daily challenges in our ever-changing work environment.

"Nan DeMars's book encourages you to evaluate your limits of loyalty, dilemmas of confidentiality and potential harassment dilemmas. It is a MUST READ for everybody! It will open the minds of its readers to the value of maintaining an ethical office environment and will provide a sense of empowerment regarding ethical conduct."

> Becky Chwialkowski, CPS
> Executive Assistant
> Seagate

"You Want Me to Do What? hits the nail on the head! This timely book clarifies what every office professional knows but is afraid to talk about."

> Kathy Burroughs
> Administrative Assistant
> Westinghouse Electric Corporation
> 1997 International President of PSI

"Nan DeMars's book has a message for the entire business community. It is an accurate report of the real world today. Readers will say to themselves, 'been there, done that'!"

> Nancy C. Shairer, CPS
> Senior Executive Secretary
> Bausch & Lomb

"If only I had had access to this succinct advice and Nan's guidelines early on in my career, I could have saved myself many sleepless nights. This book is a wonderful reminder that we are not alone. The clear, down-to-earth tools for developing and implementing a code of ethics are priceless gems."

> Patricia A. Morris
> Executive Assistant
> Anagram International, Inc.

"I cannot praise this book enough! Nan DeMars's book on office ethics was so riveting and inspiring that, once I started it, I couldn't put it down until I was finished. Reading through the examples dredged up memories of similar compromising situations I faced many times throughout my 20-some years as an Executive Assistant. I would have handled many of them differently had I had Nan's book as guidance. Her book also made me realize how fortunate I was to have worked with Mr. Dayton, who was a very ethical person. I believe this book will soon become the 'Bible' on every office professional's desk in corporate America. It should be required reading for all students before they are released into the business world."

> *Tina Carvelli*
> *Former Executive Assistant*
> *to Mark Dayton, State Auditor*
> *State of Minnesota*

"I found myself chuckling, shaking my head and nodding often while reading this fascinating book. It should be mandatory reading in graduate schools for executives and in business classes/business schools for administrative assistants."

> *Peggy Jo Danielson-Fortner*
> *Executive Assistant*
> *National Computer Systems*

"I have read many books dealing with the 'human element' in the human resource area. NONE have dealt with the issue of ethics nearly as well as this one."

> *Connie J. Schmidt, CPS*
> *Management Assistant*
> *Illinois Power Company*

"I found myself in many of the scenarios as I reviewed my own career. I particularly liked the 'Think About It' situations..."

> *Betty L. Kidd*
> *Sales Construction Coordinator*
> *Bob Meyer Builder, Inc.*
> *1996 International President of PSI*

"This book was a fun read for me — because it is about reality. The best part is that it's like having Nan in the room with you."

Gerry McGrane
Executive Assistant
Ecolab, Inc.

"You Want Me to Do What?" is one great book. It is not only interesting, fun and quick reading but, also, a great reference. I found myself copying portions and sharing with others in the office. Here are real stories from the real world."

Geri Ronningen
Corporate Secretary
Despatch Industries

"You Want Me to Do What?" is simply outstanding! I want this book to be required reading for all of today's business students."

Darlene Anderson
Business Instructor
Anoka Ramsey Community College

"Nan's book makes us realize that the focus on ethics and confidentiality must come from top management down the chain of command to all employees of an organization. If a spirit of bad business ethics and lack of concern for confidentiality permeate a corporation, the corporation will fail. If a spirit of ethical business procedures and confidentiality prevails, the corporation has an excellent opportunity for success."

Deanna A. Smith
Executive Assistant to the Governing Board
The Virgin Islands Government Hospitals

You Want Me to Do
What?
When, Where, and How
to Draw the Line at Work

Nan DeMars, CPS

A FIRESIDE BOOK
Published by Simon & Schuster

Nan DeMars is available for seminars and conferences. If you wish to be on her mailing list and/or have an ethical dilemma to share with her, please contact:

Nan DeMars, CPS, President
Executary Services
7701 Normandale Road, Suite 110
Minneapolis, MN 55435
612-835-1148
612-831-7908 (FAX)
DearNan@office-ethics.com/
www.office-ethics.com

F

FIRESIDE
Rockefeller Center
1230 Avenue of the Americas
New York, NY 10020

Copyright © 1997 by Nan DeMars, CPS
All rights reserved,
including the right of reproduction
in whole or in part in any form.

First Fireside Edition 1998

FIRESIDE and colophon are registered trademarks
of Simon & Schuster Inc.

Designed by Mike Morson, Gordon Robinson & Associates, Minneapolis

Manufactured in the United States of America

10 9 8 7 6 5 4 3 2 1

Library of Congress Cataloging-in-Publication Data is available.

ISBN 0-684-85046-X

Dedicated to
the three greatest men in my life:

Hans Wessel, my father,
Lou DeMars, my husband,
and Judd Ringer, my first boss.

These men of honor,
far ahead of their times,
proved to me it's always good business
to do the right thing.

Introduction

"So — how do I do the right thing, and still keep my job, too?"

Julie, a secretary at a Midwestern utility company, had just explained her problem to us. She was clearly upset. Her boss had asked her to do something that was "right" for the company, but wrong for the customer. She believed her promotion, maybe even her job, was on the line. She said her ethical conflict was so stressful that it was affecting her home life and her productivity at work.

Sitting around the banquet table, a dozen other office professionals and I could easily empathize with Julie. We offered our best advice. It seemed to help, too.

I remember thinking at the time: Wouldn't this kind of discussion help every office professional? Why are we having to deal with these ethical conflicts, these ethical dilemmas, more often? What are other office professionals doing about *their* ethical dilemmas? Don't we all need a new way to talk about the sometimes-murky ethics at work? And, perhaps most importantly, shouldn't our supervisors be included in this discussion, too?

That was over 15 years ago. Because I had been an Executive Assistant (and the company's Corporate Secretary) for more than 20 years, I began thinking about what strategies had worked and failed for me — and I started listening to what was working (and not working) for others. I also started looking for ways I could make a difference.

Then . . . I got lucky! I was fortunate to be serving on the International Board of Directors of Professional Secretaries International® — The Association for Office Professionals™ (PSI), which is the world's leading association of office professionals and the only certifying body for our profession. At the time I served as International President-Elect, our Board had decided to develop the first official Code of Ethics for the profession. Consequently, when I served as President-Elect and then International President, I had the opportunity to spearhead the exploration of ethics and how ethical conduct affected the functions of *all* office professionals.

In the process of this exploration, I interviewed many of the leading management and academic experts on the still-new topics of business ethics, ethics policy, and ethics training. I searched for practical, real-world resources that could help us. As a result, PSI's Code of Ethics for secretaries was written and adopted at our 1981 International Convention.

I was on a roll. I accelerated my quest for the means to develop the ethical office—the office in which both supervisors *and their assistants* could comfortably work. In addition to my ongoing interviews with leaders in the field and my writing about ethics, I began presenting office ethics seminars throughout North America and now have expanded to overseas. More and more time every year was devoted to attending meetings, presenting seminars, and hosting discussion groups to share what I was learning.

I included managers in my activities whenever possible, often working with office assistants and their supervisors together. Back then, this was considered a radical approach, but it just seemed like common sense to me. In 1985, I started a search firm for senior-level assistants, making it possible for me to interact with executives of companies of all sizes and learn about upper management's view of office ethics. The people seeking these "board-room assistant" positions are among the very best in our profession, and it has been a privilege to learn from their insights, too.

In 1991, I started writing a regularly featured column about office ethics for PSI's magazine, *The Secretary*®. Each column asks readers to help me advise an office professional on the best way to handle an ethical dilemma. This back-and-forth dialogue has been fascinating! I've caught glimpses of office environments in the public, private, and military sectors that were frantically trying to keep up with the pace of change by "re-engineering," "downsizing," and other strategies. Many of these strategies have led to levels of stress unheard of a decade ago. These stresses compound ethical dilemmas for many workers. Not surprisingly, senior managers are telling me that office productivity is slipping. Bottom line: A lot of offices are becoming not-so-nice places to work!

Finally, I felt I needed to balance my anecdotal evidence with a serious quantitative analysis. I developed a survey instrument by the end of 1994, and then asked office professionals throughout the U.S. and Canada to sound off about what was *really* going on in their offices. I've tallied the first 2,000 responses, and now I've got a pretty accurate picture of what ethical dilemmas are being encountered at work and what people are doing about them.

This book is the result. I wrote it, but it is really *all* of ours. We have each experienced our own versions of these ethical dilemmas. We have each struggled to reconcile our values with the practical realities of our job. We have each grown to be accountable for our actions, inactions, and decisions.

Many of you contributed directly by participating in the survey, a seminar, or a discussion. I am grateful for your input and feedback, and I have endeavored to acknowledge personal contributions in those instances where you were kind enough to grant me permission to use your name. And, for the rest of you, don't worry—I will continue to honor all your requests for anonymity.

Now, please—let's continue the discussion. I invite your input about various issues throughout the book. I also invite you to request a copy of my Office Ethics Survey. Hopefully, you will be moved to add your voice. You can write me at my company offices at the address below, or call and leave a message on the Ethics Hotline voice mail.

With your continued help, the vision of the ethical office will become a reality for all of us!

Best wishes,

Nan

Nan DeMars, CPS
President
Executary Services
7701 Normandale Road, Suite 110
Minneapolis, MN 55435

Ethics Hot Line Voice Mail:
    800-257-6933
Phone: 612-835-1148
FAX: 612-831-7908
e-mail: blt@skypoint.com

Contents

1

"I'd rather be right than working here!"

Think about it: *"Secretaries and other office professionals don't have to purchase liability insurance—yet," said the attorney from the podium. "But I believe that day is coming!"*

I believe that attorney.

I also believe the women (and men) who were once secretaries, or other types of office professionals, when asked what they missed most about their former jobs. Their answers are almost always the same: "I miss the action!"

By virtue of their support functions, secretaries and other office professionals are positioned squarely on the ethical hotseat. Ethics issues range from the "little white lie" on the telephone (which 88.2 percent say they do regularly, according to my 1995 Office Ethics Survey) to being asked or forced to perform illegal, immoral, and unethical tasks on the job. Between these two extremes, they must routinely make many difficult choices about their conduct at work. The consequences of their decisions almost always affect their job security, advancement, and compensation.

Julie's story

From Julie, a secretary at a Midwestern utility company: "So—How do I do the right thing, and still keep my job, too? My supervisor has asked me to fabricate a false item in the notes from a meeting with a client. He said he had to create a 'paper trail' in order to protect the company. The fact is, we made a mistake, plain and simple. Rather than admit it, he's asking me to help him rewrite history. I hate this, I just hate this! I'd rather be right than working here!"

Helen's story

From Helen, an office assistant in the Southwest: "Our office is like a quiet, desperate casino—everyone is trying to play the angles. I've got phony expense vouchers, cozy sweetheart deals with vendors, bogus time sheets and production reports—I've even got a manager who has me type fake quality control reports. At least in my department, it's 'Let's Make a Deal' every day."

Kathy's story

From Kathy, a secretary in the Northeast: "I paid workers under the table, [and] falsified government worker's compensation records and tax records. I still think about it today, even though it occurred [in 1989]. I could be taken to court! Or even worse, put in jail!"

Marta's story

From Marta, a military clerk in the Northeast: "I was groped, pinched, and teased by my supervisor. This is the military, and I wanted to make it my career, so I tried to deal with it with some common sense and a sense of humor. But then he raped me. That bastard stole five years of my life."

Jean's story

From Jean, a secretary in the Midwest: "I work for the fund-raising unit of a non-profit organization. My specialty is planned gifts and the executive I work with is an attorney. In the estate planning process, we encourage donors to seek the counsel of their own attorney for document preparation. Recently, a donor who procrastinated in having her will made out was sort of coerced into signing a will that we made out for her. My boss asked me to prepare a will and put us in it for $50,000. This elderly woman signed the will and we now have credit for this small gift. I destroyed all evidence that we drew up the will and was told to have 'no memory' of this situation. I have a good relationship with my boss and have always done as he asked. I knew at the time it was wrong; however, I did as I was asked by a trusted executive. I realize now that if the family contests this will, I could be taken into court for questioning. I was so stupid to have done this."

Stories from Florence, Gus, Angelic, and others

From office professionals in other parts of the country: "I lied for my boss about his whereabouts, expense accounts, schedules...ran personal errands...removed and destroyed damaging information... prepared documents with false and misleading information...intentionally lost information...falsified records...complied with his [and her] requests for sex ..."

These are true stories. Ethical dilemmas come in all shapes, sizes, flavors, and dollar amounts.

They are samples of the real-world ethical dilemmas office professionals face in the modern workplace. I have a filing cabinet full of similar stories from seminars, consultations, letters, and surveys. They all ask questions like: What else could I have done? What should I do now? Why did this happen to me?

Ethical dilemmas can put a person's career in crisis. Julie, for example, said her conflict was so stressful that it was affecting her home life and her productivity at work. She believed her promotion, maybe even her job, was on the line.

Julie told her story in one of my seminars with several dozen other professional secretaries. Her peers' advice was contradictory and irreverent, ranging from "sue the bastard" to "sleep with the bastard," but I think it helped Julie think through the consequences of her decision. We did not all agree on one, best plan of action for Julie to take, but she knew we would support her right to make the decision that was best for her. We did agree that this was yet another "it depends" situation that could only be judged by the people involved.

Julie decided to lie (which is why I am not using her real name). I know this because I called her several months later. She said she did it because she simply could not afford to lose her job. For her, at that time, she felt it was the right decision. But it was a costly decision. She mentally beat herself up for months afterwards by thinking, "What I should have said was..." Her boss never seemed as trusting again, and their relationship became more tense, awkward, and formal. Her relationship with her boss never recovered. But she was lucky. She is now working in another department (fortunately, it's a large company).

Could Julie have handled this ethical dilemma differently so she could have kept her integrity and her job? What are other office workers doing about their ethical dilemmas? Don't we all have to deal with ethical conflicts more often? Don't we all need a new way to talk about the sometimes-murky ethical decisions we have to make at work? And shouldn't our bosses be a part of the discussion, too?

Do you see a little of yourself in Julie? Her supervisor? No matter our positions, we have each experienced our versions of Julie's ethical dilemma. We have each struggled to reconcile our values and conduct with the practical realities of our jobs.

Do you have a problem with ethical dilemmas in your office? Take a few moments with the questionnaire at the end of this chapter.

Why are office ethics important, and why are they more important than ever right now?

Do you understand the real importance of office ethics? Let me put this in a way that even your manager can understand: *A shared understanding of office ethics promotes productivity.*

The productivity gains in an ethical office occur through better communication, mutual trust, and — you guessed it — mutual respect. Shared office ethics does wonders for morale, too. It's this simple: When there is a common expectation about how we are to treat each other and how to behave under certain circumstances, people do their best work. Office ethics show up on the bottom line as teamwork and a "can do" attitude that drives everyday tasks.

Consider what your job would be like without ethics. Lies, duplicity, theft, illicit behavior — is this the kind of corporate culture that attracts customers? Retains superior employees? Builds profits?

Ethics are important to all of us because we are accountable for our personal behavior and performance, regardless of our position on the office hierarchy. In some circles, this kind of personal accountability is the mark of a true professional.

The likelihood that you will be exposed to — or asked to participate in — behavior that is morally unjustifiable is much higher now, and it's getting higher. The situations we find ourselves in continue to astonish me. Remember Julie's supervisor and his instructions to fabricate an item in the meeting notes? This is not at all unusual. Some secretaries who are also notary publics have told me they frequently receive similar requests. They've told me about being asked to sign their names to backdated documents, attest to signatures never witnessed, and otherwise abuse their notary stamps. Those of you who handle quality assurance reports, financial information, and corporate records tell me you are also regularly challenged to resist the temptations and pressures of would-be tamperers.

The ethical dilemmas of Julie, Helen, Jean, Kathy, and the rest are typical of the dilemmas we face every day in business offices. Some of these dilemmas were resolved to everyone's satisfaction. Some cost people their jobs. Most are probably still going on, taking a daily toll in stress and lost productivity. Haven't we all felt our own version of their dilemmas? Their situations are not that different from our own, are they?

My 1995 Office Ethics Survey[1] — the first-ever survey of office professionals about ethical behavior in the office environment — provides some startling insights. Here's a preview of what the first 1,458 respondents say:

- 55.5 percent have experienced verbal harassment, and 64.3 percent observed others experiencing the same
- 31.8 percent have experienced sexual harassment
- Office professionals often see others misbehaving: 27 percent have seen coworkers falsifying expense accounts or vouchers, 32.6 percent know about bogus time sheets, 23.9 percent see others alter travel and/or lodging records, and 11.1 percent even see the official minutes of corporate meetings changed
- More serious offenses they've witnessed: sharing confidential information about hiring, firing, or layoffs (59.2%); sharing confidential information about salaries (51.7%); revealing company or business trade secrets (25.3%); preparing a document with false or misleading information (20.2%)
- They admit they are not saints: 60.5 percent of office professionals say they have taken company property for personal use, and 17.2 percent have notarized a document without witnessing the signature

Other surveys reinforce the picture of frequent misbehavior:

- The most frequently witnessed types of misconduct are lying to supervisors (56%), lying on reports or falsifying records (41%),

[1] *Nan DeMars's 1995 Office Ethics Survey,*
   ©1995 Nan DeMars, CPS and Professional Secretaries International
   c/o Executary Services, 7701 Normandale Rd, Minneapolis, MN 55435 (Tel. 612-835-1148)

stealing (35%), sexual harassment (35%), drug or alcohol abuse
(31%), and conflicts of interest (31%)[2]
- 64 percent of Americans agree with the following statement: "I will
  lie when it suits me — as long as it doesn't cause any real damage."[3]
- 74 percent agreed that "I will steal from those who won't really
  miss it."[3]
- 93 perecent said that they — and nobody else — determine
  what is moral and what in not moral in their lives[3]

Wow! What's going on here?

Whose problems are these, anyway?

Ethics are for everyone, not just upper management and obvious victims.
Left unresolved, ethical dilemmas cause an invisible, insidious drain on
the company's productivity and profitability. Consider the problems
caused by lies, duplicity, theft, illicit behavior, harassment — is this the
kind of corporate culture that attracts customers? Retains superior employees? Builds profits? No one profits from business conducted poorly.

Survey data suggest an alarming frequency of ethical misbehavior
in the office today. A corporate culture that allows this to persist is
heavily penalized. Persistent and chronic ethical dilemmas are insidious drains on productivity. It's time for co-workers in every office to
discuss their concerns and build a climate for ethical conduct.
Senior managers must continue to define the corporate conscience,
but it is up to the secretaries and other office professionals to apply a
code of ethics in a meaningful way in the practical, day-to-day world.

I passionately believe it's time for the discussion about business
ethics to move from the top of the organization to the bottom, from
the boardroom to the lunchroom. I see many companies making
long-term, costly investments to transform their cultures into more
ethical places to work; but, it appears that it took the threat of lawsuits
for non-compliance and discrimination to get the message across that
good ethics make good business. We need to democratize ethical
decision making, and to make sure the corporate conscience is awak-
ened all the way to the bottom of the corporate ladder.

Office professionals, in fact, need help right now because they are
caught in the crossfire between the company's lofty Code of Ethics and
the practical realities of office conduct. They confront questions like:

[2] *Ethics in American Business: Policies, Programs and Perceptions,*
    ©1995 Ethics Resource Center, Washington, DC
[3] *The Day America Told the Truth,* ©1991 Prentice Hall

"How do I do the right thing and still keep my job? I know what I'm supposed to do — the Code of Conduct is prettily framed right there on the wall. But if I don't take these shortcuts, I'm history."

"What can I do by myself to change things? We play 'let's pretend' in our department — let's pretend we're being fair, let's pretend we're honest, let's pretend we don't know these dirty little secrets."

"Does anyone else care, or is it just me? The path of least resistance works for my team because no one wants the extra hassle of dealing with the truth. The truth is, we've developed some pretty sloppy habits, and as long as no one squawks, we'll probably just keep cranking out bogus quality reports."

What will *you* do when your management asks you to do something you know you shouldn't, and then winks? Should you sacrifice your job for a principle? Should you risk your career for a customer? Should you help out a co-worker in a do-it-or-leave dilemma?

The executive that claims to never put a subordinate in an ethical conflict is lying to us, or himself/herself. This is simply not realistic. The notion that all is well back in the sanctuary of the office is a myth.

Speaking of sanctuaries, I'm reminded of a letter I received a few years ago when I was International President of Professional Secretaries International (PSI). As Board members, we challenged our chapters around the country to conduct at least one program that year on ethics and to write to us about any unusual stories. One woman wrote me and said, "I have worked for my executive for 16 years and he has *never* placed me in a situation involving an ethical dilemma." None of us could understand this or believe it until we read whom she works for — she is the secretary to a bishop! Maybe some of us don't have to worry about resolving ethical dilemmas, but most of our bosses are not that saintly!

Incidentally, I told that story at a seminar in New York City. Wouldn't you know it, a woman stood and responded: "I used to work for a bishop myself, and believe me, they are no different than anyone else!" I believe that woman.

Most people in business make decisions every day that require ethical judgment. Corporations discovered that ethics statements are great for business more than a decade ago (though it is unclear whether the lawsuits or the conversions came first). Consequently, our bosses get a healthy dose of ethics training at considerable expense so they can guide the corporation along the straight and narrow. Ethics provide a focus and direction for the business, and they are a great context for many decisions and actions. The public relations people and the lawyers are especially fond of ethics programs and ethics statements because they are evidence that the company's intentions are pure and high-minded.

However, I am more interested in the practicality of the real world, thank you. Most of us back at the office don't even get lip service, yet we are on the front lines of the "people side" of every business. Do I sound frustrated? I guess I am. I'm appreciative that so many people are working so hard to articulate their organization's ethics but, frankly, not many are speaking up about the ethics the staff lives with every day in the office. It's wonderful that companies now think twice before building a facility that hurts the environment or marketing an unsafe product. But there is also an ethical dimension of office life in these companies, and this needs to be examined, too. I've given seminars for a dozen years on office ethics, and I am still surprised how often I hear stories about managers running roughshod over their assistants on their way to help the company do the right thing.

At the end of the day, I believe it is the day-to-day interactions between co-workers and customers that lead to an organization's success. Why? Because, simply put, our ethics are our standards of conduct, our standards of behavior. Office ethics is all about how we treat each other, day in and day out. The multitude of these small, interpersonal interactions has a cumulative effect that ultimately defines the corporate culture. If it is to have real meaning, talk about ethics from senior executives must be supported up and down the ranks of the personnel roster.

Case in point: Through my search firm, I recently placed an executive secretary at Opus Corporation, an international development firm headquartered in Minneapolis. Opus has an outstanding reputation throughout our community. During the search process, I commented on the company's fine reputation to Judy Truex, the Executive Assistant to the Chairman and CEO, Gerald Rauenhorst. Judy matter-of-factly replied, "Opus has this reputation because it simply reflects the stature and beliefs of Mr. Rauenhorst himself; his personal code of conduct is reflected all the way down throughout the entire company."

Oh, that we could all work for such executives! But for every Opus, there are a hundred XYZ Companies that can only talk about ethics a lot, never connecting the good intentions of upper management to the practical realities down at the lower ranks.

Wait — before you rush to judgment, let me remind you of something you already know: There is no one-size-fits-all code of ethical behavior. What is appropriate for one office will be out of place in the next. We'll address all these issues in detail, in due time...

About this book...

Because of my consulting practice, I have been able to open a window into the ethical and unethical practices of many large and small companies. I've observed first-hand how office professionals and their bosses are struggling to respond to challenges to their moral judgment. I've interviewed leading ethics "experts" from the academic and corporate worlds, and discussed business ethics, ethics policy, and ethics training with thousands of business people. I've looked hard to find practical, real-world strategies and resources that can help all of us.

As I say at the beginning of my seminars, I can talk all day long "from the book" about ethics — and put you to sleep. Instead, what I'm talking (and writing) about is reality. For most people, that reality goes something like this: *"I know this is wrong, but I need to keep my job. I can't afford to hire an attorney. I don't want the hassle and the stigma of a lawsuit hanging on me for the next few years. I don't want to be branded a troublemaker. I want to do the right thing, but I also don't want to be kicked out the back door and end up on the outside looking in."*

I understand, and this book is the result. I mean it to be a compass for all types of office professionals and their managers who must navigate the morally hazardous situations of the modern workplace.

This book can help you get where you want to go but, of course, it cannot choose your direction. In other words, there will be no preaching here, no single answer, no silver bullet, no self-righteous judgment of your choices.

This book is about how to build an ethical office, because that is the healthiest, most productive environment for everyone to work in. Each of us wants to be known as an ethical person, a person who can be counted on to "do the right thing" in every situation. Most of us are able to conduct ourselves in this manner — most of the time.

This book is for those other times — those times when we may lose our moral compass and are tempted to behave in ways that are immoral, unethical, hurtful, or even destructive to ourselves and others.

Allow this book to be your key and your guide to the ethical office. Through it, you will see many others struggle with dilemmas similar to yours, so you will soon know you are not alone. I, for one, have faced the same choices you are facing, and I've talked at length to thousands of others who have, too. I want this book to be a comfort — through it, we have each other.

The approach of this book is simple: I want you to know what others are experiencing and what they are doing about it. These are your sisters and brothers from whom you can learn. I will add whatever insights I can along the way, including what I've learned about what does and does not work. Most importantly, I want to help you develop your personal ideal of the ethical and moral office so you can build one for yourself. It is my fervent wish that this book will prompt a lot of discussion in a lot of offices about what's right and what's wrong!

I challenge you to set aside your cynicism, raise your expectations, and make your personal commitment to building your version of an ethical office. If we are to regard ourselves as true professionals, and thereby enjoy the respect and compensation we are due, we each must grow to be 100 percent accountable for our actions, inactions, and decisions. Imagine the profound and cumulative effects of our efforts if we can be the spark of change regarding office ethics! If it is true that we all *want* to do the right thing (and I believe this is true), this book can be our guide.

Most of us will have to solve our ethical dilemmas ourselves. It's unlikely your boss will run up to your desk tomorrow and say, "Gosh, I'm sorry you've been forced to struggle with these burdensome ethical dilemmas! Here's a couple of thousand dollars — find a good ethics program at a fine university and help us rethink our value system and behaviors." Chances are, we are going to be largely on our own to continue sorting out our personal ethical issues. I know all business professionals need some additional help in this area, but those of us on the support staff are unlikely to receive it.

Together, let's explode the myths, shatter the secrecy and silence, and figure out how to build an ethical office that works for you. The dialogue we have to have with our manager is this: Whether we are called secretaries, office administrators, colleagues, business partners, or associates, we're all here in the same office at the same time, trying to do the best job we can for the company, right? As long as we're working together, let's agree to behave ourselves and follow some basic, fair rules of conduct that foster mutual respect!

Do I have the one and true path to everlasting righteousness? Nope, sorry. I can't offer you simple answers or get-out-of-trouble-free coupons, either. You already know that life is more complicated than that.

You also know (or can guess) that the definition of ethical behavior is certain to vary from office to office. It depends upon the people and the organization's ethical climate. Nevertheless, it is possible to discuss ethical dilemmas and communicate conclusions so there is no mystery about what conduct and behaviors are acceptable and not acceptable. This discussion must be a continuous one.

I can offer you some practical advice about how to navigate the ethical obstacle courses in your office. Much of this advice comes from my 30-plus years of experience as an office personnel consultant; much more of it comes from men and women just like you, struggling in their own ways to live with their consciences and keep their jobs, too.

A few quick notes to the word mavens among you: I refer to us collectively as office professionals in this book for the sake of the readers' convenience. I recognize that many of us are adopting new job titles to more accurately describe our new, broader responsibilities. Nevertheless, new titles can be unclear outside the context of specific organizations. Besides, I have always been proud to be an office professional, no matter what the precise title was in such and such an office. I define an office professional — and myself — in the broadest sense that most of you will find liberating and empowering. So — perhaps we can meet in the middle with this job title? Also for the readers' benefit, I use the feminine pronouns most often because, like it or not, office administration remains a profession dominated by women (sorry, guys, but you can handle it). FYI, the Bureau of Labor Statistics says 79 percent of us are women.

Finally, each and every anecdote in this book is based upon the real story of a real person. I point this out because it is important for you to know that ethical dilemmas are not theoretical abstractions or academic exercises, but rather the stuff of everyday life for many of us.

I'll never forget an evening I spent with a group of Past International Presidents of PSI. We PIPS (as we affectionately call ourselves) rendezvous annually at International Conventions and our conversations often last into the wee hours of the morn. On this particular evening, we found ourselves in a lively discussion about bosses we had worked with in our careers. I asked the question: "Have any of you ever left a job solely because of the boss?" Three of my friends resoundedly echoed "Yes!" Their reasons were interesting: Frances Jakes, of Murphreesboro, TN, said, "Because our morals clashed." Adella LaRue CPS of Kansas City, MO, said, "Because our values clashed." And, Evelynne Thompson CPS, of Rio Rancho, NM, said, "Because our ethics were not the same." Each of them said the same thing—only in different ways.

To me, office ethics—the way people treat each other at work—is critically important to business and personal success. I admit it— I'm passionate about this view of business, and maybe a little crazy about it.

Ethics are for everyone, not just the victims. Secretaries and other office professionals are in a powerful position to improve the ethical conduct of their companies. They are literally the eyes and ears of the organization—they know the truth about how it really functions. If all employees initiated a discussion with their supervisors about the ethical dilemmas in the office, businesses would be transformed: Not only would productivity shoot up, but customers would get better service, profits would rise, and the revolving doors of the personnel office would no longer spin.

> *"Make each decision*
> *as if it were the one decision*
> *for which you would be*
> *remembered."*
>
> —Walter Burke
> (Texas Instruments)
> 2/2/94

Ethical Office Discussion #1:
~~~ Nan DeMars's Office Ethics Audit™ ~~~

*Use this discussion guide to help you and your co-workers
assess the current level of ethical maturity in your office.
Each "yes" answer is a warning sign of a potential ethical dilemma.*

Yes No Do you think anyone in the office is doing
something illegal?

Yes No Do you think anyone in the office is doing
something unethical?

Yes No Is any behavior or action taking place in the
office that you would be embarrassed to see
reported in the media?

Yes No Are people leaving to go home, go crazy, go
to jail, or go to the authorities?

Yes No Do you trust your boss?

Yes No Does your boss trust you?

Yes No Do you trust your co-workers?

Yes No Have there been any incidents in the recent past that
made you ashamed of your company?

Yes No Is there anything going on in your office that you
would feel uncomfortable about explaining to your
kids? a reporter? your parents?

Yes No Is everyone — customers, co-workers, vendors —
being treated fairly?

Yes No Is there any perception of a conflict of interest?

Yes No Are there any obvious or subtle behaviors
that seem unfair, or seem to undermine the
effectiveness of the work done in your office?

Yes No Has your ability to make an impartial and
objective decision been compromised or forced
to be biased?

© 1997 Nan DeMars, CPS

2

"It depends!"

(A primer on ethical dilemmas)

Think about it: *You are given two free tickets to a lavish dinner theater by one of the vendors competing for your company's copier business. Your boss knows nothing about this, and she is unlikely to ever hear about it. The responsibility for recommending the copier supplier is yours. You worry that you may disappoint your boss by appearing to be compromised. Still, you believe you can remain objective, and your anniversary is coming up. Do you accept the tickets? Do you tell your boss?*

What do we know about ethical dilemmas?

Somewhere in the first few minutes of a discussion about an ethical dilemma, you will hear, "Well, it depends."

Teachers of ethics say that if we were placed in a room all by ourselves, *and no one would ever know the consequences of our actions,* here's what we would do when confronted by an ethical dilemma: 10 percent of us would be certain to "do the right thing"; another 10 percent of us would automatically "do the wrong thing." And the rest of us? Well, 80 percent of us will say "It depends" and act accordingly.

Here's an "it depends" situation from one of my seminars (if you're a man, just imagine how your wife or sister would respond): You apply for a wonderful job today, with twice the money you are currently earning and better hours. It's located two blocks from your home—and you adore the job description. You want this job! The human resource person is encouraging, and says an offer will be made to you next week. Then, on Saturday, you go to the doctor and learn you are pregnant. Would you voluntarily tell your prospective employer on Monday that you are pregnant, even though you fear the new job offer may be withdrawn? Or would you take the job and be "surprised" at the pregnancy after you were secure in the job — and safely enrolled in the health plan?

Boy — do I get a wild mix of answers on this one!

Another question: Your boss regularly takes off during business hours to be with his mistress. As he heads toward the door, he stops at your desk to say, "If my wife calls, make something up." You'd like to keep this job. How many of us would make something up?

How you answer these questions depends upon your circumstances and experiences. You would handle these dilemmas based on how you feel.

In the first problem, you may think you don't want to jeopardize the opportunity, it's none of their business, it won't or shouldn't make a difference, etc. The fact is, they cannot legally deny you an offer of employment because of your pregnancy, but there are some ethical considerations that may affect your decision to disclose or not disclose certain information.

What other information would you choose or not choose to disclose? Look at it another way: What kinds of less-than-flattering information do you leave off your resume, knowing that it affects your marketability? Legally, the company cannot ask questions about you that do not relate directly to the performance of the job. Yet do you choose to share more if you think it will help in the interview? Do you put a "positive spin" on certain jobs or circumstances? It's easy for these answers to end up in the "it depends" category.

In the second problem, it would be natural to respond based on our experiences: You don't like your boss's wife anyway, you don't care, you respect his personal space, you remember what it felt like to be cheated on, you have to keep this job no matter what because you need insurance for your kids, whatever. Again: If you're wise, you will think this through from the perspective of "it depends."

By the by — in the second problem, I would simply use those all-purpose words, "He's unavailable." Your boss could be in the restroom or in Europe; the point to communicate is that he's not here, now, available for conversation. At least this keeps you from lying! However, I would also pick a good time later on to have a cup of coffee with him and explain that how he conducts his personal affairs is of no importance to you (this is true, right?), and you keep all confidences, but would he please keep you out of this particular loop? If it makes you uncomfortable to be placed in the middle of a domestic situation, or in the role of co-conspirator, say so. You're a professional, so speak up!

Are there universal moral principles we can apply automatically to everyday office situations? No, but life sure would be simpler if we could. If making choices about our conduct was as simple as choosing black or white, we could set our moral compass on autopilot and relax. But there are precious few universal principles about right and wrong, and these so-called moral absolutes rarely apply directly to working in an office.

For example, we can probably all agree that murder is a poor way of resolving an argument, and senseless violence doesn't win customers! We also know it is wrong to take another's property by deceit or force, and physical and sexual abuse is wrong — period. However, since these are not usually encountered during normal business practices, the "it depends" caveat stands. Here is a sampling of other "it depends" questions you may encounter at work:

- If you are aware that a co-worker is bending the company rules in some way, do you tell your supervisor? Would you handle the situation any differently if you knew that you probably would cause this co-worker to lose his or her job?
- Are there any circumstances under which you would "look the other way" if a friend at the company was taking advantage of disability benefits?
- Do you make long-distance phone calls and photocopies at the company's expense?
  Is this always wrong? Is it a perk?
- Do you always and automatically blow the whistle on inflated expense reports when you learn of them?
- How would you respond to a co-worker who is chronically late to work and almost always leaves 10 to 15 minutes early? Would it make a difference knowing that she was a single parent with a difficult child care situation?
- If you knew something, or thought you knew something, about a job applicant's prior chemical dependency problem that would cripple his or her chance to be hired, would you speak up?

- If you know your boss is "cooking the books" to make himself look better, or to cover up for a problem, would you say something to him? Would you speak to anyone else? Would you say anything if it was likely you would lose your job as a result?
- A co-worker has been sexually intimate with her supervisor. She has confided that she was coerced into the liaison at first, but now she says, "It's not too bad. The sex is good, he's giving me more money and better assignments, and when it ends, I'll have a great lawsuit." You suspect she's putting the best face on a bad situation, yet you worry about her vengeful attitude ultimately hurting your profit-sharing plan if she sues and wins a huge settlement. What should you do about this train-wreck-waiting-to-happen, if anything?

Virtually all ethical decisions you make at work are of the "it depends" variety. You will naturally decide these "it depends" situations on the basis of what is right for *you*. Your decisions will largely depend on various needs you feel at the time of the decisions, e.g., your need for financial security, your need for self-esteem and self-respect, your need for approval from a friend or supervisor, your need to have a clear conscience, etc.

I believe there is a direct relationship between the level of a person's needs and the probability that he or she will "do the misdeed." In other words, the more pressure or pain a person feels because of one or more needs, the more likely he or she will find a way to bend the ethical rules.

This view may strike you as somewhat cynical, but I think it's realistic: Generally, it's normal for people to act in their short-term self-interests. If the moral standards need to flex, or stretch, or twist a bit to cover not-so-ethical behavior, so be it, they say. In other words, "what's right is right, *and what's wrong is right,* as long as it's convenient and suits my needs." I picture this relationship between personal needs and the influence these needs have on ethical decisions like this:

The "It Depends" Curve

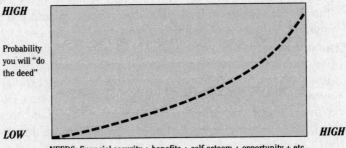

NEWS: financial security + benefits + self-esteem + opportunity + etc.

The more often you feel pain or pressure from your personal needs, the higher the likelihood you will find a way to rationalize bending the ethical rules. Also, your level of stress will rise in direct proportion to the amount of rationalization you have to do.

I continue to be amazed at people's capacity to bridge the gap of inconsistency between what they say they believe is moral and their unethical actions. If their actions happen to mesh with their core moral standards, it is only a happy coincidence.

You can see the problem. If people make all their "it depends" decisions based only on their personal needs, and do not see the satisfaction of their personal needs linked to the welfare of the team, the office environment will become unmanageable and unbearable. This selfish decision making is expected in small children at play, but not acceptable among professional colleagues in a modern office!

Of course, the rationalizations that make it possible for a person to live with what I call the "dynamic discord" of actions he or she knows to be unethical carry a cost. A personal price is paid in terms of stress and unhappiness. A price is paid by the organization, too, when this stressed and unhappy person reports for work with a bad attitude, low energy, poor motivation, poor concentration, and overall sub-par capacity to perform.

It makes good business sense, therefore, to minimize the likelihood that an employee will have to live with an unresolved ethical dilemma. This book is packed with suggestions about how you can minimize your "it depends" questions, resolve your ethical dilemmas and, in the process, build a more ethical office that supports and reinforces your natural desire to "do the right thing."

First, some definitions ...

Before we get too far along, here's how dictionaries describes the sometimes-vague concepts surrounding this discussion:

Moral implies conformity with the generally accepted standards of goodness or rightness in conduct or character; moral is generally used to describe who people are, e.g. a moral person

Ethical implies conformity with an elaborated, ideal code of moral principles; ethical is generally used to describe how people behave, act, and conduct themselves, i.e. an ethical lawyer or an ethical secretary

In other words, our *morals* are those principles and values that we have internalized. Our morals are automatic responses to situations; they are a part of who we are and our unique personality. We make moral decisions without a lot of thought because they are based on the principles and values we believe in most deeply. Some examples of decisions that are likely to be moral decisions are to: help someone who is injured, avoid pornography, trust God, tell the truth, treat others fairly, and protect our family. We learn our morals from our parents, teachers, religious leaders, friends, and experiences, and they provide the context or framework for our moral actions.

Ethics is our code of conduct. Ethics are a set of rules and standards that guide our behavior. Ethics may or may not be written down. We have personal ethics, which guide our personal behavior ("I will not lie to a friend"), and we have professional ethics, which guide our professional conduct ("I will do everything in my power to support my supervisor"). Ethics are rooted in our morals, but they are modified by group decisions, peer pressure, and circumstances ("In this department, our policy for handling this type of situation is thus and thus"). Hopefully, our ethics are an extension and expression of our morals.

When an action is in harmony with our morals, we say that the action is *ethical*. When it is not, it is *unethical*. Again, the discord, or disconnectedness, between our morals (what we know is "right") and the actions we feel we need to do causes the ethical dilemmas that cripple productivity.

In an ideal office, a set of shared ethical standards coincide with our personal morals and ethics. When the ethics in the office conflict with our personal morals and ethics, we are confronted with the classic ethical dilemma: The gap between our morals and the prevailing office ethical standards. The larger the gap, the greater the stress.

We'll take a closer look at how these terms compare with the concepts of laws and customs when we look at ethics in action at work in Chapter 7.

The stages of moral development

The good news is that we know quite a bit about how people mature morally. As they develop morally, their code of conduct — their ethics — mature, too.

Extensive research has taught us that moral development follows the same pattern as cognitive development: It proceeds in an invariant sequence of developmental stages. The stages of growth occur in order, from lower to higher stages, and no stages are skipped over.

Lawrence Kohlberg provided this breakthrough understanding of moral development in the early 1960s. Briefly, his research consisted of presenting moral dilemmas to many people with different backgrounds. During the course of extensive interviews with these people, he was able to sample their systems of reasoning, thinking, and judging ethical decisions. In analyzing these interviews, Kohlberg formed the six-stage category system shown below.

	Focus of Concern	Characterized by	Motivation	Sounds like:
Stage 1:	Self	Obedience to powerful authority	Fear of punishment	"I must do what my supervisor tells me to do, or he'll fire me."
Stage 2:	What another person can do for me	"Looking out for number one"	Satisfaction of my own needs	"You scratch my back and I'll scratch yours (but I want to come out a little bit ahead whenever we exchange favors)," and "It's all right to steal, especially if you get away with it."
Stage 3:	Meeting the expectations of groups of people, performing "good" and "the right" roles and conformity to group norms	"Going along to get along"	Acceptance as "a nice guy/gal." Affection plays a strong role	"Let's be good to each other so we look good as a group."

	Focus of Concern	Character-ized by	Motivation	Sounds like:
Stage 4:	Preserving the social order	"Doing what is expected"	Desire to follow the social rules	"On my honor I will do my duty to uphold the rules…"
Stage 5:	Free arguments and social contracts	"What is right is what the whole society decides. Society can change the standards if everyone agrees."	Desire to achieve the greatest good for the greatest number of people; there are no legal absolutes	"Where the law is not affected, what is right is a matter of personal opinion and agreement between persons." The U.S. Constitution is written in Stage 5 terms.
Stage 6:	Universal ethical principles	Principles that are general ("All persons are created equal."), instead of rules that are specific ("Thou shalt not kill.")	What is right is a decision of one's conscience, based on ideas about rightness that apply to everyone (all nations, people, etc.). These are general ethical principles, not specific rules	"The most important ethical principles deal with justice, equality, and the dignity of all people." These principles are *higher* than any given law.

The stages are defined by the major set of assumptions a person uses to think through and justify an important ethical decision. Each higher stage is "better" than the one that preceded it; and each higher stage takes into account an increasingly broader perspective, more complex and abstract thought, and more personal empathy. The higher the stage of development, the more accommodation there is to values and ethics based on principles of justice. At the lowest stages are the self-centered, relatively immature codes of ethical conduct; at Stage 6, we see the likes of Joan of Arc, Gandhi, Madame Curie, Sister Kenny, Martin Luther King, Jr., Florence Nightingale, Albert Schweitzer, Abraham Lincoln, Eleanor Roosevelt, Henry David Thoreau, Socrates, Mother Theresa, and other moral leaders.

This 6-stage category system from Kohlberg explains why some people see some ethical issues as simple black or white choices. That's also why it is possible for you to have a personal morality that is not perfectly aligned with your office's generally accepted ethics.

No one is totally in just one stage of development. Again, like cognitive development, moral development is in a continual process of evolution. This perhaps explains why a person may be in, say, Stage 4 where his marriage is concerned ("It's better to have a bad marriage than a good divorce"), but in Stage 2 at the office ("It's all right to steal, especially if you get away with it").

Another example: A boss may use a rule of fear on employees, reducing the office staff to a Stage 1 level of morality. In this way, the boss forces the company to pay a high cost in employee creativity and initiative.

I linked Kohlberg's model specifically to office ethics in my Office Ethics survey. A high majority (82.3 percent) of respondents seem to be in Stage 5, the "doing what is expected" stage. Here are the results when the respondents were asked, "When you refuse to do something unethical, which of these reasons sounds most like you?" (Multiple responses were accepted.)

Stage 1	*"I am afraid of being punished"*	*2.5%*
Stage 2	*"It is not in my best interests"*	*7.7%*
Stage 3	*"I would feel like I'd let down*	
	the others in my group"	*3.7%*
Stage 4	*"I've agreed to follow the rules"*	*6.3%*
Stage 5	*"It isn't the right thing to do"*	*82.3%*
Stage 6	*"I have to do my part to follow*	
	society's rules"	*0.5%*
	No Answer	*4.0%*

More good news: People will continue to grow ethically as long as they continue to be challenged. Again, the stages of growth are sequential, and none can be skipped, so you cannot realistically expect an excessively self-serving person in Stage 1 to suddenly behave like a saint in Stage 6. However, you can "stir the drink" to promote more moral development by asking questions and discussing specific moral dilemmas. In short: Everyone gradually learns to behave more ethically as they mature, and the more ethical dilemmas they solve, the more learning occurs.

This potential for predictable moral growth is the single best hope for building a more ethical office environment. By questioning and discussing ethical dilemmas you are experiencing in the office, everyone who participates will move a little further toward their next-highest stage of development. So there is hope! The ethical dilemmas you are thrashing out this year are helping people grow, which means you probably will not have to deal with the same dilemmas next year. There's still no guarantee that your boss will "see the light" and stop submitting bogus expense reports on her own (remember the "It Depends" graph?), but you can be reasonably confident that her ethics are improving, albeit at a glacier pace!

I have a favorite story that illustrates the process of moral and ethical growth: It seems a Midwestern father was trying to teach his son right from wrong. He came up with a novel approach. Whenever his son was naughty, the boy had to drive a nail into a fence so he could see and remember his misdeed. Whenever he did something especially good, he was allowed to remove a nail. Simple rules, right? One day the boy noticed that the fence was full of holes and looked very bad. He shared his observation with his father: "I can take the nails out, but I can't remove the holes." His father smiled and quickly made the point that, "Although we may balance our mistakes with good deeds, the mistakes still leave their mark."

What's the difference between office ethics and business ethics?

Broadly speaking, discussions of business ethics refer to the "big picture decisions" affecting the management of our organizations. Discussions of office ethics, on the other hand, focus on the "small picture choices" that comprise our personal and interpersonal conduct at work. I believe it is the day-to-day exercise of a person's office ethics that make business ethics possible and meaningful throughout an organization. Here are some of the ways these two views of ethics are interrelated:

	Office Ethics *versus*	Business Ethics
Chief characteristics	▪ focus is on personal conduct (office ethics guide our individual behavior and interpersonal relationships at work) ▪ based on long-held personal beliefs and values, which are not likely to change	▪ focus is on corporate conduct (business ethics guide corporate strategies, decisions, policies, and culture) ▪ based on the organization's customs and culture that have been successful in the past; these are easy to describe, but difficult to change

	Office Ethics *versus*	**Business Ethics**
Time reference	■ short-term decisions; office ethics guide personal choices on a case-by-case, tactical basis ("Do I or don't I?" and "What am I going to do about this?")	■ sustained mid- and long-term efforts; business ethics build corporate culture and guide strategic decisions ("What is the company going to do about our environmental problems?" and "How can we improve our customer service?")
Typical application	■ generally reactive	■ generally proactive
Who can influence these ethics?	■ each and every one of us	■ the leaders and decision-makers in the organization who: (a) establish the expectations for performance (e.g., How much will the company tolerate in order to achieve its goals?) (b) write the rules for others to follow (c) lead by their example, thereby creating the climate for the company's ethical conduct
Who is affected by these ethics?	■ every person we have personal contact with, e.g. co-workers, customers, vendors	■ employees, customers, vendors, competitors, other organizations, community leaders, media, shareholders, and others within the sphere of influence of the organization
Questions asked of ethical dilemmas	■ How am I going to handle this? ■ How do I feel about this? ■ What's the right thing to do?	■ How should the company handle this? ■ What's our policy? ■ What have we done in the past? ■ What's the right thing to do?

	Office Ethics *versus*	Business Ethics
Examples of dilemmas where these ethics can help guide conduct	■ harassment ■ lying to supervisor or co-worker ■ challenges tampering with files or documents ■ use and misuse of company resources ■ knowledge of schemes or practices that take advantage of the company ■ requests for confidential information ■ sharing and withholding-information ■ rumors and gossip ■ contributing or withholding support to the office team ■ time card reports ■ gifts, gratuities, entertainment ■ security, theft ■ outside interests ■ expense reports ■ quality, testing, financial reports ■ failure to follow through ■ selling, marketing practices ■ conflicts of interest ■ substance abuse ■ inside information	■ goals that create pressure leading to misconduct ■ downsizing ■ recruitment ■ community relations, public safety ■ compliance with the spirit and letter of environmental, employment, and safety laws ■ responses to whistle-blowing ■ customer relations ■ vendor relations ■ gifts, gratuities, entertainment ■ political contributions ■ pricing ■ substance abuse ■ selling, marketing practices ■ immigration ■ food, drug laws ■ fraud, deceit ■ tax laws ■ racketeering ■ corruption of public officials ■ antitrust

Office Ethics *versus*	Business Ethics
How do I know when I/we have an ethical office and/or an ethical business?	• "My co-workers and I are a real team. We support each other without whining, and we trust each other to be fair and honest." • "I'm proud of my company." • "I'm proud of what I accomplish." • "I respect my boss's integrity." • "I know my manager values my work and my input." • "I can talk to my supervisor about any ethical concerns I have, and I have confidence they will be taken seriously and addressed."	• The company has earned a reputation for honest communication with all its constituencies. • Sales growth is above average. • Customer and employee retention is above average. • Subordinates trust their managers, and vice versa. • Concerns about ethics are listened to seriously. • We back up the company's statements of values with meaningful action. • People who leave the company, for whatever reason, are treated fairly. • We listen to our neighbors in the community. We give something back. • We have learned to manage our business profitably while complying with the spirit and the letter of relevant laws. We strive to be a responsible corporate citizen.

Is there one ethical standard that we should all aim for? If there is, just tell us what it is — we'll tell you if we can meet it.

I once had a vehement argument with a reporter who was writing an article about my ethics seminars. He kept pushing me and pushing me, persisting with the question, "But, Nan, why can't you tell your seminar attendees what to do and what not to do?" The only way I got him to understand why I couldn't do that was to remind him, "Not even a psychiatrist tells you what to do! All the psychiatrist — and I — can do is help a person understand the ramifications of his or her actions. In the end, it's up to every person to make personal choices about what is the right or wrong thing to do!"

Is there one ethical standard we should all be aiming for?

No, no, no. Every person, and every group of people who work together in an office, have different ethical standards because they are in different stages of their own moral development. So you see, it doesn't matter what I think is right or wrong. How could I know what's right or wrong for you or your co-workers? I have no opinion about your ethical judgment. It is what it is. It will mature naturally as you challenge yourself to solve the ethical dilemmas you see.

Use Kohlberg's 6-stage model as a useful framework to understand your development and the development of your co-workers. Most people who work in offices generally regarded as "ethical" are behaving at either Stage 3 or Stage 4. Companies with formal ethics programs are at Stage 5. Churches and human rights organizations are at Stage 6.

Think about it: *At U.S. Congressional hearings on the Iran-Contra affair in 1988, Ms. Fawn Hall, former secretary to Lt. Colonel Oliver North, testified that, at his request, she shredded an 18-inch stack of documents and altered five other documents in the National Security Council files in her White House office. On her own initiative, she shredded phone logs and inter-office memos. On the day her boss was fired, she also smuggled other papers out of the White House by hiding them in her clothing. In her testimony, Hall said she was a dedicated and loyal secretary — and that her policy was to "not ask questions and just follow orders." If you had been in a similar situation, what would you have done? Why?*

Nan says: Ms. Hall appears to have been making her ethical decisions at Stage 3 (meeting the expectations of others by performing "good" and "the right" roles). Clearly, this type of loyalty that is blind to society's rules and laws can be misplaced. See Chapter 11 for more discussion.

When I discuss this case in my seminars, most attendees vow they would never do what Ms. Hall did. But let's not rush to judge someone else who obviously thought she was making the right decision for herself at the time, all things considered. Interestingly, when I discussed Ms. Hall's case at a Washington, DC seminar, and most of the attendees worked "on the hill," I got a very different reaction! Most of them said they would have behaved exactly as Ms. Hall did.

That discussion was a real eye-opener for this little Midwesterner! They started by pointing out that, although she was a civilian, Ms. Hall worked for the military. She even had a boss you stood up for whenever he simply entered the room, so consequently she was used to obeying orders. They also noted that Ms. Hall appeared to sincerely believe in Col. North's position on the Iran-Contra situation. Finally, several attendees observed that these were "last-ditch" actions, taken without a lot of time to think, just prior to North's office being sealed as off-limits to him. It would have been completely out of character, it seems, for Ms. Hall to pick that particular moment to disobey her boss.

Again, decisions with ethical dimensions are rarely black or white. The reality is, your choices will usually depend upon the unique circumstances of a given situation.

I'm old enough to remember another famous secretary who had a classic ethical dilemma: Rose Mary Woods, President Richard Nixon's devoted secretary during the Watergate scandal of the early 1970s, said she erased over 18 minutes of important tape recordings with an accidental slip of the foot.

But what would you do if you were secretary to the President of the United States and he or she said to you, "Susan — for the good of the country, would you please..." It's hard to predict, isn't it? I suppose it would depend...

> *"The time is always ripe...*
> *to do the right thing."*
>
> —Martin Luther King, Jr.

3

When does a decision become a dilemma?

Think about it: *You are the mayor of a small town in Ohio and your city staff is comprised of very effective long-term employees. Ann, your city clerk, has been with the city for 25 years. She is the key administrative person you rely on to conduct the day-to-day business of the city. She is the kind of employee you can always depend upon to put in extra time and effort when needed. She is always there in a crisis and several times she has handled situations that would have been uncomfortable for you. In short, you really owe her a lot. Recently, Ann came to you and admitted that, for some time, she has been "borrowing" money from the petty cash fund by writing false receipts. It was never much — usually less than $100 — and she always repaid it. But her conscience has bothered her so much that she had to confess. Besides, she said sheepishly, another one of the clerks caught her in the act a few days ago and threatened to tell the mayor and the newspaper if she didn't come forward on her own. Under the city's personnel policies, Ann's actions are clearly cause for immediate dismissal. What would you do if you were the mayor? Would you handle it differently if you were Ann's supervisor in a private company?*

Many people talk to me for only one reason: They know they are sitting on a powder keg of a situation that is about to blow up. Let's do a quick reality check: Are you currently at risk in a "morally hazardous situation"? Only you can say. Only you can judge your decisions or behavior as right or wrong. Your choices and conduct are yours to answer for and to live with.

I can tell you that you are not alone in your struggle to do the right thing while keeping your job. I've spoken with thousands of office professionals, and many, many of them are looking for clues that will help them answer the most basic question: "Is it OK to be doing this thing?" There are usually a few follow-up questions, too: "If it's not OK, what do I do? How do I do it anyway and not hate myself? How can I walk the highwire between what I know is wrong and what I know is right so I can keep my job?"

I notice that the questions are typically about situations the person is in the middle of, or situations they had to deal with in the past. This is understandable. When we see ethical dilemmas for what they really are, and they are heading in our direction, we rarely have a problem dealing with them.

How do you know when you are headed for trouble? What are the warning signs?

Ethical dilemmas that hurt us are the ones that fool us. This happens when we didn't know what was really going on, or we didn't appreciate the significance of our actions, or we chose to ignore the little voice in the back of our mind that keeps saying, "Watch out!" and "Don't you believe that for a second!"

Haven't we all been seduced by circumstances and situations that turned out to be something different from what they appeared to be at first? We allow ourselves to drift into difficult situations because they don't look like problems in the beginning. The occasional bending of the rules, the special person, the last-minute exception, the romantic opportunity, the short-term financial crisis, the extra-difficult client— haven't we all heard rationalizations like these for taking the shortcut, the path of least resistance, "just this once"? Eventually, sometime after the exception becomes the standard operating procedure, our ethical gyroscope rights itself and we just wake up one day to find ourselves in the middle of a first-class, grade A, category 1 ethical dilemma.

A classic example: At a recent University of Minnesota seminar, a male secretary stood and talked about a dilemma he once had with his female boss. His boss, who was married, was having a romance all summer long with a married man. His boss would say to him, "If anyone calls me, tell them I am at such and such a place. But if you need me, here's the number I'm really at." He was an unwilling co-conspirator all summer, but he went along with her charade anyway, telling himself that it was not important and none of his business.

However, he said it finally bothered him to the point where it affected his work and gave him a constant tension headache. Finally, one day he walked into his boss's office and said, "It makes no difference to me what you do with your personal life. I have kept, and will continue to keep, all confidences. However, please don't continue to put me in the middle by asking me to lie for you. It is really making me feel *uncomfortable*. [Another great word to negotiate some "wiggle room" in an ethical dilemma!] Please just give me one message — and no more." Guess what? His boss was completely surprised that it had even bothered him.

Don't you think people sometimes get so caught up in their personal, momentary dilemmas that they just don't realize how they gradually pull other people into them, too? In this secretary's case, his boss immediately apologized for putting him in such a compromising position. She kept her word, too — she never put him in the middle again.

In my Office Ethics Survey, I asked, If you do something you are not ethically comfortable with, what reason do you most often use to justify your actions? Wow! The answers were all over the map, but basically fall into three categories: I have to do it, I don't think it matters, and I made an exception. Here's a sampling of the responses (there were multiple responses to this question):

I know it's wrong, but I have to do it (person feels powerless)

"It's not in my job description, but I have to do it to keep my job."	21.2%
"This is expected in the world of work."	12.2%
"It's in my job description, I have to do it to keep my job."	8.1%
"It was a direct order."	2.2%
"It was beyond my control/ there were no options."	1.2%
"It was part of my job."	0.6%
"I fear reprisals from supervisor/ want to keep supervisor happy."	0.4%
"I'll do what I have to until I can get out of this situation."	0.3%
"I did it because of pressure to get the job done."	0.3%
"The customer expects it."	0.3%

I don't think it matters (minimizes issues or consequences)

"Everyone else does it."	8.4%
"No one is getting hurt, so why not?"	5.9%
"No one cares, so why not?"	3.0%
"I don't agree with it, but I'll do it."	1.1%
"It was the best choice at the time."	0.7%
"I'll make up for it in other ways."	0.4%
"It didn't seem wrong at the time/ I can live with it."	0.3%

Naturally, our hindsight is 20/20. Can we learn from life's negative experiences so we can avoid repeating them? I like to think so. I believe the lessons we have learned from our experiences are permanently remembered by our consciences, and we can improve our decision-making IF we can access those lessons.

The trouble is, we often refuse to examine our experiences and apply the lessons we've learned because the memories are blocked by guilt, shame, mental images that shatter our self-esteem, or similar negative associations. Don't we judge ourselves severely when we repeat an error in judgment, saying something to ourselves like, "I thought I'd already learned that lesson!" or "I learned that lesson before!"? As long as we don't think about it, the memory of the experience doesn't hurt us. Then, wham — another situation comes along and we make the same mistake again.

We make the same mistakes again if we dwell on the experience, too. Sometimes we feel so bad we can't put the experience behind us and it becomes a part of our everyday, conscious approach to coping. When this happens, we are preprogramming ourselves with exactly the wrong lesson, so repeating the mistake becomes a self-defeating behavior pattern.

Needlessly "beating ourselves up" with regret and remorse doesn't help. I'll never forget the administrative assistant who caught my skirt as I left a seminar in Pennsylvania. She said she had never told anyone her story, but wanted to tell me (I hear this often). Fortunately, my taxi to the airport was late, so we had time to sit and talk in the hotel lobby.

She prefaced her dilemma by saying she was one year away from retiring with good benefits, so quitting her job was not an option. It seems her boss went on a vacation to Hawaii the previous year and, unfortunately, suffered a heart attack while he was there. Fearful for his health, he called her from his hospital room in Hawaii, told her the location of a key to a locked file drawer, and instructed her to take a particular file home and burn it. Because she was respectful of his precarious health condition, and out of a sense of duty that comes with many years of service, she did as she was told. She said she drove into her garage, leaned over to pick up the file, and all the contents spilled out onto the front seat (it was not sealed). It was filled with pornographic photos of her boss and other adults. She was shocked, but nevertheless took them into her house and burned them in the fireplace.

Luckily, her boss recovered and returned to the office. Her very next paycheck reflected a $200-per-month raise! They never spoke of the envelope or the raise.

She was extremely upset with herself. "Nan, did I do the right thing?" What a loaded question! What would you say? I told her she must take comfort from the fact that she made the best decision she could at the time, and consequently that was the right thing to do. In fact, she had done nothing wrong — he is the one with the problem. I said, "Aren't you really asking me how — or if — you should continue to work for this man?" Bingo — she broke down, right there in the hotel lobby, and she was inconsolable for a few minutes. Imagine the burden she had been carrying for most of the past year — and could she continue to carry it until she retired?

I advised her to go to the human resource director and request a transfer to another position for the remainder of her time with the company.   If she needed to explain her request, perhaps she could refer her request to her boss. Also, I suggested she talk with a professional counselor or psychologist. She clearly needed to get on with her life and put this unfortunate incident behind her. She assured me she would take both steps, which she did. She called me a few weeks later and reported that she got the transfer and was "moving on." The lesson: Sadly, this woman should have asked for help within the resources of her organization much sooner. Carrying around the misplaced guilt and shame and confusion about her feelings for her boss was a heavy burden indeed.

The Personal Ethics Audit™

I have found a very good early warning system for situations that pose potential ethical dilemmas. I call it the Personal Ethics Audit™. It comes out of discussions with many office professionals who use a single question against which they measure their conduct. You probably have used this technique yourself in one form or another, too. For example, three of the more popular questions people ask themselves are:

> "Would you want to be treated in this same way?"
> *(Use your own version of the Golden Rule: Do unto others as you would have them do unto you.)*

> "What would my mother (or father, or spouse, or kids, or clergy person) say about this?"
> *(This question really asks, "Does this action or decision conform with the core values with which I was raised?")*

> "How would I feel if this was reported on the front page of tomorrow's newspaper?"
> *(Presuming the media will tell just the fair, unvarnished facts, without your self-serving explanations, this challenges you to imagine how society will judge you by the community's standards. This is sometimes called the "publicity test.")*

If you use one of these questions, or another single question like this, as a litmus test for your decisions, and it works for you, keep using it! I found that one question wasn't enough for me. Maybe my life is too complicated or I can't explain my choices very well. Maybe I just don't like giving the power to judge myself to someone else, no matter how much I love and respect him or her. (I certainly don't trust the media to arbitrate society's judgment of anything I do! Too often the press is just a modern-day pillory to whip up public scorn, never mind the facts. Incidentally, I live with an ex-politician, so I'm sure that affects my personal perspective!)

The Personal Ethics Audit helps me make better judgments BEFORE I get myself into trouble. It causes me to step back from the everyday situations in which I get immersed and ask myself a few tough questions about the general nature and direction of my actions and decisions.

The process of asking myself these questions helps me access the lessons I've learned from my life experiences in a way that is constructive and proactive. I suggest you try it, or try your own modified version of it the next time you find yourself in a situation that may be developing into an ethical dilemma.

Ethical Office Discussion #2
~~~ Nan DeMars's Personal Ethics Audit™ ~~~

Use this discussion guide to help you make better choices about specific situations and/or the general direction of your career. Each "yes" answer is a warning sign of a potential ethical dilemma.

Yes No Am I doing anything to someone else
          I would not want them to do to me?

Yes No Am I doing anything illegal?

Yes No Am I doing anything I would NOT want to tell the
          media?

Yes No Am I doing anything I would not want my children
          to see? My mother-in-law? My spouse?

Yes No Am I distracted and/or disorganized?

Yes No Am I depressed?

Yes No Am I disoriented?

Yes No Am I angry?

Yes No Am I feeling guilty?

Yes No Do I feel self-destructive?

Yes No Do I feel powerless?

Yes No Have I received any feedback that suggests I may be
          rationalizing too much, or perhaps overly defensive?

© 1997 Nan DeMars, CPS

Thinking about the questions

Am I doing anything to someone else I would not want them to do to me? This, of course, is the Golden Rule. Imagine yourself in the position of those who work with you. What does it feel like?

Am I doing anything illegal? This isn't as easy to know as it once was. Business is complicated these days. You may think that a comment is harmless, a conversation is innocent, and a few copies of letters or price lists are just professional courtesies, but you can't be sure. Whenever I am unsure about the legality of something, I find a way to politely stop until I have a chat with my attorney and/or the corporate legal department (NOT my boss's attorney).

Am I doing anything I would NOT want to tell the media? As I said before, the court of public opinion is biased toward circulation and viewership, not accuracy or justice. Knowing this, do any of your actions create the appearance of wrongdoing? If you answer yes, you may be holding a problem with a burning fuse.

Am I doing anything I would not want my children to see? My mother-in-law? My spouse? This is a great question because it quickly flushes out any shame or embarrassment you may be denying. If you're completely okay with everything you're doing, you'll have no trouble explaining it to those you love and those who know you best.

Am I distracted and/ or disorganized? When a person is not paying attention to her daily routines, and when she's not taking care of her daily chores, it's almost always a sign that she's struggling subconsciously with something that is unresolved. When I forget to pay the bills on time, or misplace more things than usual, I ask myself, "What a minute — what's going on here? What is it that's stealing my attention?"

Am I depressed? Depression is a chronic condition characterized by long-term dysfunction or misfunction. It is a signal that a person is failing to adapt to a situation. Perhaps I am "going along with" something I suspect is wrong, or I am avoiding a nasty confrontation that I sense is inevitable. I know I am on this path when I realize I am lacking my normal energy and feelings. When I disconnect myself from my feelings, I know I am trying to protect myself from something. In the process of trying to talk myself out of my blue funk, I ask myself, "What am I avoiding?"

Am I disoriented? The verb to orient means to set a map in agreement with the points of the compass. Our orientation as functioning people depends on us taking our bearings, or points of reference, from familiar people, places, things, and contexts of time. When we know and trust our bearings, we are confident in our ability to assess situations and act appropriately.

To be disoriented is to be lost. Momentary disorientation is normal every time something unexpected is encountered, and the unexpected is certainly a fact of life in our occupation! When we are disoriented, we instinctively look outward for a familiar relationship, routine, or other point of reference, and mentally readjust ourselves.

This mental readjustment happens so quickly that we are usually not conscious of it unless we cannot do it.

You may feel disoriented if you feel you can no longer trust your familiar reference points. Perhaps your supervisor has done something you didn't expect, or asked you to do something questionable, and this has been a big disappointment. Perhaps a co-worker has let you down, or the corporate political landscape is different from what you thought it was.

Disorientation can impair your thinking process. It can make you vulnerable to even more ethical conflict. Imagine that you've been suddenly given a new assignment that has you working with a new group of people. While you're groping for new reference points, you naturally will be hastily updating your corporate rule book. As the new person in the department, you'll be easy to lead into the forest of ethical confusion. If you feel disoriented, or know that you are working in a new environment, be on the lookout for ethical problems headed your way.

Am I angry? Anger is an emotion linked to self-preservation. It may be triggered by feelings of confusion, abuse, violation, being taken for granted, defensiveness, frustration, or similar negative emotions. Pay attention to your anger; it is a clue that you are trying to respond to something that may threaten you. Again, your most constructive response is to think about what is going on in your life or job, and try to identify the source of your anger so you can deal with it.

Am I feeling guilty? This is an obvious symptom of a conflict between your conduct and your values. Can any of us deny how we really feel for very long? I am surprised how many times I've heard sensible women and men say, "I felt guilty about doing it, but I did it anyway." Guilt is never free, and the burden can wear you down. You probably know why you are feeling guilty—is the reason good enough to drag around the extra baggage?

Do I feel self-destructive? You don't have to be suicidal to be self-destructive. If you are, or if you sense you are about to be, stuck in an ethical dilemma, you may find yourself thinking things like:

"I don't care anymore."
"It doesn't matter."
"I just wish this situation would be over."
"It figures—I deserve to fail."

If you feel this way, you will find ways to sabotage yourself in order to punish yourself. Your defeatism will become a self-fulfilling prophesy.

If you think badly of yourself often enough, you will soon believe it and program yourself for career failure.

This feeling of self-destructiveness displays itself in other ways, too, such as not taking proper care of yourself. Dramatic changes in your eating habits, an inability or unwillingness to get enough sleep, a growing dependence on alcohol or sleep medication, and withdrawing from your social life all indicate something is terribly wrong. Instinctively, you know that if you allow your normal life to drift into disarray, whatever problem you're struggling with will be made smaller in comparison to your new problems of no friends, no food in the house, poor health, etc. I suggest there are more constructive ways of dealing with these kinds of problems.

Do I feel powerless? A sense of powerlessness comes with ethical problems. How do you choose between two "right" things to do, such as loyalty to your manager versus loyalty to your company? How do you select the lesser of two evils, such as suffering a certain reprimand or risking a cover-up of a misdeed? The nature of ethical conflict almost always dictates that there is no way to resolve them without hurting someone. Think about trouble you have been in, or been a witness to: Someone steps over the bounds of what is appropriate or legal, and he or she cannot get back without facing the consequences. It's natural to feel trapped between equally unpleasant choices.

Have I received any feedback that suggests I may be rationalizing too much, or perhaps overly defensive? Like your family, your co-workers know you pretty well. If they are questioning your actions, hinting you need to reflect more often, or becoming short-tempered with your antics — well, perhaps they are trying to tell you something you need to listen to.

> *"I know there must have been*
> *a good reason why*
> *he asked me to do this,*
> *and I did as I was told."*

—Fawn Hall, former secretary to Lt. Colonel Oliver North,
testifying before Congress in 1988 about
why she altered, concealed, and destroyed
National Security Council files
related to the Iran-Contra affair.

4

Mythbusting

Think about it: *Rachel is a single mom, taking care of her three chil-dren and her elderly father. She has no insurance because her em-ployer cannot afford to provide it. The medical bills threaten to bury her in debt. She is stressed and depressed, which make her feel guilty because she is short-tempered and poor company during the precious few hours she has with her family.*

On the way home one day, she stops at the drugstore for some more medication. She suspects the check she is about to write will bounce, which will cause the bank to close her account, but she doesn't know what else to do.

On her way into the drugstore, she sees a fur-clad woman emerge from a Cadillac and hurry off in another direction. Rachel notices that the woman drops her leather purse, and she instinctively scoops it up. She is amazed that it contains a number of hundred dollar bills. Rachel has only an instant to decide whether to chase after the woman or slip the wallet into her own purse. What would you do?

Up until now, we have been talking about office ethics in the abstract: Here is what they are, this is the role they play, here is how to recognize an ethical dilemma, and so on. In the following chapters, we're going to be focusing on practical strategies that you can use to improve the ethical climate in your office.

Before we do, I want to use this chapter to dispense with some common beliefs about ethics that I have found to be untrue. We will be better at spotting potential ethical dilemmas and then coming up with good resolutions to those dilemmas if we set aside some of our naiveté about ethics in organizations.

Frankly, if we are going to improve the ethics in our respective offices, we must learn to see things as they really are, not as we want them to be. Most of us tend to be optimistic, even idealistic, when it comes to ethics. We tend to give the other guy or gal the benefit of the doubt, for example, and take things at face value. As professional support people, we instinctively try to help others do their jobs, trusting that they share our "all for one, one for all" attitude.

Well, it's time for a reality check, folks. Not everyone is as nice as you are. Remember: You, your boss, and your co-workers *can* learn to make better ethical decisions *if* you question and discuss specific dilemmas you care about. Growing from Stage 3 to Stage 4 (see Chapter 2), for example, is possible as long as there are plenty of opportunities for discussions about the tough questions. Who's going to ask those questions? Probably you, right? If you're going to be an effective challenger to the status quo ethics in your office, you're going to have to get used to asking the tough questions.

Let's take the next step toward the more ethical office by setting aside a few of the most common myths I keep hearing over and over from otherwise reasonable office professionals.

Myth #1: "I can trust my boss to always be fair."

Wrong. Your supervisor is a human being, capable of mistakes in judgment. His or her managerial skills may be an exceptional match to your personality and needs, or they may not be. Or, perhaps your supervisor has some personal problems that affect his or her judgment at times. This person has a lot of power over you, so make sure you have a realistic understanding of him or her. You can predict that there will be times when you have to talk through some thorny ethical decisions, so you will need to cultivate an open, free-flowing communication style with him or her.

Myth #2: "I can trust my company to always be fair."

Wrong again. "The Company" is neutral about your sense of right and wrong; it doesn't have feelings, a sense of justice, a memory, or a conscience. However, the decision-makers who direct the company and speak for the company try to be fair, I think, if for no other reason than it's just a good business practice to stay out of court and stay out of the media's limelight. So who are the people running your organization? What are their names, and where are their offices? How "connected" do you feel to senior management? If you are struggling with an ethical dilemma, and it's affecting the performance of your office in your corner of the company, who among the company leaders is going to care? Brace yourself for some rough-and-tumble discussions if you choose to challenge the prevailing corporate culture. The Company isn't a faceless, nameless entity that runs itself; it's an association of real people who generally make the best ethical decisions they can — and they are no more and no less fair than anyone else might be. So you're going to have to be prepared to take some chances. When the tough decisions have to be made about minimizing legal settlements, trimming the payroll, protecting their star performers, and optimizing profits, normal business people will be making the decisions.

Myth #3: "I have to do what I'm told to keep my job."

I have heard this a lot. The script goes something like this:

Supervisor: "I want you to do this thing, and do it like this."
Secretary: "I disagree" or "I have a better idea" or "I object to doing this thing."
Supervisor: "Look, I'm the boss. Do what I say, or I'll replace you with someone who will. I don't care if you choose to stay or go — but if you stay, you'll work by my rules."

The coercion isn't always that blunt, but many of us have gotten the same message, loud and clear. Again, this is reality! Unless you have a signed employment contract with your company (which most of us do not), you can be fired "at will." Here's what I think about this: The supervisor has more power than you do, but that doesn't mean you don't have any power. Assert yourself and push back as much as you dare when he pushes you. Speak up with your best ideas and alternative approaches. Depending on what you are being asked to do, there may be others in the organization who would be interested in hearing about this guy's pressure tactics. Look for a middle ground. Talk it through — get that long-overdue dialogue about office ethics started.

Of course, if your supervisor's a real jerk, and there's no room for discussion, you may have to leave, and sooner is better than later. Some supervisors *should* be committed to institutions for the managerially impaired, and there's nothing else for you to do but to take care of yourself. Sooner or later, these guys with revolving personnel doors pay a huge price for having chronically "new" people on the office support team.

However, there is nothing that pulls my chain more than when I hear an assistant say he or she left a firm due to the unethical behavior of the supervisor! In other words, that assistant has to leave a good job — with good benefits, salary, friends, reputation, etc., and start over just because some turkey did not know how to manage. I would rather see you work out the problem and come to a more fair resolution to your dilemmas. So, keep reading!

Myth #4: "I really made a big mistake. I'm a bad person."

No, you are a good person who made a bad choice. You may believe that lapses in ethical judgment are terminal, but I prefer a more forgiving view. *See Chapter 18: Misdeeds and second chances.*

Myth #5: "What others do is none of my concern."

Yes, it is! Leaking confidential salary information, abuse of privileges, playing games with the time clock — you'll read more about these in the chapters coming up. Suffice it to say right now that no office professional can be successful with an isolationist, blinders-on, Lone-Ranger, I'll-just-do-my-job attitude.

Myth #6: "I'm the only one who sees what's going on, and I'm the only one who cares."

This is doubtful. Ethical dilemmas cost the company in lost productivity, public relations points, and hard-earned profits. Someone else cares. Can you find out who that someone else is, make your case, make a change, and still end up with your job? We'll use the rest of this book trying to help you make that happen.

Myth #7: "An action is either right or wrong. There is no middle ground."

See Chapter 2: "It depends!" A primer on ethical dilemmas.

Myth #8: "It's not my job to police my boss."

Yes, it is. He or she needs you to help maintain the ethical standards that work for your office. It's very much your job to keep your boss from getting careless and taking shortcuts. Most executives I've worked with appreciate and value the tactful reminders and reinforcements they receive from their support staff.

Myth #9: "I can't change this place."

Yes, you can. Keep reading!

Myth #10: A person cannot be talked into greater moral courage.

This is not true. Effective ethics programs have demonstrated that the development of a person's moral judgment is ongoing and continuous. This development is stimulated by examination and discussion of relevant ethical dilemmas. The best way to conduct this examination is through a process of asking supportive and challenging questions. Ethics training that has been found to be most effective (effective being the graduation from one level to another) is when it asks questions that help people think through situations. Lecturing, sermonizing, telling, or reading about moral dilemmas have little impact. Likewise, shaming someone at the point their hand is in the cookie jar, so to speak, yields little. It is when people actually discuss relevant moral dilemmas that they care about with people they care about—that's when change occurs. That's why I'll offer numerous suggestions throughout this book for you to do precisely that: Discuss your concerns with those with whom you work.

Be advised, however: You may take some satisfaction in getting your boss or co-workers to move in the right direction, but you may be disappointed in how fast they change. It is true that people cannot be talked into doing anything before they are ready. The good news is, the support and encouragement of a trusted friend at just the right time—say, just before he or she makes an ethical decision requiring unusual courage—may be all they need to "do the right thing." Most changes are modest and evolutionary, not revolutionary.

Myth #11: You are born with your morality—you believe what you believe, and you will cling to it throughout your life.

Wrong again. People grow up. They mature because of their experiences and opportunity to reflect and examine their decisions.

At one seminar, a woman stood up and told us of the company officer she worked for who had "one wife and three mistresses." She said she "kept them all straight"—no one ever learned about the others — and, in the process, she never had a better job, better salary, better bonuses, or better raises than she did in that position. Then I asked her — because I *had* to know — was it all worth that extra effort, and would she do it again? She didn't hesitate for a second: "No way!" she said. Thankfully, we can learn and make better choices next time.

Myth #12: Women have a more developed sense of ethics; they are more moral and more principled.

Wrong. Researcher Carol Gilligan charged Kohlberg's 6-stage model as sex-biased in her controversial 1982 book, *In a Different Voice*. Subsequent research has not supported her criticism. The most frequent finding is that there is a universal sequence of the stages of moral development for both sexes.

Myth #13: People just naturally "do the right thing" when presented with a moral dilemma.

What's the "right thing"? Moral growth has been found to be, in the words of the researchers, an invariant sequence. That means that people mature in their moral judgments in a predictable sequence, with no reversals. The best way I've found to explain the differences between a child's self-centered ethics and the altruism of a Gandhi, Mother Theresa, Joan of Arc, Eleanor Roosevelt, Martin Luther King, Jr., Abraham Lincoln, Thoreau, or Socrates is Lawrence Kohlberg's Stages of Moral growth. *See Chapter 2 for this discussion.*

 Texas Instruments shared their interesting view on this with me. TI has been an award-winning, international leader in the movement for corporate ethics programs, and TI's corporate Code of Ethics has been a model for countless companies for the past 35 years. To his credit, Glen Coleman, manager of TI ethics communication and education, has not rested on the fact that his organization is more ethically mature and sophisticated in relation to other companies; he is continually pushing himself to look at new ideas and new approaches so his organization can be ready to respond to new types of ethical dilemmas. Some of these challenges, he says, are coming from new lifestyle pressures on the employees; others are prompted by the rapidly changing technology in his industry.

 Coleman sees three types of people:

Type 1 — Ethical people who strive to always "do the right thing." The world would be a better place if it was made up of only these people, wouldn't it? The problem is, Coleman says, ethical dilemmas aren't always just black and white. What would this person do when confronted with two, equally compelling, "rights"? For example, would this person tell the truth when asked for his or her opinion about a friend's dress, no matter what? "If you can't say something nice, then don't say anything," is the common advice this person follows, but this is more easily said than done.

What about stealing food to feed a starving family? Or stealing medicine for a sick child? What about Rachel's problem at the beginning of this chapter? This is dangerously close to "the end justifying the means," which is a slippery slope of logic.

Would you violate a personal commitment to keep information strictly confidential if you discovered revealing it might prevent a violent act? Suppose revealing it could harm your personal credibility so much that you could no longer do your job effectively?

Even under the best of circumstances, an ethical person can be confronted by two rights that are in conflict. Can you always choose the "higher" principle to follow? This is not always easy — and it's difficult to know if you've made the right choice.

Type 2 — Unethical people who are willing to intentionally do the wrong thing because it serves their interests, sometimes at the expense of others and the risk of their reputation.

Type 3 — Non-ethical people who may not ever think about the ethical implications of a decision or action. For this person, the ethical dimensions are never even considered. These people may be completely unfamiliar with an environment that builds personal character and/or challenges principles and values.

Myth #14: Good employees don't do bad things. People act unethically because they are selfish, stupid, bad, or all of the above.

It's not that simple. From the ethics hotline at Texas Instruments come these most popular reasons for unethical performance:

a) *Pressure* —
  ■ to meet schedules, deadlines, milestones, and shipping dates

- to meet overly aggressive financial forecasts
- as a response to peer pressure
- to create billings
- to accomplish tasks within time and money constraints
- to complete a task faster than it is possible
- to accomplish perceived unrealistic goals
- to alter data to make the program (and hence the boss) look good
- to meet perceived expectations of superiors

b) *Retaliation* — to get back at the company for perceived reductions in benefits, etc.
c) *Inattention* — when moving too fast to get things done correctly, ethics suffer
d) *Ambition* — personal gain
e) *Doing it for the Company* — a misplaced sense that anything is OK as long as the company gets ahead
f) *This is What's Rewarded* — this is the "go along to get along" justification
g) *Path of Least Resistance* — "if you don't confront, you don't suffer"
h) *Office Politics* — turf issues, image issues, MUST win attitude

When people were asked how they justify committing unethical acts, the most common explanations were:

"No one will notice." (This seems to reflect Kohlberg's selfish Stage 2)
"Nobody cares." (Stage 3)
"It's only a _____. The company can afford it." (Stage 2)
"As hard as I work, the company owes it to me." (Stage 2)
"Everybody does it. I deserve it, too." (Stage 2)
"He did it. Why shouldn't I?" (Stage 2)
"I did it for the good of the company." (Stage 4)
"I didn't know it was wrong." (Stage 2 or 3)

Myth #15: Ethical management means ethical organizations.

Codes of conduct don't guarantee ethical behavior, either. The lower a person's rank in an organization, the more likely he or she will encounter ethical dilemmas and hold negative views about ethics.

This is partly a function of the person's lack of power, and partly due to a lack of ethics training. Office professionals do not receive ethics training, yet they must interact every day with customers, suppliers, and other employees who are well motivated to promote unethical conduct.

What myths do you have about ethics, morals, and "doing the right thing"? I encourage everyone to begin having discussions among their co-workers about real or hypothetical ethical dilemmas, because an unexamined ethical framework is fragile and brittle. The more you rehearse what you would do in specific situations, the better prepared you will be.

> *"Promises may get friends,*
> *but it is performance*
> *that must nurse and keep them."*
>
> —Owen Feltham in "Resolves"

5

Bring your own coal

(and other trends)

Think about it: *You are a secretary to Ms. Nordby, an attorney. An elderly client comes into your office to develop his will. He is accompanied by several members of his family. While they are waiting to see your boss, you overhear their conversations and conclude that the family members are exerting too much influence on him. You even suspect they may be coercing him to change his will to their advantage. After they have met with Ms. Nordby, she calls you into her office and asks you to witness the signing of the gentleman's will. Because you feel something unfair or inappropriate is occurring, you wish to decline. Do you have the right to do so? Can you, practically speaking? What, if anything, should you say to your boss?*

I am always asking former secretaries who have moved on to other positions within their companies, "What do you miss most about the secretarial profession?" They almost always reply, "I miss the action!"

This is why office professionals are among those in your company who encounter ethical dilemmas most frequently — because we ARE where the action is. We often see, hear, and get involved in many activities that other professionals do not. Our assignments often have us crossing the boundaries between specialists, departments, and functions, so we usually have a pretty good idea what's going on. We are part periscope, part listening post, part clearinghouse, and part switchboard. Because of our unique role, some legal scholars are predicting that we will even need our own professional liability insurance in the near future!

Until recently, we used to be among the "silent professions." The silent professions are comprised of the employees in every organization that are seemingly so much a part of the background (and so low on the hierarchy of importance) that they are virtually invisible.

A wait person in a restaurant is an example: You're sitting in a restaurant with your best friend discussing something most personal and confidential. The wait person serves you more coffee, and what do you do? That's right — you keep on talking! Or, you are having a confidential business meeting in a hotel meeting room and a hotel employee enters the room to change the light bulb or linen. What happens? Everyone keeps on talking as though that person was not even in the room. Ask these people about the conversations they overhear on the job; I think you'll be surprised.

The same thing used to happen in the office — stenographers, secretaries, clerks, and many other office professionals were regarded as "silent" and "invisible" — essentially, they were "non-persons."

A limousine driver in New Jersey was the first one to make this point to me about the "silent professions," and his observation made me start "seeing" staff people differently. This particular driver said I would be shocked at the conversations that take place in his back seat as if he didn't exist. He said officers from international conglomerates leave board meetings and travel together to the airport, continuing to talk about the most confidential subjects. He said he has actually been embarrassed for them! He said, "If I wanted to, I could sell all kinds of trade secrets."

What happens at your company when you walk into a meeting in progress? Do people stop talking until your role is explained? I hope so. To me, this is a positive sign. It is an indication of the increased respect and appreciation others have of the professional assistant's role today. You are "in the know" — and other people know it!

It wasn't always this way. If you were an office worker a hundred years ago, you probably would have had to bring your own coal to keep the office warm. You would have had to also endure low pay, low status, and low-brow humor about your gender and physical appearance. You would be expected to dress like you were going to church.

Your boss would have been a man. Your duties would have included meaningless busywork, making coffee and copies (by hand, of course), and gossip control. Your primary function would be to keep your boss organized, protect him from his own foolishness, and keep him out of trouble with customers and others.

You might have even been a man. It's true — male secretaries used to be quite popular, especially in some industries. The railroad industry is a good example. Years ago, secretaries for the railroad often traveled with their bosses on the rails; and (heaven forbid) you can't have a female secretary traveling with a male boss (and they were all male bosses in those days). Consequently, male secretaries were hired and — surprise, surprise — they paid the males more money because they were the breadwinners raising families.

How far have we come as professionals? You be the judge. In 1954, World Publishing issued this advice in a secretarial service manual:

> *"Perhaps because they are comparative newcomers in the business world, women frequently have more difficulty in their personal relations with employer and office associates than men do. On them is the burden of proof that they are really interested in their jobs and not primarily in finding social companions or husbands; that they can be trusted with responsibility and can keep to themselves information not for general distribution. They must prove that they can work congenially and efficiently with superiors, but at the same time be respectful, reserved, and matter-of-fact. Likewise, they must be able to work smoothly with other employees, but have the ability to claim their respect, good will, and cooperation when necessary.*
>
> *"And, very important, they must prove that they can free their minds of all social or domestic matters and give their work all the attention it requires."*

New pressures, broader roles have led to new titles

I've seen a lot of wonderfully positive changes in the office support profession since the women's movement kicked into high gear in the 1970s (I'm still proud to call myself a feminist). Back then, secretary was one of the three obvious occupations for women (the other two were teacher and nurse). I'm proud to say that many of our sisters who were the most progressive in their attitudes about equal opportunity for women could be counted among the ranks of these three occupations.

Ironically, secretaries, nurses, and teachers became symbolic of what was wrong with opportunity for women. One of the mantras of the women's movement became, "You don't want to be *just* a secretary, do you? Why not be the boss?" For purposes of opening up more employment opportunities, it became convenient to reduce and simplify our profession to a few negative characteristics like subordination and service to others (usually to managers who happened to be male), low levels of responsibility (the stereotypes of Girl Friday à la Robinson Caruso's native helper, Friday — who, incidentally, saved Robinson's biased behind more than once!), and jobs that had to be "dummied down" for intellectually impaired females (blonde bimbos, coffee-and-copier girls).

This was troublesome for me and a lot of other progressive women. We happened to *love* our jobs as office support professionals, and regarded our participation in the work force as pretty potent evidence of the coming revolution.

I eventually had the opportunity to voice my frustration over this simplistic and unfair "blight" on our profession. The time was 1980, shortly after I became an officer of Professional Secretaries International; the place was New York City at the office of *MS.* magazine editor Gloria Steinem, one of the founding mothers of the feminism movement. I still remember how my knees shook in the elevator on the way up to her office. I wanted to tell her I (and many other "just secretaries") supported all she was doing, but the women's movement was inadvertently *trouncing* our profession and our career choices. We felt like second-class citizens, or worse.

Gloria was and is very wise about the process of social change. She said she understood my concern and agreed that secretaries were being reduced to a cartoon-like symbol. "But, Nan," she said, "the process follows the path of the pendulum. Women are way over here on one side right now and it is totally unbalanced — they have almost no career opportunities open to them. We have to make some radical moves — like burning the bras — to make a clear statement and push the world over to the other side. In the process, some predominantly female professions like secretaries, nurses, and teachers will catch the flak for awhile. But, you watch. We *will* be successful; and, in the future, more and more opportunities will be open to women. Consequently these traditionally female professions will be narrowed to the true professionals and, as a result, they will be even more respected and their salaries will rise accordingly."

You know — Gloria was right! Fifteen years later, I see a completely different landscape in my search and recruitment business. The qualified office professional is a significant and valued contributor, recognized and compensated for his or her specialized education and training.

How many of us remember those days when every one of us felt like a pioneer? I remember two skirmishes over TV ads that blatantly patronized the secretarial profession. The first ad was from a copier manufacturer that used the copy line, "This copier runs so easily that not even your secretary can screw it up!"

Another ad, this one from a well-known floral marketer, ran during Professional Secretaries' Week®, which is in April every year. The ad showed a woman stepping into an elevator with a bouquet of flowers. Another woman in the elevator asks her where the flowers came from, and she smugly replies, "It's Secretaries' Day and my boss gave them to me." At this point, the poor second woman burst into tears, suggesting her boss did not recognize or appreciate her.

Pretty sick, huh? (The gesture with the flowers was so patronizing I hurt when I saw it.) These were both big-production ads by the best (obviously male) brains of big-name ad agencies. I'll spare the companies the embarrassment of naming them because their good sense prevailed in the end. Here's what happened: Professional Secretaries International geared up to oppose these demeaning ads via an aggressive letter-writing campaign of protest to the advertisers. When blistering letters started arriving from all over the U.S. and Canada demanding a more respectful portrayal — and threatening a boycott of the products — the companies got religion in a hurry. Within days, the ads were pulled and shelved forever, I hope, in the large, large Blooper Warehouse at the end of Madison Avenue. Kudos to PSI and all of you who were members at the time for these two successful campaigns!

We have not been well served by the rest of the media, either — although this is probably a complaint that all women can echo. Carol Burnett's "Mrs. H'Wiggins" and Miss Buxley in Beetle Bailey are classical caricatures of the "intellectually challenged" assistant. I enjoy a good laugh at myself, too — but, where are the serious portrayals that make these so funny? I got excited when I saw the Roxanne character on "L.A. Law" a few years ago because she appeared to be an up-to-date assistant. But I guess I goofed — when I mentioned her in a seminar as a good TV role model, the class jumped all over me, objecting to the fact that she slept with her boss! I think the only Hollywood product that ever came close to showing us the way we see ourselves was Della Street, Perry Mason's secretary, who actually was expected to think and got credit for it besides.

Interestingly, when the term secretary became symbolic — and began carrying the negative baggage attached to it — many companies felt compelled to distance themselves from it. This resulted in many new and creative titles like executive assistant, administrative assistant, coordinator, specialist, office assistant, etc. One human resources director told me his company was trying hard to completely eliminate the "S" (secretary) word! This attitude actually has been a plus for our profession, too, because it has caused many people and organizations to rethink our job descriptions, our roles, and our true contributions. Nowadays, when someone is called a secretary, it really means something. The title of secretary is not at all a casual description anymore for "the girl out front" — instead, it is a professional job title backed up with a professional job description. Your pendulum is still swinging, Gloria!

(I continue to welcome men into this predominantly female profession. Why? Because salaries go up, and we can all benefit from that. Is this fair? No, but it's reality. In 1993, the median annual earnings for a full-time woman employee in the U.S. was only 71.5 percent of the median earnings of a full-time male employee.)

Incidentally, it was during this time that I coined the word "executary." I think it captures the spirit of professionalism we should always aspire to, and so that's what I named my company.

Another bit of historical trivia: Did you know that "type-writer" was first used to describe the person, not the machine? "Copier" was likewise used until 1956 when Xerox introduced the first machine.

To say it simply, our jobs — no matter our job title — have "grown up" and, in the process, they have become more complicated. We are now involved in aspects of the organization in ways that our mothers and grandmothers never dreamed. We have assumed broader responsibilities and expanded roles. What we do, or don't do, can make a significant difference in the effectiveness and profitability of our company. We have raised our expectations and, along the way, adopted informal rules of conduct. In short, while we have always felt we deserved to be treated as true professionals, now we are being recognized by everyone else as professionals, too.

For the record, a professional secretary, according to Professional Secretaries International, is:

> *An executive assistant who possesses a mastery*
> *of office skills, demonstrates the ability to assume*
> *responsibility without direct supervision, exercises*
> *initiative and judgment, and makes decisions*
> *within the scope of assigned authority.*

Take note: Professional secretaries assume responsibility... exercise initiative and judgment...make decisions. These are important, permanent enhancements to what we do and how we do it. Our fundamental support function may be unchanged, but we are now valued as key contributors to the successful organization. We expect more of our careers, and more is expected of us.

But these are complicated jobs we have. They are getting more difficult to perform well because business is becoming more sophisticated and faster-paced. There is little time to deliberate about what is right and wrong. Just getting the job done is a big challenge! We have to start thinking and communicating clearly about our ethics if we are to avoid being victimized as innocents on the way up the corporate ladder.

So — are office professionals today dealing with more ethical problems than their predecessors? And are they more complicated problems than ever before?

Yes, there are more ethical problems today than in the past, and yes, these dilemmas are more complicated. This is because our expanded roles and new technology have us doing more different types of work with many more people. But what is radically different today is how we are responding to these problems. We are true professionals, fully accountable for our choices and actions.

We have new ethical dilemmas, too

I count many potential ethical dilemmas in our new, expanded roles. I call these "morally hazardous situations" because they put our morals at risk. These situations, and many other potential dilemmas, are unique to our jobs in the company.

For example, we are expected to be loyal to our supervisors, but not blind in our allegiance. We are expected to earn their trust and support their efforts. Yet, what do we do when our feelings of loyalty to our boss conflict with the interests of other employees, customers, the company, and even the general public?

We encounter daily many other potentially compromising situations. Some of these are caused by our manager, some by others inside and outside the company, and some are caused by our own actions or inactions. How many of us have been:

- tempted by the vendor who wants "inside" information about pricing, schedules, names, inventories, etc.
- remorseful that we provided sexual favors involving physical contact in return for advancement, increased compensation, or preferential treatment (yes, it happens — more often than you think)
- confused by contradictory messages about employee confidentiality (i.e. employee assistance programs often promise to not tell anyone about an employee's marital, financial, health, or substance abuse problems, yet this information is often used to deny worker's compensation benefits)
- angered by apparent double standards (some workers get to consistently arrive late and leave early, while others must account for every minute and make up lost time)
- ashamed that we conspired to make someone else look bad
- upset when asked by a supervisor in another department for sensitive information that may compromise our boss
- remorseful that we shared confidential information about salaries, company secrets, layoffs, or hiring and firing
- uncomfortable with routine practices of lying on the phone to screen calls
- frustrated by a co-worker's incompetence or indifference, yet directed to ignore his or her poor performance

Do you recognize yourself or co-workers? Haven't we all worked in offices where these problems cropped up? We are on the ethical hotseat. It is an occupational fact of life.

Spend a few minutes with the next catalog mailed to your boss offering management development training. You're likely to see one or more courses on "Management Ethics in the Workplace" or something like it. Suddenly, managers have discovered ethical practices are good for business (and, coincidentally, an insurance policy against legal troubles). As noted trend-watcher Faith Popcorn observed, the 1990s are the time of the 3 E's: Education, Environment, and Ethics.

Well, I say it's about time. The fact is, office professionals have always been struggling with business ethics. We have been right in the middle of the ethical crossfire for a long time, and the situations are rapidly growing more serious.

It's only logical that we are in the thick of things. We know more about the office's filing system, so we are the ones asked to circumvent it. We know what the computer files are named because we wrote them. We answer the phones, so we tell the little lies that protect our bosses. We know the clients and vendors, so we become the gatekeeper to all sorts of information.

Most office professionals wouldn't have it any other way. We like being in the middle of the flow of information and people because it's just simply more interesting. Being in the middle of things also provides some job security — don't we all secretly suspect that our office would be thrown into confusion if we weren't there?

The good news is that we continue to gain more and more responsibility. Now we administrate — we manage — we supervise — we budget — we plan — we orchestrate. We've earned our additional job responsibilities by demonstrating that we are capable of handling them. We can do the work — and then some.

I call this the Rosie Promotion, after Rosie the Riveter, that famous feminist symbol of World War II. This was before my time, of course, but my mother (who was a secretary, by the way) told me that women had to step into all types of factory jobs when the men left to fight overseas. Many of these jobs required tough, dirty work — like hot-riveting steel — and consequently they redefined what women could accomplish in the workplace. Women didn't ask for these jobs, but found it within themselves to rise to the challenge and somehow they got the work done. By most accounts, the women did excellent work and kept the country running .

In the past decade, many of us received Rosie Promotions when our companies were "downsized" due to poor economic conditions. There have been bone-cutting layoffs of personnel, and middle managers took the hardest hit. But still, the duties of these middle managers had to be handled. Who did senior management ask to fill in and take up these responsibilities? The secretaries and assistants, of course. Just like Rosie the Riveter, we did the work because no one else was there to do it. Somehow, we kept the paper flowing, phones ringing, and the copier working. Once we demonstrated that we could do the work, the secret was out that we are highly capable professionals.

The "glass ceiling" still keeps us from some positions in some industries, but that's their loss. In most industries, and most companies, we have broad opportunities with meaningful career paths. Again, once allowed the opportunity to prove ourselves on a level playing field, we can be proud of the responsibilities we've earned.

Personally, I think these trends are moving us in the right directions. We are becoming colleagues within the office, all cooperatively focused on achieving the corporate objectives.

We must remain vigilant and continue to point out antiquated attitudes and policies when we find them, however unintentional or benign they seem. A case in point: I got into trouble once at Boise Cascade in Boise when I stated, from the podium, that some corporate policies purposefully or unintentionally demean us as professionals. I cited the example of the experienced secretary who had to "requalify" herself by taking a typing test when she moved to a new position. Well, one of the male executives in the back of the class (they always hover near the exits—they never want to take a high profile seat up in front of all those women!) challenged me. He said, "How do I know she can type if I don't give her a typing test?" So, I repeated my point: "An experienced, qualified secretary who has evidence that she's held responsible, professional positions should not have to go back to square one to prove herself on the keyboard just because she makes a move to advance herself."

This manager persisted: "But, until I give her a typing test, how do I know she can type?" So I asked him, "Excuse me, sir, are you an engineer?" Yes, he said, he was. I asked, "Were you handed a slide rule in your job interview? And have you been required to take out that slide rule and demonstrate you can use it again every time you interviewed for a promotion?" That brought the house down. The engineer responded with class—he saluted me. My point stands. You don't give a professional chemist a chemistry formula in the job interview and say, "Would you please mix this right now?" We have to get beyond these stone-age policies that don't acknowledge even our basic competencies.

A wonderful change was implemented at a GTE plant as a result of a discussion of this issue. At lunch during a two-day seminar, several of the attendees and their bosses were discussing changes in the secretarial profession. The secretary to the human resource director picked up the ball and ran with it. She said, "Do you know, George, I've been with GTE over 20 years. If I was to apply for a transfer, even just a lateral transfer within the company, I would have to take a typing test." He was astonished—he apparently was unaware of the policy. He wisely said, "That's utterly ridiculous. We have to change that policy." A couple of weeks later, the secretary wrote me to report the policy was eliminated. Core competencies like typing, and credit for demonstrated experience, should be recognized and "portable" to new positions for us, just as they are for other professionals. But, until you start talking about these out-of-date policies and put the underlying issues on the table, no one thinks to make the changes.

Incidentally, the best comment I heard about these entry-level typing tests came from Terri Steinhoff, CPS, a veteran of many managers. She said, "That time I took a typing test to get my first job was the last time in my life I had five minutes of uninterrupted typing."

Sometimes, however, the real world continues to lag behind. I am angry and sad when I think about the conditions some of us have had to put up with just to keep our jobs. I think some companies and certain managers should fess up to the culture of muddy ethics they have fostered in their offices. Let's see—what would those recruitment ads say if they told the truth? "Sexy babe who knows how to dress wanted for fun and games at work. Must smile a lot, organize manager's personal life, demonstrate saintly patience, and type 130 wpm, no errors. Flexible morals preferred."

Even Hollywood refuses to "get it," and I'm beginning to doubt that they ever will. I hear from PSI members in the entertainment industry that these creative producers are really very conservative and very chauvinistic when it comes to portraying new roles for women.

Do you remember the movie, *9 to 5*? That movie was released the year I was President of PSI. I loved the actresses, but hated the premise—but at least it gave me the chance to plant a few ideas in people's minds. When asked for my thoughts about the movie during media interviews that year, I always said, "Any secretary who is treated in such a disrespectful, demeaning way should just walk across the street and find another job!"

Then I received a call from a secretary at General Electric. It seems the movie had done some good for her. After a particularly frustrating experience, she angrily suggested her boss go see it. Shortly afterwards, he called her into his office and apologized profusely for his previous behavior. He said he went to the movie and "got the picture" of how often and casually bosses take advantage of their secretaries' time and plans, and he was guilty. This led to the conversation they should have had years before, and they both "lived happily ever after."

Still, I wonder how much good really comes from negative portrayals, albeit as an absurd spoof. Do most people see it that way? A decade later, Hollywood gave us *Working Girl*, set in a present-tense investment house. All the secretaries in this movie were stereotypes from the 1960s — short skirts, high heels, wild hairdos, stuffed animals on their desks, chronic gum popping, and ding-a-ling dialogue. In a not-at-all subtle contrast, the female executives were portrayed as consummate professionals. Duh! What were these producers thinking?

The Ethical Office is under construction

Bosses and office professionals need some more help in the ethics department, now more than ever. The age-old battle for mutual respect is still being fought, according to thousands of office professionals I talk to every year. My 1995 Office Ethics Survey reflected 55.5 percent of respondents experienced verbal harassment, 31.8 percent experienced sexual harassment, 54.2 percent experienced emotional harassment, and 7 percent even experienced physical harassment. Respondents reported even higher percentages when asked if they witnessed these types of harassment being inflicted on others.

This is pretty basic stuff to be worrying about at the turn of the century, isn't it? How can we ever make meaningful progress toward greater productivity if we can't work together like adults with mutual respect for each other? Bosses still abuse their secretaries too much, and ask them too often to do things they shouldn't. Office professionals still wage silent wars against their bosses and their companies when they feel forced to choose between their values and their security. Everyone still plays blame and shame games as a way to deflect criticism and protect their self-esteem.

In the real world, ethical dilemmas are up-close and personal, sometimes subtle, sometimes shocking, and usually prompted by someone who knows exactly how far he can go before you, the victim, run out of patience or money. Court action is a clumsy and complicated remedy, worthwhile only as a last resort for the most outrageous actions. Most of us will never file a lawsuit against our employer or potential employer. Most of us will have to muddle our way into and out of murky ethical situations, beyond the meaningful reach of the law.

The problem is, many office professionals say, that we are the ethical ones, while the manager—well, he or she is just *something else.* The not-so-subtle assumption here is that the secretary is somehow the ad hoc corporate conscience, and without her or his moral fortitude, the whole shebang would slide down the slippery slope of shoddy behavior into the hellfire of damnation.

Excuse me? The Survey indicates that office support professionals commit their share of misdeeds, too, ranging from sharing confidential information and falsifying reports to trading sex for advancement and stealing.

This seems to be the Age of Rationalization, doesn't it? Everyone has an excuse that lifts the burden of personal responsibility from them. True, our job has gotten tougher, but your supervisor's job has gotten tougher right along with yours. After all, the ranks of management have been permanently thinned, so he or she is making many more difficult decisions with less time and information, yet the penalty for a mistake is even more severe. Who should be promoted? Who should be laid off? Which vendor gets the order? What does he have to do, and who does he have to please, in order to keep his job? Temptations abound to cut corners, do it the easy way, look the other way, and use mirrors instead of the truth.

I recall a recent case I presented in an article: What if you and seven of your co-workers in the human resources department overhear someone in your group sharing confidential salary information? I invited readers to respond. I was saddened with the number of readers who replied they would "do nothing—because it was not my responsibility." This is not what the Ethical Office is all about. We have to hold ourselves to the same high standards we are holding others. We must commit to getting involved with and resolving these ethical dilemmas because they affect the profitability of our companies and the productivity of our offices.

We're in this together. We work side by side with each other in the office for eight to ten hours a day. Doesn't it seems like a smart investment to build an ethical office that promotes mutual respect, trust, and integrity? The anti-discrimination, anti-harassment, and other "politically correct" laws have gotten us thinking in the right direction. Morality cannot be legislated beyond broad guidelines, however. There are no laws that say we have to be nice to each other.

Still, I'm hopeful. Here's how I compare the traditional approach to office ethics, which we are moving away from, and the new ethical office, which we are moving toward:

The traditional approach to office ethics...	The new Ethical Office
From: Conspiracy of silence regarding unethical behaviors (*Sounds like*: "I can't believe she's doing that! And I can't believe no one is saying anything to anyone about it, either.")	*To:* Culture of empowerment and permission to frankly discuss conduct of self, others, and organization (*Sounds like:* "This is wrong, and we all know it. Let's figure out another way to deal with it.")
From: Acceptance of "house rules," regardless of rightness or wrongness (*Sounds like:* "I have to do this thing because my boss said I had to. If I don't, I'll be fired. So what can I do? I'm powerless.")	*To:* Acceptance of personal responsibility and accountability (*Sounds like:* "This is my company, too — we have to do better than this.")
From: Learning rules of acceptable conduct indirectly by observation (*Sounds like:* "If it's okay for them to do that, it must be okay for me to do it, too — and, as long as I've come this far, why not try to get away with this other not-so-nice thing, too?")	*To:* Frank discussions about difficult situations that are likely to arise in the future (*Sounds like:* "Let's talk about what we should do if ... or when ...")
From: Chronic distress due to unresolved ethical dilemmas (*Sounds like:* "Now what? I feel horrible, I can't concentrate, I'm sleeping poorly. I hate this place.")	*To:* Enthusiasm and energy for the people and the job (*Sounds like:* "I can't wait to get to work.")

(continued)

The traditional approach to office ethics ...	The new Ethical Office
From: Diminished self-esteem and low respect for co-workers (*Sounds like:* "Am I as bad as they are?")	*To:* High morale (*Sounds like:* "This company brings out the very best in me.")
From: Reduced productivity and job satisfaction (*Sounds like:* "I hate my job because of what I have to do and how it makes me feel.")	*To:* Increased productivity because of higher job satisfaction, confidence in ability, and willingness to advocate for the company's objectives (*Sounds like:* "I believe in what this company's trying to accomplish, and it deserves my full support.")

The fact is, *improving ethical decisions is everyone's responsibility.* Ethical behavior is needed in every office, every day, not just in church. We need a way of talking about our ethical conduct at work that brings out the best in all of us, regardless of our job. The company needs us to do the right thing, and we need to be able to trust each other to do the right thing.

We need a new way to talk to with our bosses, suppliers, customers, and co-workers, and I believe it is the language of office ethics. You see, the discussion about office ethics is about conduct, about how people behave with each other when they do their jobs. We need this new language to equip us to deal with the increasing complexity, sophistication, and responsibility of our positions.

So — I think we're going to get better at our jobs and do more for the good of our companies as we develop as professionals. The danger is that we get in over our heads. Are we prepared to deal with the ethical challenges we are going to meet? Can we make the tough choices — AND keep our jobs, friends, and professional relationships intact?

The answer is, yes, we can — *if* we can manage to work in an ethical office environment. What that ethical office looks like, and how we go about building it, will be the focus of the following chapters.

> *"When schemes are laid in advance,*
> *it's surprising how often circumstances*
> *fit in with them."*
>
> — Sir William Osler

6

Welcome to the
Ethical Office: the vision

Think about it: *A customer service representative at a printing company in the Midwest became very angry when she learned her company had been secretly monitoring her phone conversations. The company management admitted that her calls, and those of 12 other representatives, had been tape recorded for the past six months in an effort to "improve customer service."*

Three of her peers quit immediately in disgust and anger. The others remain very upset, and morale has hit the floor.

She asked if this practice of taping phone conversations without the caller's knowledge was illegal. I said, no, not in her state—but it was certainly unethical.

This bungled effort to improve customer service—if that's what it really was—had the net effect of widening the gap of trust and communication between the representatives and management. This secretive approach made the employees feel betrayed, violated, and not trustworthy. It also shot a hole through the heart of the representatives' enthusiasm for the company, which previously had been very good. These negative feelings are bound to show up in the voices and level of service provided over the phone.

If the printing company described above had addressed its customer service concerns in an ethical way, it would have treated the representatives with genuine respect and trust. But precisely what would that look like? Well, at the very least, the representatives would have been told in advance that they would be monitored and taped, and why. The message from management to the representatives then becomes, "We care about how you handle customer calls," instead of, "We don't trust you to be doing your job correctly, so we're going to 'get you' by catching you doing something wrong." Had they been told about the monitoring in advance, the representatives would have likely been pleased to see management's concern about the difficulty of their jobs, and they probably would have performed at their best because they would have known they might be recorded. In any case, the results would have almost certainly been a more positive attitude and higher performance.

The fact that this monitoring went on so long without any constructive feedback going to the representatives suggests management was simply fishing for something else. Maybe this exercise had something to do with customer service, maybe not. The point is: *Performance is hard-wired to employee motivation and loyalty.* Ethical office practices support motivation and loyalty, and unethical practices discourage them.

In previous chapters, we looked at some of the ethical dilemmas faced by contemporary office professionals. We also defined our terms, explored some of the reasons ethical dilemmas are more frequent and more complex when they occur, provided some self-assessment tools to help you audit your office ethics, debunked some myths about office ethics, and put ethical dilemmas at the office into a historical context.

Now, I want to begin expanding on the vision of the ethical office. This chapter will broadly describe the vision of the ethical office, and the following chapters will explain how to achieve it and the payoff that makes the effort worthwhile. Believe me . . . it does pay off!

Let's start by looking around an ethical office. Imagine visiting Copy Cat Sales, Inc., a hypothetical sales office for copying machines. As we walk through the front door, we are struck by the high level of energy. Every employee appears busy. When we walk around, we overhear comments that suggest each employee is focused and productive, trusting of his or her co-workers, feeling confident and valued, and generally happy to be at work and doing his or her job. "What a great team to work with," we think to ourselves.

I know many of you know exactly what I'm talking about. An office is like a home — it has a distinct nature, a unique energy vibration, that a visitor can sense intuitively. If you're looking for them, you can soon map the office dynamics — who's working well with whom, who's "in" or "out" of the group, who wields the real power, who's happy with their position and who's not, and so on. The presence of this dynamic "personality" of an office is understandable; after all, these people work together at least eight hours a day and share many common experiences.

The ethical office's chief feature is its high level of productivity. Quantitatively, ethical workers outperform all others. They sell more product, receive fewer service calls, and post superior profit margins. Qualitatively, the "personality" of an ethical office is healthy, energized, forward-looking, confident, creative, and resourceful. Copy Cat Sales, for example, is a real "can do" place to work.

Why? Because the workers in the ethical office have a cohesive understanding of their shared values, and this understanding—this code of ethics for their office—guides their conduct. The ethics framework provides the opportunity and the mechanism for everyone to communicate with each other. These people are working near the top of their potential most of the time because they are not confused about what is expected of them, they are not stressed to distraction with unrealistic goals, and they are empowered to take responsibility and to be accountable for their performance. They trust each other. They are honest with each other. They place a high value on personal integrity. They communicate loudly, clearly, and often about "doing things right" and "doing the right thing." If something doesn't pass the "smell" test (as in, "This stinks!"), everyone involved will talk about it until they resolve the dilemma. In short, they have: (a) learned to communicate about their values, (b) identified some form of collective conscience, and (c) made a commitment to help each other stick to it.

Just lofty words? Not at all—it's much more than lip service. These ordinary workers are turning in extraordinary results because they are taking the time to talk through their ethical dilemmas, and then get consensus and commitment from each other to handle them in certain ways. This is not rocket science—it is the practical work of applying basic group decision-making processes. But it is uncommon for this familiar process to be used to resolve ethical conflicts.

On the other side of the freeway, directly opposite Copy Cat Sales, is a competing copy machine sales office named Fat Cat Sales. Walking into their showroom, your instincts tell you that something isn't quite right. People seem hassled, uncomfortable, uncertain, and frustrated. When you ask a question, the response is evasive and along the lines of, "that's not my job." The support people in the office admit they are in conflict because they are expected to "work miracles" with too little time and too few resources. Consequently, they are cutting corners. The customers are getting less time, no one has the energy or desire to get the new billing software up and running, call backs and quotations aren't happening fast enough, and the other bread-and-butter activities of their business are getting only token attention. The office staff sounds cranky and secretive about what they are doing and why. You intuitively know that this is not a happy group, and you wonder how many came in early this morning to make copies of their resumes. This office isn't ethical; it's borderline dysfunctional.

Opening the door of the Ethical Office

It is my belief that we are in the process of inventing something new called the Ethical Office. It has three chief characteristics:

- a corporate conscience, which is a shared understanding and agreement of what the standards are for acceptable and unacceptable behavior,
- a commitment to hold yourself and each other personally responsible and accountable for those standards, and
- an ongoing discussion or system of honest communication about ethical issues that promotes trust and fairness.

To put it another way, the ethical office features clear communication about an organization's commitment to a specific, agreed-upon code of conduct based on the organization's guiding moral principles. This communication creates an expectation of conformity to this code of conduct, thus making it routine to discuss ethical dilemmas and resolve them in a way that is aligned with the code of conduct. Note that this kind of code of conduct is not the garden variety to be framed and hung on the wall — instead, it is a dynamic, living part of the organization's culture. People working in an ethical office believe they have a right and an obligation to their work group to identify and discuss ethical dilemmas when they come up.

Essentially, people working in an ethical office say to each other, (1) "We all know the difference between the right thing to do and the wrong thing to do (this is the corporate conscience)"; (2) "We have agreed to commit to doing the right things (commitment to accountability)"; and (3) "We will communicate like crazy whenever we encounter an ethical dilemma (it's okay—and expected—to talk about ethical concerns)."

The ethical office is a metaphor for any place or space where people work together. It is not limited or defined by specific sets of people and their relationships, although these people are a part of the community of people moving in and out of the office. It is a place with rules of behavior, just like a theater, school, church, museum, or stadium. The visitors to these places cannot be expected to follow the same rules of behavior after they leave but, while they are on the premises, they agree to abide by the rules. Likewise, people who choose to earn their livelihood in the ethical office are expected to abide by the office's code of conduct.

Here's how I suggest you think about the ethical office: You, your co-workers, your customers, and your suppliers comprise a business community with its own rules of conduct. You have all agreed to check your most extreme personal beliefs, problems, and feelings at the door in order to work together with some degree of harmony and productivity. Now, rather than leave those rules of conduct undefined, I am challenging you to initiate a discussion about them.

Why start the discussion now? Because when you and/or your group are in the middle of an ethical conflict, it will be too late to be constructive. Whoever gets named as the "bad guys" will almost certainly end up leaving the company... and that could be everyone's loss.

The three characteristics of the ethical office—conscience, commitment, and communication—don't just happen naturally, or materialize out of the fax machine. The ethics of your office—your office's code of conduct—has to be explicitly discussed and developed by you and your office mates. If my prior experience is any guide, these will be among the most interesting and personally rewarding discussions of your career. This book will help you start these discussions.

What's the difference between office ethics and business ethics? Which is more important?

Briefly, office ethics are a subset of business ethics. (Refer to Chapter 2 for a review of the basic differences.) Each is a code of conduct. Business ethics guide the "big picture" strategies and policies of the company; office ethics are tactical guidelines that specify reasonable and acceptable conduct toward our customers and co-workers.

While business ethics are the conscience of the corporation, office ethics guide our interpersonal behavior. Business ethics are broad, generic statements of general principles; office ethics are personal, more frequently applied, and unique to our situation.

In my mind, business ethics and office ethics are equally important to secretaries and other office professionals. Business ethics, which are articulated in your company's code of ethics, provide the context, the platform, from which you can act. Office ethics are your personal applications of the company's principles of conduct.

Business ethics and office ethics are mutually dependent and mutually supportive. Umbrella business ethics pushed down through the organization by senior management do not become "real" — they do not "live" — until someone like you chooses to apply them in a particular situation. As guiding principles, business ethics affect you. As one of the arenas where lofty principles meet the real world, office ethics affect you, too.

Our office already seems like a pretty ethical place to work. At least, it has always seemed that way to me. Is this additional discussion really necessary?

Well, you decide. Are you certain everyone is in agreement about the corporate conscience, meaning the standards of conduct? Presuming they know what they are, is everyone committed to them? And finally, if an ethical issue comes up, is there an ongoing dialogue or communication process that can be utilized to talk it through and get it resolved?

Think about your office. It already has a set of acceptable and unacceptable behaviors, even if they have not been explicitly identified as such. For example, in your office, can you:

- make long distance calls of a personal nature?
  what are the "reasonable limits" on these calls, if any?
- make copies for your son's scout troop? how many can you make, and how often? can you make them during business hours, or do you have to come in early or stay late and "keep it out of sight"?
- make copies and phone calls for the professional association you belong to?
- raise your voice at a co-worker?
- trade gossip at the coffee machine?

- use profanity?
- bring your kids to the office for a few hours?
- "tattle" on a co-worker?
- harass a co-worker, either verbally, emotionally, or physically?
- send personal faxes?
- lie about someone's whereabouts?
- share information with outsiders, such as news about who is submitting a bid, what the competitor's price is, financial information about the company, new products, names of project managers?
- falsify administrative records? falsify date stamping?
- run personal errands?
- sign someone else's name to routine personal correspondence?
- notarize signatures without actually witnessing the signing?

Intuitively, you can probably categorize which behaviors are and are not acceptable. Or can you? If you're like most of us, you've learned the rules of conduct informally, by paying attention and observing others. "If they do it, it's okay," you conclude. Some are easy, but what about those that happen behind closed doors, on the telephone, and out of earshot?

Building the Ethical Office sounds like a lot of work. Knowing my co-workers the way I do, I can predict some resistance to talking about right and wrong conduct. Is all this effort really worth the trouble? What are the real benefits of the Ethical Office?

I want to suggest that there are solid personal and professional reasons to bring the discussion about office ethics "aboveground." This does not have to be complicated, but it may prompt you and your boss (and possibly your co-workers) to discuss mutual expectations for loyalty, confidentiality, and questionable duties and tasks.

The corporate culture that does NOT promote the ethical office is heavily penalized: *Persistent and chronic ethical dilemmas are insidious drains on productivity.* When office professionals feel pressured to do things they don't want to do because of the unrealistic expectations of their supervisors, or because they must compensate for the effects of "downsizing," what do we do? You know the answer. Cutting corners with less-than-ethical conduct frequently appears to be our only, or best, or least offensive course of action if we want to stay promotable or keep our jobs.

The lack of a strong ethics culture makes us do crazy things. For example, 17.2% of the respondents to my Office Ethics Survey say they have notarized something without witnessing the signature, and 30% say they've observed others doing the same.

Secretaries and other office professionals still have to endure the most negative aspects of the boss-subordinate relationship. Nearly one-third of the survey respondents—31.8%—say they have personally experienced sexual harassment, and 37.6% say they have observed such behavior in others. Furthermore, 55.5% say they have experienced verbal harassment; 64.3% say they've observed it. Finally, 54.2% report experiencing emotional harassment, and 57.1% say they've observed it.

Even more alarming, respondents say they have observed other employees providing sexual favors that include physical contact in return for advancement (17.4%), increased compensation (15.6%), and preferential treatment (19.3%).

Lacking an ethical office culture makes other people do crazy things, too. Among the misdeeds the survey respondents say they've witnessed are: Preparation of a document that contains false or misleading information (20.2%), falsification of expense accounts (27%), and falsification of time sheets (32.6%). Although they have observed these infractions, it was gratifying that less than 5% of the respondents said they had ever committed these offenses themselves.

What's the benefit of an ethical office? Consider the importance of confidentiality in your company's business. Confidentiality is another defining ethical issue office professionals must confront regularly. In fact, safeguarding information—both written and oral—has always been one of the secretary's key responsibilities.

However, the survey suggests that office professionals often stand alone in their respect for confidentiality. Over 59% of the respondents have observed others sharing information about hiring, firing, and layoffs; 51.7% observed others sharing salary information; and 25.3% observed others sharing information about company or business trade secrets.

The survey data suggest an alarming frequency of ethical misbehavior in the office today. It's time for each of us to discuss our concerns with our supervisors and co-workers, and then build a climate for ethical conduct. Senior managers must continue to define the corporate conscience, but it is up to us, the secretaries and other office professionals, to apply a code of ethics in a meaningful way in the practical, day-to-day world.

What is it like to work in an Ethical Office?

Let me give you an example of what it's like to work in the ethical office. A friend of mine — let's call her Lori — is a secretary to a busy buyer for a large retail clothing store. Her boss easily could be your boss — say, a busy executive in real estate, utility, or healthcare industry.

"Lots of people want to talk to me," he said when Lori applied for the job. "Their livelihood depends on getting through to me. They need to pitch me on their latest proposition that I-just-can't-afford-to-live-without. This is a problem, because if I talk to all these salespeople, I can't accomplish what I really need to get done." Lori nodded her head — yes, she understood.

How can she help? "Tell everyone I'm out of the office, no matter what," he instructed her. "Ask them to leave a message. Then, if their name is on this short list of people I want to talk to, tell them I just now walked back in and put them through." Only a man could think this up, Lori thought.

Wait a minute, said Lori. That means I'll be lying to just about everyone, doesn't it? she asked. "Technically, yes," said her boss. "But it's what works around here. We think of it like a game, and the really good salespeople know the rules. If they're smart enough and persistent enough to get through you, I want to talk to them."

"So I'm the gatekeeper?" she said.

"Basically, yes. Have you got a problem with that?"

Well, Lori did have some problems with that, but she needed the job. How bad can it be? she thought. She quickly found her own ways to keep the rabble on the other side of the door. Sometimes, "He's not available," was sufficient. Her boss objected to this at first: "That response makes the situation worse, in my humble opinion. These sales guys are like hound dogs, and that phrase is like laying down a scent. They ask you, 'Oh, that's too bad — so when WILL he be available?' or 'When would he be more likely to be free?' Then they put you on a call-back list and they never give up. Don't encourage these poor saps, Lori — it's cruel."

Lori said she thought her boss was giving the average sales person too much credit. "Most are not that persistent," she said. "This is one of MY ways of dealing with pesky people. It has been MY naive experience that most of these folks give up rather quickly, so they go away." Her boss shrugged and pointed out that it was her problem to solve, and he would be satisfied as long as he didn't get surprised with a sales pitch he didn't want when he picked up his phone.

Lori came from the purchasing department in the medical products industry. She thought that was a competitive, rough-and-tumble environment but, in comparison, the retail clothing trade was a war zone. She quickly came to appreciate her boss's need, although she was uncomfortable telling a lie to virtually everyone who called.

Lori's best, and most professional, reply was, "Mr. Wagonfaggle is unavailable right now [this is the truth — he may be in the restroom or Europe, but he's certainly not here, available to talk]. May I take a message, or may I try to help you?"

This response didn't always work, however, so she experimented with other types of hurdles and obstacles to protect her boss from unwanted sales calls, including the truth. With some, she had to even become borderline rude:

- "I'm sorry, I know he's not interested in considering any new vendors/ventures /offers /proposals this month."
- "You can hold if you like, but I won't be able to check back with you. May I please take a message?"
- "The procedure we use in this office is to only accept written materials, not phone calls."
- "I'm sorry, but today turns out to be not a good day. Can you mail something or leave a detailed message on his voice mail — then he can call you if he's interested."
- "I sympathize with your desire to set up an appointment, but I can assure you his calendar is absolutely full through the end of this month. Would you like to check back later?"
- "Could you please explain to me why you want to see him, and I'll see if I can get you a quick response."

Lori became skilled at responding in ways that satisfied her boss's need for control over his outside interruptions, her need to be ethical (in other words, conduct herself in a way that was fair and honest), and the salesperson's legitimate need to promote.

We've all experienced our own versions of this same situation, haven't we? In a so-called normal office, where ethical dilemmas are not talked about, Lori would not have had the opportunity to put her boss on the spot.

That's the difference in an ethical office: It is a part of the culture to discuss conduct. When someone encounters conduct that makes them feel uncomfortable because it conflicts with their morals or values, it's okay to talk about it in order to define what is the right and wrong way to behave. Lori needed to find the alternative responses she did in order for *her* to do *her job* to the best of *her* abilities. It's clearly in the company's best interests, and hers too, for her to be comfortable in her job.

The definition of ethical behavior is certain to vary from office to office. It depends upon the people and the organization's ethical climate. I know other people, equally professional as Lori in their attitude and skills, who would have no trouble with Lori's dilemma. They would share the boss's view of the situation, and they would easily agree to use the "always gone" script. They, on the other hand, may have been embarrassed and humiliated by a request to run the boss's clothes to the dry cleaner—a task that Lori didn't think twice about

The point is, you and your boss need to agree on the set of ethical conduct rules that work for both of you in your version of the ethical office. *It is possible to discuss ethical dilemmas and communicate conclusions so there is no mystery about what conduct and behaviors are acceptable and not acceptable.* Frankly, it doesn't matter what the rules are, as long as you both are in agreement. This discussion must be a continuous one.

We do not sit in judgment of each other. Each of us brings our unique personal code of conduct to work at the ethical office, so we should expect some differences between our lists of what we will and will not do to keep our jobs.

The 4 greatest rewards of the Ethical Office

Raising the ethical standards in your office is no small feat, but it's well worth the effort, both personally and professionally. I mention this now because I want you to associate distinct benefits with the vision of the ethical office.

You need not tear apart your relationships or remake the corporate culture in order to begin receiving some of these benefits. From the first time you say, "No," or, "I'm uncomfortable continuing to do this," you and your organization will derive tangible rewards for your pursuit of the ethical office.

With my deep appreciation to those of you who shared your

insights and stories at my seminars during the past 10 years, here is my summary of the top benefits of building a more ethical office:

Reward #1: Self-respect

You feel better about yourself when you do the right thing. Even when you are trapped in a less-than-perfect situation, you can earn back a portion of your self-respect by finding a way to stop doing something you regard as unethical. Even the small things add up — ending abuses of the time clock or the phone are things you can do today that will affirm your professionalism and value to the company. Making a tough decision to do the right thing makes you proud of yourself, and motivates you to make the next tough decision, too.

Reward #2: Positive reputation

"A reputation is a jewel whose loss cannot be recovered" is one of my favorite proverbs. It applies to each of us personally and professionally, and it applies to our company, too.

What's it worth to be known as a fair person (or fair company)? Trustworthy and dependable? Honest and honorable? Our reputations are the collective memories of our prior associations. We can't control what others remember of us — but undoing a misdeed, and living with a remembered misdeed, is much harder than living with respect and admiration!

A local printing company has earned an enviable reputation with me. It has consistently delivered a superior product, on time and on budget, and always with a smile. When I ask a question, I get an honest answer I can plan a budget and a schedule on. When there's a problem — and there have been a few — I've been treated fairly and with respect. From my perspective as a customer, this is an ethical business. As far as I'm concerned, it has a sterling reputation, and consequently, it has my continued business.

Loyal customers like me are a great source of new customers, of course, because we refer others. Could I buy my printing at a lower price? Probably — with about 1,000 printers in the metropolitan area of the Twin Cities, it's a buyer's market. It's not the quality that keeps me loyal, because high-quality printing is virtually a commodity here. It's the service; and, *ethics are the heart and soul of customer service*.

Sadly, people tend to remember the negative longer than the positive. I sometimes tell myself that I don't care what people think of me, but I do. I want people to like me, to love me, to send me their business. The older I get, the more I appreciate the value of my reputation, and the greater a treasure it has become. I'm sure this is true in your organization, too. Your reputation for doing the right thing, even when it isn't convenient or necessary, can only help you.

Keep doing the right things! You will stay happy with yourself, stay promotable, and keep your customers happy and loyal!

Reward #3: Retention of high-quality people

The old adage is true: "A business is only known by the employees it keeps." How long do people choose to stay at your company? The optimal situation for the company is to keep all the high-quality people it needs, as long as it needs them.

Business is still about people, especially for businesses that provide a service. Finding new people to help grow the business is an expensive proposition. Recruitment costs vary, but most companies I work with expect to pay many thousands of dollars in direct and indirect costs to get a new secretary or office professional to work on her first day. The direct costs include recruitment ads, search firm fees, and enrollment costs for payroll, benefit plans, and insurance plans; the indirect costs are personnel costs to screen, interview, test, and check references. Once hired, the company must invest additional time and money in the new hire's orientation, training, and unproductive learning time until she is actually earning the amount she is paid. Generally, if an office professional leaves in less than two years, the company has lost money.

Think about what it means to a company to have a low turnover rate and long-term employees. It can avoid many of the costs of going out into the job market to find qualified applicants. It can choose the best of the crop, because ethical companies are almost always well-managed, and they are magnets for the most capable candidates. And best of all, a company like this will benefit from the long-term development of its employees. As service becomes more important to a business, the relationship between customer and employee can make or break a company. Who is the first face and the first voice a customer gets to know? An office professional, of course.

Reward #4: Higher productivity

Here is the most important reason to continue striving toward an ethical office: It's just plain-ol'-fashioned, money-making good business. An ethical business climate yields high employee morale, high positive energy, self-confidence relative to decisions and actions (a.k.a.

empowerment), and fewer distractions. The cumulative effect of
these positive features in the office environment is increased productivity and profitability.

Perhaps nothing makes this point better than a look at the absence
of ethics at work. We have already discussed some of the findings of
my 1995 Office Ethics survey. Similar results come from a 1994 survey
that included 497 administrative and salaried office professionals
and 807 hourly employees in other job functions by the Ethics
Resource Center in Washington, DC. This survey reported the most
common unethical acts observed are:

- lying to supervisor   56%
- lying on reports or falsifying records (improper
  charging of time, falsifying quality statistics, etc.)   41%
- sexual harassment   35%
- stealing /theft   35%
- alcohol or drug abuse   31%

Note that in both surveys, the respondents report their own misdeeds at a much lower rate than that which they saw others do. Nevertheless, if even just half of these numbers are accurate, imagine the
waste and inefficiency these companies must endure!

There is further evidence to suggest that some companies are paying costly penalties indirectly due to unethical behaviors. A Fortune
100 company shared the following excerpts from its ethics hotline.

According to the hotline director who tallied the results, the most
common ethical dilemmas heard are:

- faking sick days— "the mental health days" ...not reporting personal time off to run errands
- coming in late, leaving early— not working the full day
- long lunches and breaks
- wasting time on personal reading, phone calls, computer
  games, working out, socializing
- falsifying time cards
- allowing personal appointments, business to override work-
  related business

How pervasive are these offenses? I'm sure they vary company to
company and office to office. The point remains, however—the
greater the tolerance and acceptance of low standards of ethical conduct, the lower the organization's productivity.

One more observation about the link between office ethics, productivity, and profitability. In their classic survey of companies viewed as excellent and innovative, authors Tom Peters and Robert Waterman discovered that the most profitable companies were those pursuing *a larger purpose*. These companies consistently outperformed those that made profit their primary goal. The "larger purpose" refers to the successful companies' values, beliefs, and basic philosophy. When the larger purpose is communicated by a consistently visible senior management team (not necessarily charismatic, but always a good model) throughout the ranks of the company—right down to the people working in every office and every shop floor—the company almost always excels.

"Every excellent company we studied is clear on what it stands for, and takes the process of value shaping seriously. In fact, we wonder whether it is possible to be an excellent company without clarity on values and without having the right sorts of values." ... "Virtually all of the better-performing companies we looked at... had a well-defined set of guiding beliefs." (From *In Search of Excellence*, 1982, pp. 280–81. New York: Harper & Row.)

Peters and Waterman note that most business people are loathe to write about, talk about, or seriously promote explicit value systems, *yet the most successful do exactly that*. In fact, their legendary list of eight attributes that characterize excellent, innovative companies includes two that solidly endorse ethical behavior: *productivity through people* ("The excellent companies treat the rank and file as the root source of quality and productivity gain"), and being *hands-on, value driven* ("We are struck by the explicit attention they pay to values, and by the way in which their leaders have created exciting environments through personal attention, persistence, and direct intervention—far down the line"). Today, these links between values, ethical behavior, productivity, and profitability are more obvious than ever.

Today, almost every office professional admits to feeling more heat as they sit in the ethical "hotseat." Yet in spite of the increasing pressure from ethical conflict, most manage to resolve their ethical dilemmas and enjoy a high level of trust with their supervisors. When asked whether they plan to be working for their current employer five years from now, 70% of the respondents said "yes." This shows a commitment to their jobs, their supervisors, their organizations, and their profession.

Secretaries and other office professionals today are in a powerful position to improve the ethical conduct of their companies. They are literally the eyes and ears of the organization — they know the truth about how it really functions. If all office professionals initiated a discussion with their supervisors about the ethical dilemmas in the office, businesses would be transformed: Not only would productivity shoot up, but customers would get better service, profits would rise, and the revolving doors of the personnel office would no longer spin.

This chapter has offered a vision of the ethical office in miniature. This vision will be expanded throughout the rest of the book by addressing specific ethical issues and coping strategies. I hope you continue to find the discussion interesting and useful!

> *"He who excuses himself*
> *accuses himself."*
>
> — French proverb

7

No regrets,
no shame

Think about it: *Reba's widowed mother is hospitalized with an ill-ness that will require long-term medical attention. She wants to moni-tor her mother's care via daily phone conversations with the doctor. This requires long-distance phone calls during the work day. Reba decides that she can make the calls from her desk on the company's WATS line for a small cost. She reasons that because the phone logs are rarely checked, her chances of doing this without detection are good. Reba tells herself she will "pay the company back" by putting in some extra time over the weekend.*

Would this be an ethical dilemma for you? Is Reba's reasoning sound, or is it just rationalization? If you were in Reba's position, would you explain yourself to your supervisor in advance, or just do it and keep a low profile?

Getting from the reality to the vision: There is almost always more than one answer to an ethical dilemma

"It's easy to be an iceberg in the frigid zone," Bishop Fulton J. Sheen used to say on his television show. He meant, of course, that it was easy to act in an ethical way if one already lived in an ethical envi-ronment.

The vision of the ethical office presented in Chapter 6 is a pretty picture, isn't it? In the ideal, ethical office, we wouldn't even encounter ethical dilemmas because we would have done such a good job of communicating our expectations for ethical conduct to everyone around us. And if by chance we did have an ethical dilemma thrust upon us, we would only need a little ethical chat with our boss to straighten it out, right?

Hello? Is this the vision — or fantasy — of the ethical office?

You and I live in the real-world offices where good people still do bad things, at least occasionally, and, bad things do happen to good people. We've all had first-hand experiences with not-so-ethical conduct in the workplace, and these experiences will not be our last.

But — *there is hope!* No matter how unethical your office environment is right now, you can take immediate steps to make it more ethical. No matter what low point you are starting from, no matter how poorly you are prepared, no matter how checkered your personal history, you can take action that will begin building a new, more ethical office culture. Who knows? Once you get the ball rolling, you may be pleasantly surprised at how close you get to Chapter 6's vision of the ethical office! In this chapter, we'll begin bridging the gap between the real office you are working in now and the ethical office you imagine.

Let's start with another story: At a seminar in Canada, a woman I'll call Ronnie stood up to take issue with one of the cases we were discussing. The particulars of that case are not important here. What struck me was how emphatically she made her points, saying "I would do this, but I'd never do that." It seemed no one in the room agreed with her, but she stuck to her position. "I know it wasn't illegal, and it wasn't even unethical, but I just feel strongly about this issue." I was impressed with her because she knew her own mind on this issue, and she was willing to stand up against the tide of popular thought to defend her principles.

Then I got the surprise of the week. At the end of the day, Ronnie came up to me and said, "Nan, I have another ethical dilemma case for you." I thought, great, I'm always looking for cases. Here's what Ronnie told me: "A year ago, my boss went to Saudi Arabia for the first time to start a new business relationship between our company and a Saudi partner. Once there, he learned that part of the customary hospitality offered him included the services of a prostitute. I thought I knew my boss better than I guess I did, because he felt he had to partake of this hospitality out of respect for his host. I thought he'd be able to sidestep that situation if he really wanted to.

"This year, just recently, the Saudi Arabian gentleman came here and he expected reciprocal arrangements to be made. My boss really felt obliged to return the favor. The problem was, my boss asked me to make the arrangements." I asked, "What did you do?" She looked me square in the eye and she said, "I think my boss wanted me to volunteer for the night. I just know it.

"But I didn't let him win. I fooled him by doing exactly what he asked me to do. I didn't know how to find a hooker, but I figured it couldn't be that hard. So I put on my coat and hit the streets. It was horribly embarrassing, and eventually laughable, but I got it done, I made the arrangements." I had a momentary image of this naive, plucky woman making inquiries at sleazy bars. How does one go about finding a suitable hooker, anyway? The Yellow Pages?

As curious as I was about the details, I was more interested to hear Ronnie explain herself. I said, "A few hours ago, you were in front of several hundred people arguing about something that wasn't illegal, immoral, or unethical. Now you tell me just did something that was all three of the above."

"I know," she said. "And I'll never do it again, especially after today's workshops, but Nan"—she was crying now—"I really believed I had to do it to keep my job."

Ronnie learned a lot from that experience about what her boss thought of her and what he felt he could ask her to do. She was dismayed to learn that her workplace wasn't quite the ethical environment that she thought it was. She went on to tell me what she should have said to her boss and what she should have done to avoid compromising herself to this extent. The next time something like this comes up, I'm certain she'll take the opportunity to advance the discussion about ethics with her boss. I'd love to see that!

Ronnie's story illustrates how much we can be affected by the practical pressures of our job. Ronnie is a single mom. She rents half a house with another single mom, and by most visible measures, she says she has a pretty comfortable lifestyle. But she is chronically worried about her financial security. She told me she is never more than two or three paychecks away from serious cash flow trouble, and there is always something that kicks her back when she starts to get ahead. "What would happen to my kids?" she said. "There is no other option. I have to work, and for now, this job is my best ticket."

Ronnie is my kind of everyday hero from whom we can all learn something. Here was a person who obviously thinks about "doing the right thing" more than most people, feels strongly about her principles, and actually has the intestinal fortitude to walk the talk, at least among her peers. Yet even she is not beyond intimidation. There are many of us who have experienced similar situations where we felt we had to do something we knew was wrong.

Doesn't it feel hopeless sometimes? The people in your office are like your family—you can't get away from them, no matter how badly they behave!

The most difficult situations are the ones involving a boss who doesn't listen or doesn't care. Bosses like this never see themselves as the bad guys, of course—they just keep pushing us, not thinking or not caring, self-satisfied with their own goodness and completely confident the company's Code of Ethics framed on the wall covers all contingencies. Co-workers can be just as bad, or worse—especially those who seem to view the workplace as a battleground. The worst of these so-called "team members" only view the world from their narrow personal perspective, think only in terms of winning and losing, and believe the only rule is Don't Get Caught.

The practical realities of our jobs probably aren't going to change any time soon, either. Our offices are too dynamic to be completely predictable or controllable. Ethical dilemmas are not dropped on us accidentally every great once and awhile; they regularly come after us like heat-seeking missiles! About 18 percent of respondents to the Office Ethics survey say they have to make ethical choices they are uncomfortable with at least once a month, once a week, or every day.

We cannot get out of the ethical hot seat. We're stuck. Ethical dilemmas come with our job. The pressures that breed ethical dilemmas are always present—new deadlines, new competition, new market conditions, and new personnel problems, to name just a few. And it's not enough that we have to deal with these pressures as they come up—we're usually the lucky ones who have to explain the insanity to newcomers! Like Ronnie, we have to deal with these ethical pressures in a way that really works for us, or find a different job. For many of us, it's that simple, and that important.

Sure, you can always leave and find another job, but why should you have to give up a good job and start over somewhere else? It's been my experience that every office has some ethical problems anyway, so what's the point of running away? Your address may change, but your reality will stay the same.

So what can we do? The vision of the true ethical office features nice, well-meaning co-workers, reasonable bosses, and lots of communication when ethical dilemmas crop up. In the real world, our co-workers are frequently crazy (at least, it seems so), our bosses don't listen or don't care, and any suggestion that the policies and tactics used by the company are less than fair or honest is met with hurt feelings and hostility.

Can we somehow find answers to ethical dilemmas that are practical and workable in the real world?

Yes! Keep reading!

The good news is that in the real world, *there is almost always more than one answer to an ethical dilemma.* The challenge is to find the "right" answer for you before you are overwhelmed by the ethical dilemma — and, as we'll see in a minute, that "right" answer can be any answer you can live with.

Ronnie learned this valuable lesson. True, Ronnie didn't think about her options until after she had done the deed, but she apparently needed that jolt to get her oriented to the real situation between her and her boss. Somewhere between quitting and pimping, Ronnie now knows she could have resolved this dilemma.

You could have, too, although your way of resolving it would probably be different from Ronnie's. Perhaps you would have gladly quit the job; or perhaps you would have hired the prostitute without a second thought. Or, perhaps you would have found a way to say "no" without losing your job. It all depends — remember the "it depends" curve we looked at in Chapter 2? — on your personal values and how important you think it is to apply them to the situation at hand.

Where do you look first for answers to ethical dilemmas?

Codes of ethics have become popular as evidence that an organization's heart is in the right place. Personally, I like the idea of codes of ethics — mostly because I have seen them used very successfully by some companies to create and reinforce vital, dynamic cultures of ethical behavior. I *don't* like the way some companies have developed them and used them. Here are some of the *wrong* reasons to adopt a code of ethics:

- As a substitute for overdue discussion or action, as if to say, "There, we've done ethics, and taken care of the ethics problem."

- As a "feel good" exercise, as if to say, "We're so proud we're so ethical. Just look at our fine code of ethics."
- As window dressing to conceal poor business practices the company has no real desire or intention to change
- As a begrudging settlement of a lawsuit
- As a "me-too" response to other companies
- As a whim of senior management, developed in isolation and presented to the employees as a finished document
- As a strategic, fig-leaf defense for imminent legal action, i.e. harassment suits

Codes of ethics are meant to be beacons that guide policies, practices, decisions, and personal behavior at work. They should answer the questions, "What do we believe in?" and "How do we believe we should conduct our business affairs?" The process of developing a code of ethics is a formal way of promoting discussions and consensus about the important questions surrounding ethics. Codes of ethics are supposed to be the result, the distilled summary, of a reflective process involving most employees. They are supposed to provide the guiding principles that will help everyone up and down the corporate ladder work together with similar attitudes of respect, trust, and integrity.

"It's better than nothing!" Unfortunately, that's about all you can say about the codes of ethics developed via shortcut routes, i.e. without a formal process that included everyone in ways that built "ownership" and understanding among employees. Incredibly, some companies attempt to deliver codes of ethics developed solely by the legal department, public relations department, or an outside consultant. These codes are generally just poor uses of plaques and frames because they lack the understanding and support of the people who are expected to be guided by them. At its best, a prefabricated code of ethics is ignored and has no effect; at its worst, it is a source of confusion and disappointment.

Texas Instruments is one organization that has done it the right way. TI penned its corporate code of ethics more than 30 years ago, long before it became fashionable, and long before it became a requirement of suppliers to the defense industry.

"Texas Instruments will conduct its business in accordance with the highest ethical and legal standards." This statement was published in TI's first corporate ethics book in 1961, and this fundamental principle remains the cornerstone for the policy today.

What makes the TI code of ethics an effective guide for this large, widely dispersed, international company that competes so successfully in numerous complex market niches is summed up in one word: commitment. There is simply no doubt in anyone's mind that TI is serious about having every employee know and live by the code of ethics. TI ethics training is organized so every employee learns the company's mission, basic principles, and values. The connection between good ethics and good business is impressed on everyone early and often. Most importantly, the code of ethics is brought to life by making it practical in the real world of experience. This is done through a series of "where to go for help" and "what to do IF..." resources like booklets, phone networks, brochures, training programs, formal and informal discussions with senior management, electronic mail, hotlines, suggestion programs, etc. Underlying this approach is the explicit understanding that the company knows every employee is going to have to (1) make ethical decisions in their day-to-day tacit and (2) be personally accountable and responsible for their ethical decisions.

However, most ethics codes offer little or no help in the practical world. In the first place, there is typically a lot of "wiggle room" between a code of ethics — which naturally has to be a general statement about doing the right thing, trust, integrity, etc. — and the assorted personal morals we and our office mates bring to work. Our office mates can usually be counted on for specific opinions about any particular ethical dilemma, but they have a disconcerting tendency to shift wildly depending upon the circumstances and the people involved. (For example, it's okay for Jennifer to come in late, but Sandy's tardiness is inexcusable.) The chances that there are clear connections between the lofty code of ethics and the nitty gritty conduct of employees running the office are less than slim.

What about seeking an answer to an ethical dilemma in the *legal system?* This is a high profile means of resolution that I recommend only rarely, and only as a last resort.

Laws are the bare, essential requirements that maintain social order. They apply to everyone. They are attractive because they are actually written down. *But laws are poor substitutes for either moral or ethical choices.* To conform to a standard that is simply the minimum standard for behavior is hardly an achievement.

Laws make a poor guide for conduct at work for two reasons: First, you cannot possibly legislate all aspects of the interpersonal relationships that comprise an office environment. If someone in the office is going to treat someone else unfairly, he will find a way to do it. Second, you can satisfy the letter of the law even while committing an act considered unethical or immoral by most reasonable people. It may be technically legal to accept a gift from a supplier, but does that make it the right thing to do? Still, it's tempting to let our ethical judgments gravitate toward a simple, minimal legal standard for our conduct. When called to account for our questionable behavior, how many of us would hide behind the flimsy statement, "I did nothing illegal," or "What I did was perfectly legal," as if legality equals "rightness."

The legal standard is the minimal standard — it provides the outer boundaries of conduct ("If you go beyond this point, you risk going to jail"). It tells you what you *can't* do, but provides no positive guidance about what you *should* do. Offices that are guided by the law alone tend to be negative, petty, and mean-spirited. Naturally, we must comply with the law, but it's not enough.

Ethical standards are the next step up on the hierarchy of standards. Ethical conduct is the set of behavior standards established for a group of people working together in the same place, same group, or same profession. There may be differences between corporate ethics, professional ethics, office ethics, and personal ethics, depending upon your situation.

Moral conduct implies the highest standards of conduct guided by personal principles, values, and virtues. If the law is the minimal standard, and the ethical code a reasonable expectation, then a moral code is the highest personal standard.

In short, *the law tells you what you should not do, ethics tell you what you should do, and morals tell you what you should aspire to do.*

Along this hierarchy or continuum, there are usually several answers to ethical dilemmas. I don't want to be the one to suggest you lower your standards, but I have to tell you the truth: In the practical world, sometimes the best you can do is choose the answer closest to your personal moral aspirations.

Still true after all these years

Nearly 2,500 years ago, the Greek philosopher Aristotle wrote the first systematic treatise on ethics, called the *Nicomachean Ethics*. He observed that we all seek happiness, though we pursue a variety of means to attain it. Some people think they will be happy if they are rich, so they pursue wealth. Others pursue power, or pleasure, or status, or things. Aristotle concluded that the excess of any one thing or activity ended up being as burdensome or as painful as the deprivation. Therefore, his recommendation was to pursue a course of moderation in all things if you wanted to be happy. This guiding principle of his is called the "Doctrine of the Golden Mean."

Besides moderation, Aristotle held up other virtues that we still aspire to: courage, liberty, pride, friendliness, truthfulness, wittiness, good temper and honor. Benjamin Franklin restated these virtues some 200 years ago, and they have been echoed again and again by the modern self-help industry. If these virtues were practiced every day amongst our co-workers, wouldn't our work life be grand?

Back to reality. Aristotle said that achieving happiness is difficult, usually requiring the better part of a lifetime. Attempting to be perfectly virtuous all the time, every day, was viewed as immoderate by Aristotle, and therefore a path leading to even more difficulties and unhappiness. For example, strictly speaking, no part of our personal life should ever be allowed to "steal" the company's time or other resources — which means we should never receive or make a personal phone call, make a photocopy for our personal use, always tell the truth, etc. Personally, I believe this overly rigid approach imposes unrealistic expectations on the workplace. Not everyone shares the same ideas, values, beliefs, priorities, or philosophies. To insist on sainthood standards from ourselves and those around us would inevitably lead to more conflict with our co-workers and become a serious obstacle to cooperation and productivity.

The virtues of Aristotle (and Franklin and the rest of the gang) are made palatable by the test of reasonableness, also called "golden mean" judgments. Aristotle challenges us to use our common sense and apply virtues in a reasonable way. We may call our personal "golden mean" test our common sense test or reasonableness test. By exercising our common sense, or judgment for reasonableness, we are actually applying the virtue of moderation.

This does not mean we can excuse ourselves willy-nilly to suit the convenience of the situation (this response is sometimes called relativism or contextual ethics, and it does not serve us well). Our values, beliefs, and principles must stay whole and intact, but we may find ourselves varying the degree to which we apply them.

I am reminded of the importance of ethical constants in the following from Thomas Watson, Jr. as he reflects upon his experiences at the head of IBM in his book, *A Business and Its Beliefs:* "I firmly believe that any organization, in order to survive and achieve success, must have a sound set of beliefs on which it premises all its policies and actions. Next, I believe that the most important single factor in corporate success is faithful adherence to those beliefs. And, finally, I believe if an organization is to meet the challenge of a changing world, it must be prepared to change everything about itself *except* those beliefs as it moves through corporate life.

"... Technological or economic resources, organizational structure, innovation, and timing ... weigh heavily in success. But they are, I think, transcended by how strongly the people in the organization believe in its basic precepts and how faithfully they carry them out."

In other words, you are obliged to always act as ethically as you are reasonably able, basing your decisions on your knowledge of your personal values and the values of your organization. You may not always be able to live up to all your standards, but the standards remain the same nevertheless. It would be wrong to change your ethics or values to match the situation just because you felt disappointed in your choices or the consequences of your actions.

In the next chapter, I'll introduce you to the Ethical Compass and we'll practice applying the common sense test for ethical action.

> *"... The Golden Rule*
> *was meant for business*
> *as much as for other*
> *human relationships."*
>
> —J. Cash Penney, founder,
> JCPenney Co. Inc.

8

Which way now?

Using your ethical compass to resolve ethical dilemmas

Think about it: *You are the assistant to the chief surgeon at a leading medical school. The chief surgeon is visited by several people from a drug company (you know this because you arranged the appointment). Soon after the meeting, you see invoices from the drug company coming directly to your boss. Your boss acts oddly when you show the invoices to him, but a day later he tells you to write a check from his personal office account and pay them. This departure from routine also strikes you as odd, but it's a busy day, so you do it without asking any questions and forget about it. Besides, there's no question in your mind what your job goal is: When you were hired, you were told explicitly that your job was "to keep the good doctor happy."*

At the end of the month, you are processing your boss's reimbursement request form when you notice he has several new items. The amounts seem familiar to you, and he has coded them as "miscellaneous," so you go back and check his checkbook. Yup, there they are—you wrote the checks to pay those invoices from the drug company directly. You also remember that you signed the checks and mailed them, which is the routine procedure for this busy man's personal office account. Now it is clear that he expects the medical school to reimburse him for the amounts he asked you to send to the drug company. You are getting very worried—because those checks have your name on them.

Because of this man's long and sterling career with the medical school, you know his requests will not be questioned, so the reim-

bursement request will doubtlessly be paid. This doesn't look or feel at all right, but what can you do? You genuinely respect and admire your boss — in fact, you derive a lot of satisfaction from helping him be successful. Furthermore, from a financial perspective, your job as the assistant to this world-class surgeon is the best job you've ever had.

You're in conflict between your instincts to help, support, and comply with your boss, yet you are smart enough to see a bad situation developing. Compounding this dilemma is the schedule — the reimbursement requests have to be in by the end of the day or wait until the following month. You feel you need to talk to your boss, fast — but he's attending a conference overseas, and he won't return for six days. At the last minute, you submit the fraudulent reimbursement requests.

Several months later, you are talking to an attorney investigating the misuse of funds by the good doctor. It's the truth, but your explanation seems weak: "I was afraid I would be chastised if I didn't do it. I guess the bottom line was, I didn't want to make the doctor angry."

It's time for another reality check, okay? In the previous chapters, I've presented the ethical office as an ideal workplace environment, a worthy goal deserving your persistent efforts. I've also encouraged you to approach these high ethical standards within the context of your own test for reasonableness and common sense. So far, so good — as long as you are more or less in control of a situation that you decide is an ethical dilemma. Now, I want to give you something to help you in those times when you may not be in control of the situation.

The fact is, much of our job duties keep us in a reactive, not active, frame of mind. I know, I know — all those requests from all those people keep us pretty active! What I mean to say is that when someone says "jump, please," our job description specifies our prompt and attentive response. Sure, we all like being assigned to work autonomously, but it's also fun to be in the thick of things, pulling rabbits out of your bag of tricks on demand (and don't we just love it when we can save someone's sweet behind, and thereby earn their undying gratitude — for a little while, anyway!).

Reacting under pressure is usually not conducive to making reasonable decisions. It's a challenge to even recognize fast-moving ethical dilemmas before they overwhelm us, and even more difficult to make a common-sense decision about how to resolve them. Basically, we have to react according to our instincts and trust our internal gyroscope. If we are in close touch with our core values, morals, and principles, and if we have discussed some of the hypothetical problems already so we have the benefit of some advance thinking, we can usually trust ourselves to do the right thing, even though we may only have a few minutes or a few seconds to respond.

These dilemmas would require quick-thinking on our part:

- sexual propositions
- lies to unexpected callers with questions for which we are not prepared
- "hand grenade" comments or instructions of all kinds from our boss (these are the "just do it/ just get it done" types of comments, and the thoughtless comment or remark causes us to ask, "What did he mean by that?")
- instances of physical, emotional, verbal, or sexual harassment
- instances of unfairness or harassment that we witness
- unexpected "discovery" situations (overhearing an incriminating conversation, coming across an explosive file of compromising documentation)

The Ethical Priority Compass™ for making ethical choices

To help you with the "quick reaction" categories of ethical conflicts, I want to equip you with my Ethical Priority Compass™ for making ethical decisions. This provides you with a fast, simple, hierarchical approach to any ethical dilemmas you may encounter. I developed it after listening to thousands of people pose "what if" questions to me at my seminars; I think you'll find it a fast and effective way to orient yourself to any ethical dilemma and thereby be better able to make the right decision.

© 1997 Nan DeMars, CPS

First — Take care of yourself. No matter what, you have to protect yourself from physical and emotional harm, legal action, financial disaster, and related problems. Do not confuse character with compromise. If it is necessary to compromise, it may be acceptable as long as you communicate your ethical position to the people with whom you need to compromise.

Second — Take care of your company. Your company's interests are subordinate to your own. However, if something — anything — affects your company, or your ability to do your job, you must speak up and attempt to resolve the dilemma. Ethically, your organization deserves your loyalty because it has provided you with your livelihood. Practically, your organization can demand your loyalty because it is more powerful than you, your manager, your co-workers, your union, your customers, and your suppliers. Long after you and your problem have gone away, the company will remain. In a dispute, your company will be your best friend or worst adversary. It isn't always fashionable to take care of your company, but it's the right thing to do — up until it can be demonstrated that the company no longer deserves your support.

Third — Take care of your supervisor. This is a personal relationship that merits a lot of your loyalty, but it's not blind loyalty and it's not unconditional loyalty. You share a history, and he or she probably holds considerable power over you regarding compensation, the benefits of mentoring and networking, advancement, resources, scheduling, work assignments, and the quality of your work life. Your supervisor is also a normal human being with warts, worries, and other flaws. He or she is neither angel nor devil. If he or she is part of an ethical problem, do not leap to the conclusion that he or she is the enemy. After listening to literally thousands of stories about trouble with supervisors, my counsel is to make the extra effort to mend and preserve this relationship. This person has more power, and more options, and more resources than you do — and you will quickly approach the point in a dispute where you may win the argument, but lose your job. And let's be honest about this — even if you have the protection of the courts against retaliation, say for whistle-blowing, your supervisor can make or break your quality of life. If the damage to your relationship with your supervisor cannot be repaired, it is only a matter of time and convenience before your relationship ends.

I urge you to memorize the sequence—*self, company, manager*—because it will provide you with a stable point of reference. When confronting an ethical decision requiring a fast decision, use my Ethical Priority Compass at the end of this chapter to help you decide what to do.

The chart at the end of this chapter demonstrates how to use the Ethical Priority Compass. The questions below will help you think about the three steps to the Ethical Priority Compass. A few of these will probably become favorites of yours because they conjure especially powerful images, or they help you recall something your mother said, or some similar response.

- Is this an ethical problem or communication problem?
- What — exactly — is the ethical problem?
- How serious is it? Can you live with it?
- Do you believe the "rightness" of a decision is "relative"?
- Do you decide which action to take based on which course of action harms the least number of people?
- Do you believe an unethical act is justified if it causes another unethical act to cease?
- How would you feel if this dilemma appeared on the evening news? (This is the "publicity test.")
- Can you explain your actions to your kids?
- Who will be affected by this decision?
- What are the harms and benefits to those affected? (what are their needs, wants, values, expectations?)
- Whose rights will be affected? Who has entitlements that must be accommodated?
- What are the alternatives?

I have one final set of model questions for you to consider using yourself: Texas Instruments has simplified their ethics test to three simple guidelines they call the *"TI Ethics Quick Test"*:

If you know it's wrong, don't do it.

If you're not sure, ask.

Keep asking until you get an answer.

> *"You can't ride in all
> directions at one time."*
>
> —Yiddish proverb

Nan DeMars's
∼∼∼ Ethical Priority Compass™ ∼∼∼

*Use these examples as a guide to help you
make ethical decisions you can live with.*

Description of the ethical problem	*First...* Take care of yourself	*Second...* Take care of your company	*Third...* Take care of your supervisor
Your supervisor is harassing you.	You document this incident, then talk to your supervisor. Give him a chance to reform and clear up any possible misunderstandings.	Talk to the company; it may be liable for your supervisor's conduct; give it a fair chance to resolve the problem.	It's probably too late to save him from himself; be professional, but do what you have to do, including legal action, to resolve the problem.
You see a co-worker stealing.	You document this incident; you decide you must take action to protect your interests in the success of the company.	Report the co-worker's actions according to the company's procedure. In this case, the legal department and the human resource department will likely become involved.	Probably does not apply, unless you wish to seek his counsel or he is a part of the reporting procedure.
You are frustrated seeing a co-worker come in late, leave early, and perform poorly.	You document these incidents; you decide you must take action to protect your interests in the success of the company.	Report the co-worker's actions according to the company's procedure. In this case, this will probably involve your supervisor.	Does not apply, unless the supervisor allows the co-worker's behavior to continue. In that case, you have a different problem.
Your manager asks you to lie for him.	You document this incident and discuss your objections with your manager; if he persists, insists, or threatens retaliation if you don't comply, go to the company.	Explain the situation to the human resource department, the legal department, and perhaps even your supervisor's supervisor.	Why bother?

9

How can I say "THAT"?

Ground rules for discussions about ethics

Think about it: *You are Mr. Wilson's secretary. Mr. Wilson is a senior-level engineering manager with whom you have worked for more than five years. During that time, you have assisted him in both his professional and business activities. This was what you expected — your job description specifically included responsibilities like handling his personal financial records, his appointment calendar, his personal and professional travel plans, and duties related to his commitments to outside boards, trade associations, and civic organizations. You share a high regard and respect for each other and enjoy a professional working relationship.*

Mr. Wilson told you — in confidence — about six months ago that he was planning to divorce his wife within the next year. He asked that you not discuss this with anyone else, and you promised him you would not.

However, you have recently become concerned. Within the scope of your secretarial duties, you have assisted him in the transfer and changing titles of ownership of several major assets, opening new bank accounts, and setting up trust accounts for his children and several other people with whom you are not familiar. All of these activities appear to be technically legal, but you have concluded Mr. Wilson is using you to help him hide his assets in preparation for the impending divorce.

You have applied your ethics compass and your common sense test.

You have concluded that this situation is a bona fide ethical dilemma
for you that is affecting your work. You know you have to talk to Mr.
Wilson about this before you do anything else.
   How do you begin this awkward conversation — what do you say?

The very first person you should talk to about an ethical dilemma at
work is your boss. (If he is part of the problem, see Chapter 10.) An
open channel of communication between a supervisor and the
office professionals with whom he works does not guarantee a good,
productive work team — however, without this communication, you
and your boss are doomed to fail. Give your supervisor a fair chance
to respond and help you. In return, don't let him be caught unaware —
anticipate the ethical problems headed his way and grant him the
professional courtesy of giving him a "heads up" conversation.

The importance of feedback

Robert MacGregor, president of the Minnesota Center for Corporate
Responsibility, says he has a special kind of discussion with every
assistant soon after he or she is hired. The conversation goes something like this: "I'm going to be going 100 miles per hour to do my job.
You will be going 120 miles per hour to stay ahead of me. In my haste
to get a job done and meet a particular deadline, if I ever appear to
be cutting corners or sliding into unethical practices in any regard, I
WANT you to stop me and call it to my attention. I want you to help
me monitor our processes, and I insist that you call to my attention
ANY potential ethical problems you come across." That kind of a
conversation — at the beginning of their working relationship — is a
model for the kind of discussion that should take place between
every supervisor and employee.

   Ethics discussions are difficult to have, so it's no surprise that many
office teams do not have enough of them. Ethics questions fundamentally challenge others in ways that make them uncomfortable. It's
difficult to raise an ethical issue without suggesting that the other person has somehow disappointed you by lying, cheating, etc. Isn't the
natural reaction a mixture of defensiveness and denial? I know that if
someone suggested or even hinted that I was guilty of misconduct, my
first instincts would be blind and childish — I would revert to what
worked for me when I seven years old and say something like, "It's not
so! And if it is, my brother, Brian, did it, too!"

A conversation about ethics should be the logical starting point for resolving a dilemma but, if done carelessly or thoughtlessly, it could also be the beginning of the end of your relationship with this person. *When you initiate a discussion about ethics, you run a high risk of offending someone — and consequently jeopardizing your relationship with him and your job security.*

Intuitively, we know this, don't we? However you sugarcoat your language, or tiptoe around the point, the core message of a discussion about ethics will come through: "I have a problem with your behavior, and I'm talking to you because I want you to help make this problem go away."

Think back to your conversation(s) with your soon-to-be-boss when you were interviewing for your position: You were both on your best behavior, right? Each of you were selling yourself to the other as a team player committed to communication, empowerment, and all the rest. You certainly didn't dwell on all of the possible conflicts that could arise between you. You each took a leap of faith that you were fundamentally in agreement about what was right and wrong. You were willing to take each other at face value on the ethics questions because you were already in agreement on the more important questions of skills ("Can you do this job?") and compensation ("How much does it pay?"). Anyway, you just about had to trust your instinct and first impression that this boss was okay because it's unlikely you could ask about the office's dirty little secrets!

After you accepted your job, when you learned where the bathroom was and how to make the coffee, your boss started to direct your activities. As you began to work together, a process of discovery began. You discovered what your job was all about, while your supervisor discovered what you can be counted on to do well. Like a new marriage, there were some happy and not-so-happy surprises for both of you.

After a short honeymoon period, you learned a lot more about what it means to "provide support" (I am 99 percent certain that this phrase is on your job description) to this person who holds so much power over your life. You may not like it, but doesn't your success largely depend upon the success of your interpersonal relationship with your boss? If you work well together, great; but if you don't, you are probably miserable.

You cannot change the fundamental power relationship with your supervisor. This is just a simple reality. But the good news is that the interpersonal dimension of your relationship is very elastic. You can improve it by changing how you talk to each other, treat each other, and work with each other.

I suggest you have this kind of conversation with your new boss while you're still in the "honeymoon days" of getting to know each other: Before any conflict starts, tell him or her, "I would like to have an honest and direct style of communication between us. I hope we can have the kind of relationship whereby we both feel free to compliment and constructively criticize each other. I want you to let me know when I have done something well, and I want you to tell me when I have not met your expectations. I would like to hear these things right away, instead of saving them all up for my six-month performance review. That kind of feedback helps me get better at my job TODAY. Likewise, I would appreciate it if I could give you feedback about when we are and are not working well together..." You get the idea. What manager is not going to want this kind of high-quality communication?

One of my favorite cartoons shows a woman flat on her back on the office floor, passed out cold. Two people are standing over her, and one says to the other, "Someone complimented her on her work today, and then someone else said thank you. It was too much for her."

Isn't it true that no one has died from too much praise; but lots of employees become spiritually "dead" because they never get any recognition for their work?

Truthtelling discussions are not easy

Discussions about ethics are messy affairs, aren't they? They are difficult to keep focused, full of words that everyone defines differently, and plagued by the syndrome of "let's-hurry-up-and-get-this-over-with." Ethical issues can be so volatile, so explosive — once we've started the discussion, we have to finish it, however messy and destructive it becomes. We can't very well say, "Oops! Sorry, boss. On second thought, and after observing that you're not taking this very well, I've changed my mind and decided that I am completely comfortable with your obnoxious behavior."

Ethical discussions are difficult, so we avoid them, so they remain difficult. That's why we hold back, why we don't confront the issue, and why we continue too long in our role of supportive helpmate.

When we finally get to the point where we're boiling up inside and we have to say something, we're rarely as rational or as professional as we need to be.

A cornerstone of the ethical office is being able to communicate about ethical concerns as they surface in ways that are positive and constructive. As tough as it is, we have to learn to initiate and conduct these conversations about ethics. This becomes easier as the culture of the ethical office takes root, but the first few discussions are usually difficult.

Yet we have to learn to do this. In this chapter, we'll lay the groundwork for productive conversations about ethics that resolve the dilemmas at hand, clarify group understandings about the office's ethics so future dilemmas are avoided, and do it in a way that enables you to keep and enhance your job and relationships.

Think again about the case of Mr. Wilson and his hidden assets at the beginning of this chapter. If you started a discussion about this dilemma in an unplanned, emotional way, you would be essentially calling him a liar, a thief, and a scoundrel of a husband to boot.

I have received this same dilemma in various forms numerous times. In each case, the secretary was certain her boss was using her to help "bury" his assets. And, in each case, the secretary was really bothered by this situation — probably because she knew the boss's spouse, too. What's troublesome about this situation is that the secretary's activities are technically legal and within the scope of her job description.

What would happen if a secretary stifled her frustration and worry about this situation as long as she possibly could, then finally stormed into her boss's office to confront him? Her boss quite likely would respond with defensiveness and denial, saying something like, "What in the world are you talking about?"

So, what can you do?

You can choose to simply do your job, keep mum, and let the situation unfold. (Of course, you can only do this if you are certain the things you were doing for your boss were legal. If he is asking you to do something illegal, you have a different problem that requires the advice of a lawyer. Use your ethical compass, and do what you have to do in order to take care of yourself before you go any further out on a limb for your boss. As good a boss as Mr. Wilson is, it is unlikely that he is putting your best interests before his own in this situation.

Taking care of yourself may mean talking to an attorney, either yours or the company's — NOT his.)

Your other choice is to take direct action to resolve this dilemma by discussing it the *right way* with your boss. Set aside your frustration and give Mr. Wilson the benefit of the doubt until you learn how he wants to deal with this ethical dilemma of yours. Again, sometimes people get so caught up in their personal situations that they don't realize they are drawing other people too far into their plans.

Here's what I suggest: Pick a good time, and sit down for an honest conversation with Mr. Wilson. Say something like this: "You have told me you are planning to divorce your wife sometime in the future. I have kept this confidence and will continue to do so. However, in the past few weeks, you have asked me to handle a lot of financial transactions and similar matters. Here, I've made a list of them. These activities are starting to make me feel uncomfortable (again, a *great* word!) because, sometimes in divorce proceedings, the secretary is subpoenaed. And if I ever was, I would be bound to reveal the things I've assisted you with. I'm worried and distracted by this situation, and it's starting to affect my job performance." Believe me, this has happened more often than you can imagine.

I guarantee that a light bulb will go on in your boss's head and he'll pull you right out of the equation. When it is pointed out to him how much you have been involved (it's preferable to do this in written form), he will appreciate your position and accordingly back off.

Notice: You haven't accused Mr. Wilson of anything. You have not judged him. You have not been confrontational, but merely said you are "uncomfortable." You've presented the situation as you see it, which for you happens to be an ethical dilemma, as a practical problem for him. Your feelings of vulnerability, guilt, etc. are *your* feelings, not his feelings. It is not reasonable to expect him to change his behavior just because you feel badly. He will, however, remove you from the situation if you "package" your dilemma as an unnecessary risk to his interests.

What's the bottom line? As difficult as it is, you have your best chance of resolving the dilemmas that involve or affect other people if you find a way to discuss the problem with them. All of your alternatives — filing a lawsuit, quitting your job, complaining to the human resources department, etc. — are more costly for you. Talking is a logical first step that lets everyone get a fair chance to tell his or her side of the story. If everyone is honest, respectful of each other, and behaving like adults, you have a good chance of resolving the dilemma and repairing any hurt feelings or damaged relationships.

A candid discussion is generally a logical, fair, and respectful way to bridge the foggy "ethical free zone" between people. An ethical free zone is an aspect of your relationship where there are no ethical rules yet. Until a situation comes up, you may not even be aware of your different behavior standards. What do you do if you think some conduct is okay, but your coworker disagrees? What do you do if you both know something rotten is going on, but you differ in your remedies to fix the situation? You'll almost always end up negotiating a one-of-a-kind, mutual-tolerance-and-respect understanding with the other person.

You can't sugarcoat a discussion about ethics. Ethics are too personal to be treated like a simple misunderstanding or communication problem. To even raise the suggestion that someone is doing something unethical is to attack them in a most personal way. Mincing your words, or trying to tiptoe around the problem, just seems to make matters worse. Imagine how you'd feel if a co-worker came up to you and said, "Excuse me? I've noticed you've been doing such-and-such, and I have to tell you that I'm very uncomfortable with your behavior because I think it is hurting the department." Wham! Wouldn't you feel defensive, maybe even angry and resentful that someone else would dare judge and convict you?

Somehow, you have to get to the point of truthtelling, and do it in a way that preserves your job and your relationships. The case of Mr. Wilson is an example of one way to talk about one type of ethical dilemma. In this case, the discussion was with your boss. It could just have easily have been with a co-worker, a customer, or a vendor.

The first, best answer is more talking and listening

Are we in agreement that clear, frequent communication is the best protection against, and remedy for, ethical dilemmas in the office? The most important first step is *to start the discussion about ethics at whatever level of comfort you can.*

With my tongue firmly in my cheek, I think there are basically four kinds of conversations at work that can be counted on to NOT deal with ethics well:

A "Handy" Guide to
Everyone Else's
Ethical Discussions

"Hand me the dice" — *You're very lucky. Everyone understood what you meant. The dilemma is resolved, and you get to keep your job. High Five!*

"Hand me the salt" — *You're eating crow. You got your facts wrong about the situation and now you're sorry you ever stirred the pot. Sit in the penalty box by the water cooler.*

"Hand me a shovel" — *You're digging yourself into a deeper hole. You made a serious mistake by raising an issue before you checked your ethical compass or applied your common sense test. Now you sound wishy-washy and confused, uncertain as to why this situation is a dilemma. You were not able to answer the question, "Why are you worrying about THAT?" You're embarrassed, and your co-workers are looking at you funny.*

"Hand me a hand grenade" — *You've blown your chance to talk about the dilemma. You were angry, and you decided to share your feelings with your boss, so you confronted him in an unprofessional, I'm-not-interested-in-listening manner. This incident may be the beginning of the end of your job.*

The hand grenade discussion has the worst possible outcome. It is caused by a lack of planning and preparation. I will stress again and again that you must be mentally prepared before you initiate these discussions, or else you will lose your focus on need for the resolution of your dilemma.

The unplanned, "hand grenade" ethics discussion goes something like this: "Hi, boss? Got a minute? Listen, I've been stewing for a month about the way you behaved at the client reception. You are a chauvinist pig! I'm mad as hell, and I'm not going to take it any more! I demand satisfaction, and if you don't give it to me, I'm heading straight for my lawyer. Got it?" A discussion like this is short, explosive, and almost impossible to stop once you've pulled the pin and thrown it onto someone's desk.

Interestingly, the better we are at masking our feelings, the more of a surprise the dilemma is to the person with whom we are having a problem. This surprise will immediately put him on the defensive, possibly making him angry and feeling unfairly judged. In this kind of an emotionally charged conversation, things will be said that cannot be retracted, making it highly likely that you have done precisely what you hoped to avoid — the early termination of your career, your relationship, or both.

Back to basics: This is reality

Here's a quick refresher to set the stage for your discussions. We know this much already going into these situations; these are the "Reality Cards" every subordinate has been dealt to play:

- There are some things that you will absolutely never do, for any reason.
- Your first goal is to keep your job. While quitting is always an option, you want to leave on your terms and your timetable.
- Your second goal is to behave in a professional manner and thereby retain your self-respect.
- Your third goal is to maintain a good working relationship with your boss. Making him feel angry or embarrassed, or shameful, or vulnerable to a lawsuit, is counterproductive to this goal.
- You and your boss share the goal to improve productivity and profitability.
- Finally, once an ethical dilemma arises, your relationship will change for either better or worse. It will either be the beginning of the end of your relationship, or you will be able to discuss the potential dilemma and thereby build more trust and confidence in each other. The latter, of course, is preferable because this leads to a more ethical office.

With these points about your reality in mind, let's imagine how you might discuss the following dilemmas with your boss.

- You win a contest from a vendor and accept a free trip for yourself and your family. Under what circumstances would this be acceptable? Unacceptable?
- You notice a supplier of business forms is getting business from your company via a co-worker, even though you know this supplier did not have the lowest bid. You observe your co-worker is

unusually friendly with the supplier. Is there anything wrong with this?

- A co-worker runs a small real estate business on the side and spends a significant time on the phone. His work does not appear to suffer. Is this wrong?

What would you say to your boss, and why? Do you see the link between your ethical standards, and what you might end up having to do?

Keep in mind that perceptions are reality when talking about ethics. We can't read each other's minds, and we can only guess at each other's motives and intentions. If something looks unethical, the facts may be irrelevant, depending upon your co-workers' willingness to keep an open mind and hear your side of the story.

If the situation is perceived as real, it will be reacted to as if it were real. Its consequences will certainly be real. Steps must be taken to explain the situation ahead of time, making the point that this information is being communicated to avoid precisely the problem of misperceptions. Allow an opportunity to discuss the situation, if possible, so no one has any lingering suspicions.

Interestingly, the size of your office will also make a difference in your discussions. A smaller-sized office means more confusion, more people doing more things beyond their job description, fewer guidelines, and fewer boundaries. Chances are, you also will probably have a more personal relationship with your boss in a smaller office.

Ruth's story

Discussions with our boss are one of the most frequent types of ethical discussions — because the boss is the boss. In the following example, Ruth is having a heated discussion about office ethics with her boss. What's wrong with this picture?

Ruth: "Look, it's right here in the employee manual: 'Every supervisor has an open door policy about concerns you may have regarding conduct unbecoming a co-worker who is a company representative.' Then it goes on to say, 'Your supervisor is trained and empowered to investigate your concerns and take any steps he or she deems necessary to remedy a problem with a co-worker.' I've explained that I think Connie is taking unfair advantage of the flexible schedule. I think it's high time you did something about it because it's driving the rest of us nuts."

Ron: "Hmmm. I understand your concerns, but . . ."

Ruth: "But what, Ron? This is the third time we've had this conversation. I've documented her comings and goings for the last month, just like you asked me to. We've all been patient. We want you to act, and act now."

Ron: "You don't think you're making too much of this?"

Ruth: "I'm beginning to resent your patronizing attitude. I think you're making too little of it. I think you are not living up to what is written in the manual."

Ron: "Now, wait a minute. *Your* attitude is becoming a problem here..."

Ruth was frustrated because her manager did not take action to fix a problem that she felt was legitimately affecting the morale of the office and the productivity of the office. By all accounts, including the "official" employee manual, he should have taken action before now.

But he didn't, did he? And after the above exchange with Ruth, do you think he was moved to action? Probably not; no one responds well to pressure like that.

I can hear some of you say, "I could *never* talk to my boss like Ruth did." Yes, you can. And it won't be just your boss and co-workers you'll discuss ethics with, either—you'll probably have occasions to talk with customers, suppliers, and many other outsiders, too.

Real rules, real life

What determined whether Ruth was successful in her attempt to talk her way to a resolution of her dilemma? Ruth did not follow the "Real Rules of the Office." The rules governing interpersonal dynamics in the office are impossible to document for all combinations of people and circumstances, but they always provide the context for the ways we work together. Who gets to say what, to whom, are prescribed by the complex interactions of experience, personalities, and customs.

Ruth was correct that the manual preached open-door communication and textbook-perfect supervision. But that's not the whole story. In this company, Ron knew that no one gave critical feedback to Connie except her mentor, who was a manager in a different department. Furthermore, Ron knew that most of the managers, including Connie's mentor, viewed flexible scheduling as an experiment that merited some additional time to debug. No one ever stated it explicitly, but it was understood that all negative experiences were to be saved up for the management review in a few months. Why? Because flexible scheduling is a pet idea of the company president, and any detractors would be labeled naysayers and negative thinkers who were not giving the idea a chance to work.

Is her boss going to explain all of this to Ruth? Certainly not. Maybe he doesn't want to admit he's playing a political office game. Maybe he's worried about appearing too wimpy or petty to Connie or her mentor. Maybe he can't articulate his actions, which are largely intuitive. Or maybe he thinks Ruth and her co-workers are "out to get" Connie, and are tattle-telling biddies who need more work to do!

In the real world, success is not determined by who does the best job of following the written policy statements. Nor does success automatically go to the smartest, most creative, or hardest working. Success is almost always the reward for people who have the ability to discover and follow the real rules that operate in the office.

Most people act on reflex, doing what they want to because that's what is convenient, or expedient, or least uncomfortable, or what we know best, or what we believe to be true. We usually are not aware of the rules we follow or expect others to follow. Even if we are consciously aware that we are not following the script, we have an inexhaustible supply of rationalizations for reacting to a situation in our own unpredictable way, then explaining it after the fact.

We learned this lesson in school when we discovered the best route to good grades was to mirror the teacher's biases, pet ideas, etc. Rare is the teacher that really values confrontation and intellectual challenge, even though that's what they say. Likewise, I've never once met a company that didn't endorse the manager who didn't espouse a strong commitment to teamwork, either. Does this mean, "the team makes the boss look good" or vice versa?

The real rules of the office reflect and cater to that which is most important to the people making the decisions. An ethical corporate culture is rooted in the example set by the decision-makers, too. If ethics are genuinely important to senior management, it's likely everyone else in the organization will care more about ethics, too. How ethical the corporate culture is depends at least indirectly upon the personality of the boss. Few corporate cultures are strong enough to override this basic pattern.

Implications of the Real Rules for us on the professional support staff are profound. Your power to influence your office culture is limited. You had better learn to pick your battles, and be prepared to live with a loss (you may be forever stuck with an unresolved dilemma). Your only satisfaction may come from the fact that you tried your best to resolve the dilemma, and managed to keep your job, your self-respect, and your relationships intact in the process. And who knows? Because you raised an ethical issue today may plant the seed of a new behavior standard that will ultimately prevail.

Start talking about ethics

Clear, frequent communication about ethics is a valuable tool to both prevent and cure ethical dilemmas. The important thing for you to do now is *start the discussions*.

I organize ethical discussions into four types:

	As an inoculation to PREVENT ethical dilemmas from developing in the first place	As an antidote to CURE existing ethical dilemmas
Informal	One-to-one hypothetical discussions covering a broad range of topics to explore "what if" situations, thereby sharing beliefs, expectations, experiences, etc.	Focused discussions describing specific, observed behaviors, the problems associated with those behaviors, and possible resolutions
Formal	The corporate ethics awareness or ethics training program; Code of Ethics; Mission Statement; personnel policies, etc.	Structured, recorded discussions with lawyers, HR representatives, etc., in order to comply with due process

Informal ethics discussions can PREVENT ethical dilemmas: The informal Real Rules of the office are fully engaged when you have informal discussions, less so with formal discussions. If you can establish some simple agreements about conduct and talk through some hypothetical dilemmas, you can establish some baseline expectations for behavior with your boss, co-workers, vendors, and customers. These ethical baselines will prove to be useful guides for everyone in many different situations. You will agonize less often over decisions like, "I wonder if it's okay to say this, or do that," and the Mr. Wilsons of the workplace will think twice before asking you to do something that might be questionable.

Don't worry about prescribing acceptable ethical behavior to everyone in advance of every possible problem. People are smart enough to make the connections, reasoning that, "We talked about such-and-such as a group, so I just know that if I do this thing, it will really raise people's eyebrows. I think I'd better not do it."

Informal ethics discussions can RESOLVE ethical dilemmas: In my experience, talking things through in a hypothetical context is a good, preventative starting point, but only a start. Of course your boss is not going to tell you to your face, in advance, that he expects you to do something unethical or illegal. Most of the ethical dilemmas will have to be dealt with on-the-spot as they come up, or shortly after. If you have had some discussion beforehand about ethics, at least you will have a context, a frame of reference, on which you can base your reaction.

Finally, formal ethics discussions are beyond the domain of this book. What will be said to whom, and in what manner it will be said to them, will be determined by your human resources department, company lawyers, and similar policy and decision-makers. By the time the formal discussions take place, the informal discussions have failed. The formal discussions about ethics are always costly to the company to resolve (due to attorney fees, settlement costs, etc.); the informal discussions are preferable because they are a faster, less complicated and less expensive response.

Ethics discussions are conversations, not inquisitions

Okay, let's go to work and apply what we've discussed. Imagine you are going in to the office right now ... what can you do differently, today, to make your office a more ethical (and thus a more productive) place to work? Can you and your boss (or co-workers, customers, vendors, etc.) talk about existing or hypothetical dilemmas? If not, how can you begin the discussion? Can you use your new insights about your professionalism, your personal morals, and the scarcity of absolute rights and wrongs to remedy an ethical dilemma you are currently stuck in, or preempt some impending difficult situation?

I offer the following discussion guidelines to get you started on the next step of your personal journey toward a more ethical office. These have also been called "conversation starters" and "brain starters" by my seminar attendees. They work, so give them a try. My intention is not to script your discussions, but simply to give you a starting place.

I know your job satisfaction and your job security may hinge on the success of your attempts to discuss ethical conflicts at work. My experience is that you can get the ball rolling with just one or two questions, then hang on for the ride while the conversation goes after the pressing topics in your office. Start the discussion with a question from the most appropriate list below. If the discussion lags or becomes awkward, go on to the next question.

Keep in mind that many, many people have trouble talking directly about the ethics of their conduct, so be prepared to be patient — the person you're talking with (or maybe you, too) may have to talk around the edge of the central questions, tell lots of anecdotes, persist in discussing other tangents, etc., before they get to the point of making a decision or commitment to remedy the dilemma.

BEFORE INITIATING ANY ETHICAL DISCUSSIONS, review your job description. Does your job description explicitly or implicitly refer to the ethical dilemma in any way? Most of us haven't looked at our job descriptions in years. The company probably hasn't either. Many are written purposely vague so the manager can have some flexibility to adapt your job to keep it updated. If you are dealing with an interpretation of the job description, you better know BEFORE you start rocking the boat with a serious discussion. For example, if it makes you uncomfortable to be an "office wife" — which usually means taking care of your manager's personal affairs, such as ordering gifts, running errands, etc. — be sure it isn't in your job description before you voice your concerns.

If you want to conduct a general ethics "check in, check up" with your boss and/ or co-workers, use the Ethical Office Discussion #1, the Office Ethics Audit. We first used this in Chapter 1 for a personal assessment, but it is useful in a group setting, too.

If you want to prepare yourself mentally for an upcoming discussion by getting in touch with your feelings, I suggest you review the Ethical Office Discussion #2, the Personal Ethics Audit. Knowing what you feel and why you feel it will brace you for attempts by others to minimize, trivialize, or avoid the dilemma you are discussing. "Going public" with your feelings opens the door for others to admit they feel the same way, too — and, believe me, if you feel there is a problem, you are probably not alone! The Personal Ethics Audit is discussed in Chapter 3 in detail.

Discussions to PREVENT dilemmas

If you want to have a discussion with your boss, co-worker, or someone else to PREVENT an ethical dilemma, start with the following questions:

- "Do you believe the 'rightness' of a decision or behavior may change with the situation, or do you believe right is right and wrong is wrong, no matter what?" *This is an abstract, philosophical question that is always revealing, even if he has a poor answer for it!*
- "What is your personal definition of 'professional ethics'?" *Definitions will range from the simple to the sophisticated; getting other people's views will enhance your own:*
  a) Performing your duties within the context of your moral values without adversely affecting those around you.
  b) Doing the "right thing." This means the right thing cannot change due to changing circumstances. If it is right, it is always right.
  c) Conducting your job with the trust and confidence of your executive without being asked to do anything which is against your morals or better judgment.
  d) Doing your work with honesty, reliability and integrity.
  e) Being 100 percent personally accountable for your performance. Your performance is the work that you accomplish and the behaviors you use to accomplish it.

- "How often do you face ethical dilemmas at work?" *Each person needs to appreciate the other's position. Everyone has their own dilemmas to confront.*
- "Tell me about one situation or decision at work that was, or continues to be, an ethical dilemma for you. How did you or will you decide to handle it?" *Discuss a specific situation. The answers will also provide some insights into how the person approaches and resolves ethical dilemmas.*
- "What's changing in our office or business that make ethical dilemmas more or less likely to occur?" *As a boss-secretary team, we have to confront some situations together, e.g., working on a special bid that must be kept strictly confidential, even from other officers. Some circumstances can be controlled, others cannot.*

- Ask a few hypothetical questions, like:

    a) "If I come across confidential information while filling in for someone at the front desk or in another department, and it will have a direct impact on you as my supervisor, will you expect me to tell you what I've learned?" *This is a classic conflict between loyalty to the company or a co-worker versus loyalty to her boss.*

    b) "Imagine I get an advance look at the list of employees who will be laid off soon. You, my supervisor, remind me this is confidential information and will not be made final until the monthly sales results are reported. Meanwhile, a good friend of mine who works with me here at the same company excitedly tells me about the dream house she and her husband are planning to buy. My friend is on the list of people about to be laid off. I know that she cannot afford the house without the income from her job. What would you expect me to do? Should I protect my friend from a horrible financial mistake by telling her about the company's plans, and take the risk that the information about the impending downsizing will NOT travel quickly on the company grapevine? What are the practical limits on loyalty and confidentiality? What policies does our company have that are relevant to a situation like this?" *The obvious answer here is that you should say nothing. It's your job to keep confidential information confidential, no matter what. To do otherwise is grounds for dismissal. Besides, what if the friend is never laid off? Do you want to be responsible for her losing a good house?*

    c) "Do you think a job applicant is ethically bound to reveal she is pregnant?"

    d) "Tell me what you think: If a secretary is occasionally directed by her boss to sign his name for him, such as when he is out of the office or when a large number of form letters are being sent with his name on them, when does this practice cross the line between convenience for her boss and bad business for herself and/or the company?" *Many secretaries are willingly assuming more responsibility. What are the net benefits if she is granted this authority? What are the limitations and/or safeguards within your supervisor-secretary*

team? What guidelines can you suggest if she is told to sign:
1) routine client correspondence?
2) unique client correspondence?
3) solicitation and marketing correspondence?
4) price quotations?
5) legal documents?
6) internal administrative documents (e.g. check requests, expense vouchers, time sheets)?
7) correspondence/forms common to your business?

Ask your boss: When is it appropriate to sign his name for him? How should this be handled? We all know that when you must sign someone else's name to a document, you should put your own initials next to the signature indicating you are the signer. However, there are times when supervisors wish you to sign their name without your initials (even just the first name) to correspondence when they are out of town so it looks like they personally took the time to sign the letter. If this occurs, my suggestion is to type a To-Whom-it-May-Concern note on your company stationery, put a date to it, and say "I give authorization to my assistant, Nancy Jones, to sign my correspondence on my behalf," and then, have your supervisor sign the note. Tuck the note away in your file drawer and hope you never have to use it. If you do have a problem some day, at least this note will offer some protection. Of course, this applies to just normal correspondence. If you sign for your boss on a legal document, you MUST initial it. Assistants are sometimes given Power of Attorney to cover these situations. For example, when I was an executive assistant, I had the legal authority to buy and sell stocks for my boss in his absence. For this, I was bonded, however. Other suggestions: Ask your supervisor to use a signature stamp for large quantities of form letters. Or, use a stamp with these words: "This letter is being mailed in my absence to facilitate a prompt response."

e) "Here's another 'what-if' question: A secretary in your company is given a report to type that will summarize costs for a client's project. The report will be the basis for the company's compensation. Based on the secretary's knowledge of the company's actual expenditures and accounting procedures, she realizes the numbers are incorrect. When she takes her concerns to the person who prepared the report, she is told the numbers are correct. Should she do as she is directed and type the report? Or should she take her concerns elsewhere in the company? As my boss, what would you expect me to do?" *Are "empowerment" and "quality customer service" a part of your corporate vocabulary? What do they mean in your corporate culture? Does your supervisor support your approach to handling this?*

f) "What if: You, my boss, oversleeps one morning. You call me from home and ask me to tell your client you were delayed in another meeting and will miss the meeting." Is this an understandable and acceptable request? *Would you make the call, and if so, what would you say? In general, what are your limits on the "little white lies" you are asked to tell? Does your boss understand and accept these limits?*

g) "Let's imagine your boss wants to search your office for 'something' — she won't tell me what it is. How should I handle this? Make an issue with security? Escort her out? Remain in the office under the pretense of 'helping'?" Again, your supervisor's answer to this hypothetical situation will be revealing.

- "Are we, as a boss-secretary team, doing anything that we would NOT want to tell the media? Are we doing anything you think might be illegal, immoral, or unethical? Is there anything else I should know?" *Give him plenty of opportunities to tell you the Feds are going to shut the office down if such-and-such occurs. You can't help — or protect yourself — if you don't know.*

- "Is anyone else concerned about an ethical dilemma?" *This is a wild card because these discussions ought to be strictly confidential. Offering yourself as a sounding board may help, though. But if he tells you all about someone else's problem, he's going to be talking about yours tomorrow to someone else.*

- "What is the best way for us to find a solution that will be acceptable to both of us when faced with an ethical dilemma in the future? How will we know we have resolved this dilemma to our mutual satisfaction?"

- "What is your opinion or policy about sending personal faxes from the office? Making copies for a non-profit community group? Are there any explicit limits on this behavior?"

Discussions to RESOLVE dilemmas

If you want to have a discussion with your boss, co-worker, or someone else to RESOLVE a specific ethical dilemma, start with the following questions:

- "Please, may I take a few minutes to clarify a few points with you?" *Here, you are making a COGNITIVE assessment of the facts and circumstances as you know them. This gives you an opportunity to correct any misunderstandings you have been laboring under. It also starts the discussion by having you both focus on the same facts. This is a good way to open a discussion because it is safe (you can retreat if you see the situation is so sensitive you have to use a different approach), respectful of the other person (you are courteously asking permission to take time to talk about this), giving everyone the benefit of the doubt (many people do not recognize an ethical problem until they step back and analyze it), not making any judgments or accusations, and being professional (you are seeking data as the first step to correcting a problem).*
- "Are you aware that this situation is affecting my job performance?"
- "Are you feeling as uncomfortable about this situation as I am?" *Then describe your interpretation of the situation or events, and briefly express your feelings, opinions, and concerns. Do NOT make a long speech at this point — you are simply opening up a topic for discussion. Also, do NOT use a tone that could be taken as accusatory, judgmental, or otherwise negative — it'll get you off on the wrong foot and set up the expectation that there MUST be a "bad guy" to blame.*
- "What is everyone else feeling and thinking?" *Find out. It will help if others offer new information, corroboration, and their insights in the process of "going on the record." This question usually eliminates the possibility that "it's just your imagination" and it avoids making this "your" problem by making it an "our" problem.*
- "How serious is this to you?" *This simple question is important to cover. It gives you a chance to say something very important: "This dilemma/situation/problem is affecting my job performance." This is corporate-speak that identifies a problem as*

important enough to resolve for financial and legal liability reasons. Be prepared to describe your feelings of stress, embarrassment, awkward communication, fear, shame, etc.

- *"What can we do about this?" Seek consensus around no-fault resolutions. Let everyone walk away with their dignity intact. Remember, the challenge is to resolve the dilemma between expected behavior and actual behavior — the challenge is NOT simply to make everyone feel better. Probe with follow-up questions like these:*
  a) Who will be affected by our decision? (are they nameless, faceless?)
  b) What are the harms and benefits to those affected? (what are their needs, wants, values, expectations?)
  c) What are the alternatives?
  d) What is the solution that will be acceptable to both of us?
  e) How will we know we have resolved this dilemma to our mutual satisfaction?

Summary

Initiating and conducting a constructive conversation about ethics among your co-workers is difficult. The art of managing these conversations that are potentially awkward is a key skill, and I want to give you as many insights, guidelines, and conversation starters as I can to help you.

It has often been said that World War II was the one war most Americans felt patriotic about. This was true in large part because of our leaders' ability to articulate *why* the U.S. was fighting the war. The message was communicated simply and clearly from President Franklin Roosevelt, through General George C. Marshall, on to the soldier sitting in the trenches and the stateside volunteers. Everyone knew we were doing the right and necessary thing, difficult as it was. Imagine how much less successful our war efforts would have been if we had become confused about our purpose because we perceived our leaders as inconsistent, hypocritical, manipulative, whimsical, impetuous, vulnerable to human temptations, or otherwise prone to human failings.

I don't mean to imply your office is a battlefield (although some offices I've visited made me feel like I was crossing a mine field!). My point is that nothing can be accomplished in the way of building an ethical office without clear communication from the top of the chain of command regarding what is and is not acceptable. What is true in a wartime crisis is true in the mundane workplace, only we don't have symbolic, larger-than-life leaders to invest our faith in — all *we* have is the manager down the hall with the stain from a jelly donut on his tie.

I often say in my seminars that an open, honest channel of communication between the supervisor and the assistant does not necessarily mean an effective working relationship has been established. However, *without that open communication,* there isn't a prayer for an effective working relationship! John Gardner, president of Common Cause, said it this way: "There must be not only easy communication from leaders to constituents — but, also, ample *return* communication — *including* dissent..."

We already know that one-way pronouncements from management are predictable, we'll-always-take-the-high-road stuff. Your job is to push back with questions and challenges based on your experiences in the practical world. Then, somewhere in the middle of that spirited discussion, you and your boss will come up with resolutions to your ethical dilemmas that you can both live with.

Think back to your most recent ethical dilemma. After applying your "common sense" test and ethical compass questions, you'll know what kind of an ethical dilemma you're in.

If it's a problem of your own making, and you're still in control, you hopefully can stop what you're doing wrong and find a way to unravel the mess (i.e., remove the pirated software from your computer, stop making personal long-distance calls at work and reimburse the company for money owed, refuse any more gifts from vendors, etc.).

But if someone else is involved, you'll want to try to talk it out. Discussions about ethics are either informal or formal, and they are intended to either prevent ethical dilemmas from arising, or resolve an existing dilemma. Conversations ought to be attempted as soon as possible, before pent-up emotions, unintended consequences, legal costs, and similar obstacles become too costly.

It would be accurate to say that an ethical office environment is in a perpetual cycle of construction and repair. While our personal and corporate values and principles stay constant (even though they may not be exactly the same as our co-workers), changes are always occurring in the people we work with and the daily pressures of our jobs. Our ethical behavior is the conduct that results from this dynamic interaction. We cannot always transform the conduct of our office mates — it's a simple reality that only the boss can unilaterally raise or lower the behavior standards of an office — but we can certainly talk about it in a way that starts the process of change started. This discussion must be an *ongoing* discussion.

> *"One of the most difficult tasks*
> *an office professional has*
> *is making the boss realize that*
> *'no' is a complete sentence."*

— Nan DeMars

10

The trouble with the boss

Think about it: *You love your job, and you work with a great boss. The problem: Your boss doesn't seem interested in having any discussion with you or anyone else about his sometimes-questionable ethical behavior. The last time you asked for a few minutes to talk about some concerns you had "about how we do things here," he bluntly stated he was "not interested in wasting time with that." It's almost as if he believes he is somehow exempt from normal rules, so he makes up his own rules to fit his needs as he goes along. He certainly does not want to open himself up to being judged by anyone else, and you cannot imagine him ever coming down off his high horse long enough to say things like, "I was wrong"; "I'll change the way I handle that next time," or "I'm sorry." Happily, he's a pretty good guy and usually does things by the book, so significant ethical dilemmas — the kind that make you stop, hold your breath, and try to forget — only come up two or three times a month. Is there any way to give this otherwise superior boss a wake-up call about paying attention to ethics?*

Guess what — bosses are human, too! An administrative assistant of 20-plus years for the same boss once said to me: "My boss and I have a wonderful business relationship. I LOVE working with him; but, I could never be married to him! And," she said, "his wife LOVES being married to him; but, she could never work with him." Now — there's the perfect match!

In this chapter, I'll address the unique nature of your relationship with your boss. I have one simple, important message that I want you to take away from this chapter, and this is it: *You have more power than you think to affect your boss's unethical decisions.* This is the "get tough or get out" option, and it is the logical step to take if you fail at the ethical discussions I proposed in the previous chapter.

In 1993, *Industry Week* magazine surveyed 1,300 middle managers working in medium-sized and large companies with at least 500 employees. The purpose of the survey was to answer specific questions about how managers were grappling with ethical issues like stealing, lying, and discrimination at work.

Have today's managers, most of whom were in some way influenced by the attitudes and standards of the '60s, created a more liberal, progressive, and tolerant organizational environment for themselves and their direct reports? Or have they chosen to adopt the more conservative views and "old boy" behaviors of previous managerial generations?

In a nutshell, the managers answered straightforward questions about clearly right-or-wrong ethical questions (Would you ever steal? Would you ever discriminate? etc.) with steadfast virtue. But when presented with cases that reflect real-life dilemmas between conflicting values, loyalties, goals, and the desire to do the right thing, rationalizations for shady behavior began to show up in the manager's decisions.

To be sure, managers have their share of tough choices. The *Industry Week* survey is one more confirmation that they, too, experience some conflict between what they *want* to do because it's the right thing to do and what they *actually* do because of whatever pressures or temptations they encounter.

Your imperfect boss is the hinge that swings many ethical dilemmas

Imagine you are unmarried, and you work in the marketing department of a large insurance company. You take a liking to the cute customer service representative on the third floor, and the two of you start dating. What will your manager do if he or she finds out?

When asked about this case of co-workers dating, 12 percent of the respondents to the *Industry Week* survey said they would disapprove, but take no action. The next 10 percent said they would disapprove and take whatever action they could to thwart the budding romance; and, 5 percent said they would disapprove, but decide whether or not to take action only after considering the lovebirds involved and the degree to which the relationship affected their work. Fully 73 percent of the managers said they would be indifferent to the relationship.

The dilemma becomes more complicated when the coworkers are married, however. Almost two-thirds (64 percent) of the managers object to intimate relationships between married co-workers.

But wait — there's more! When asked about their own behavior, *one in five managers say they have had intimate relations with a co-worker,* and among those individuals, one-half were involved in relationships in which at least one of the partners was married. Is this evidence of a double standard? Sure. Among those managers who have had intimate relations with a co-worker in which at least one of the partners was married, 39 percent say they object to others in their organization engaging in the same behavior.

I often give seminars that include both managers and their assistants. I once posed this true-life moral dilemma to such a class: How should the secretary react if she returns to her office late at night to retrieve something she forgot and walks in on her boss (a male) on the office couch in a compromising position with a woman from the organization (whom the secretary also knows). EVERY manager in the class immediately responded by saying the secretary should do nothing about the situation. They said things like, "Simply ignore it — it's not your concern — it's his life," etc.

The assistants in the class seemed to agree with their managers. However, I sensed they felt a bit intimidated because their managers responded so strongly. Then, I reversed the situation and asked the managers the same question: What would they do if they walked into their office late at night and found their secretary on the couch in a compromising situation with someone? The class was silent, so I directly asked a gentleman sitting close to me at the podium. How should he react? He looked quite startled. I repeated the question: "If you walked in on Susan (his assistant seated next to him) on the couch, etc." He frowned, looked quite thoughtful, and then responded, "Well, I think that would be a discipline problem. I would have to talk with her the next day." Wow! The entire class — especially the assistants — came down on this poor man! He immediately blushed. He had inadvertently confirmed what we have often observed and experienced, albeit unfair: Managers tend to hold themselves to ethical standards that are different from those to which they hold their employees.

I use this example to illustrate how thorny the negotiations with a manager over an ethical conduct point can become. Bosses are people, too, with all the inconsistency, whims, and weaknesses as the rest of us. Yet, as we discussed in Chapter 9, a boss IS different from us because he or she is the dominant influence in an office's code of conduct, and he or she sets the ethical standards.

What's an office professional to do when talking doesn't work?

In Chapter 9, we took a close look at the ethical discussion. This is a conversation where you can muster your courage and, with a little tact, broach the sensitive issues that are causing your ethical dilemmas. The informal ethics discussion should always be your first attempt to remedy a dilemma because it is usually off-the-record, less threatening, quicker to do, allows everyone to keep their pride intact, and costs virtually nothing because the lawyers have not yet been called. In short, it is the lowest-risk approach to solving the dilemma without losing your job.

In a perfect world, the genteel conversations described in the last chapter would be enough to solve all our ethical problems. All bosses would be basically nice people, logical and reasonable, sharing common values with you, and just as interested as you are in doing the right thing. But what do you do in the real world when your manager, George, is:

- a part of the problem.
- indifferent or hostile to change because it raises his level of discomfort, exposes him to various risks, or simply means more work and responsibility for him.
- philosophically opposed to your position, or the principle of change.
- pressured to maintain the status quo, however unethical it is, by calling it a "common practice" (this is an institutionalized bad ethics practice, e.g., routinely waiting for the second or third request before paying small suppliers, thereby having use of the money for an extra 60 to 90 days; does your company care that this policy creates cash flow headaches among your suppliers, perhaps adding to their stress at work and home?).

Stay tuned. In a moment, we'll look at what other options you have when simple, informal conversations like those outlined in Chapter 9 don't work. But first, let's take a close look at the problem.

Is your boss a part of the problem?

Because you work so closely with your boss, George, it won't surprise you that many ethical dilemmas you encounter involve him in some way. We talked about this in Chapter 9, too. In fact, the manager sets the ethical standards in the office, and he or she is directly or indirectly involved in many, perhaps most, of the dilemmas simply because he or she is at the top of the office food chain. Think about all the ways your manager can affect the ethical environment in your office:

Your manager starts the problem. I know from the Office Ethics Survey that many of you have been asked to do things you consider unethical by your boss, such as:

- help submit bogus expense reports.
- delete potentially incriminating computer files (the "electronic paper trail").
- conspire against another employee.
- conspire to mislead a customer, supplier, or another manager.
- support incorrect views.
- sign false documents.
- overlook wrongdoings.
- do business with his friends.
- overbill a customer.
- take care of personal business on company time with company resources.
- charge personal purchases to the company or a customer.
- or something equivalent (I've listened to these horror stories for 12 years, and I am still surprised at the stunts that some bosses try to pull!).

Your manager tolerates the problem, thereby making it worse. There are several song-and-dance routines managers commonly use to sidestep the managerial responsibility to uphold and promote high ethical standards. Perhaps you've heard some of them when you've brought an ethical dilemma to your boss's attention:

- "It's not your job to worry about this."
- "It's not my job."
- "The law does not require us to do that."
- "I have [or have not] been ordered to do it."
- "It's company policy."
- "I can't because _____ [fill in the excuse]."

- "This is the way we do things around here." [similar to: "We've always done it like this before," and "We never used to have problems until you came along."]
- "I'm paid for getting the right results, not using the right process."
- "I do not want to rock the boat. We have to go along to get along. This company is my career, and I don't want to become known as a troublemaker."
- "It's just the way it is."

Your boss ignores or minimizes the problem, pretending that it doesn't exist. This response is one of denial and/or attacking the messenger (that would be you, sweetheart). Here's what this attitude sounds like:

- "I don't believe you."
- "It's not that bad."
- "If it's such a big deal, let HR handle it." ["Upward delegation," or passing the buck to anyone else, still works for many managers]
- "I don't know what you're talking about."
- "Are you sure you're not imagining this?" [Similar to: "Are you sure you're not overreacting to this?"]
- "Why are you making an issue of this? What's your agenda?"

Your boss sets a bad example. We all pay attention to the explicit and implied cues sent by those we work with, don't we? We naturally look to managers for guidance about what is and is not acceptable. They communicate through their actions what the real work standards are, what behavior is expected in the workplace, and what it takes to get ahead.

We tend to mimic the examples the managers set. These examples are stronger than any written policy or set of notes from an ethics program. When a manager denies his responsibility to be an ethical leader and ethical standard-setter, he is abdicating his authority and turning his back on an opportunity to create a positive ethical environment. People notice what managers do and don't do about ethics violations, and their talk about it sounds like these comments from a discussion group:

- "My supervisor is not communicating her expectations clearly. I am confused, because I get mixed messages from her."

- "There are stories on the grapevine of how managers got away with beating the system. This depresses me."
- "My manager is a good talker — he does things that are unethical, then justifies them to soothe his conscience. But he's so transparent about it, we're laughing at him."
- "My peers and supervisors sing the 'we-are-so-ethical' song and then, when they think no one is watching, do the exact opposite."
- "Managers are so cynical. They believe that everyone else is doing the same as them and that it's OK to do so. They expect the basest, worst possible behavior out of us."

Why do they do it?

No surprises here. Managers are not automatically stupid or foolish; nor are they ignorant of their influence on the ethical environment. But they're people, too. They react to pressures and temptations just the same as other people. In the Ethics Resource Center survey cited earlier, managers said these were the principle causes of the pressures they felt to compromise standards of ethical business conduct:

1. Meeting schedule pressures	54%
2. Meeting overly aggressive financial or business objectives	39%
3. Helping the company survive	26%
4. Advancing the career interests of my boss	24%
5. Peer pressure	19%
6. Resisting competitive threats	16%
7. Saving jobs	14%
8. Advancing my own career or financial interests	9%
9. Other	9%
10. No answer	1%

The Fallback Plan: You DO have the power to build a more Ethical Office, in spite of your boss

Clearly, your relationship with your boss is the centerpiece of a more ethical office. Equally clear is the fact that talking about the problem may not yield a satisfactory resolution in those cases where your boss is a part of the problem. You need a plan B.

You say, "Well, what can *I* do? The office is a reflection and an extension of the boss, so he sets the ethical tone." This is true, but it's an incomplete view. You are an important part of the equation. Here is a more formal approach to take after you've tried the gentle persuasion suggested in Chapter 9.

Step 1: Recommit to resolving this dilemma. You are about to up the ante on this issue. The consequences are about to get more expensive for everyone. Re-examine this issue, and be sure you are prepared to pay the price. Do you really want to fight this battle? Are you prepared to press forward, no matter what the friction? Are you prepared to lose your job, as it might get to this point? Revisit the Ethical Audits (Chapters 1 & 3) and the Ethical Compass (Chapter 8) we used earlier. They will remind you what your core personal issues and values are.

With some help from Rockwell International, we have a set of parallel questions I think constitute a Situation Ethics Audit (let's call this one Ethical Office Discussion #3) that are useful at this juncture:

Ethical Office Discussion #3
∼∼ Nan DeMars's Situation Ethics Audit ∼∼

Use this to help you make better choices about specific ethical dilemmas. There are no right or wrong answers; these are open-ended questions that stimulate thinking and discussion. Feel free to share your thoughts with a neutral partner.

What is the problem?

What caused the problem?

Who is affected?

Who will be harmed?

Who will benefit?

Are someone's rights involved?

Who can help?

What are the alternatives?

What action needs to be taken?

How can this problem be avoided in the future?

Step 2: Ignore it. Based on your analysis, can you do this? If you cannot, you must continue.

Step 3: Collect evidence and document your position in writing, simply and clearly. You'll need this numerous times as you begin "shopping" the dilemma to others who may be interested in helping.

Step 4: Talk to another supervisor, preferably someone at or about your supervisor's level. Talk to someone else with more, or different, authority. A boss's power is ultimate, but not absolute. It is limited to his sphere of direct and indirect influence within the organizational chart. Try to gain your supervisor's assent to this — reassure him that you are simply on a mission to discover other alternatives, not to assassinate his character or competence.

No matter how well you try to finesse it, you may as well face the fact that this action has a high probability of wounding your relationship with your boss. By going around him, he will worry that you have embarrassed him before others in the company by saying something like, "I'm talking to you because my immediate supervisor won't or can't do anything. He therefore must be weak, unethical, a scaredy cat, or all of the above."

You can try not to let this happen by presenting the third-party option to your manager first. You may be able to package this as a win-win option by saying something like: "I realize this puts you in an awkward position, and your hands may be tied, even though I know you wish it were different. May I suggest something else: Why don't I take this situation to the HR department and get their input? That takes it off your desk, and makes the HR staff person look like the ethics policeman, so you do not have to upset any other working relationship because of this situation. How does that sound?" If your manager perceives you to be committed to resolving the problem, this may be an acceptable approach.

The prospect of you starting to talk to others about your concerns may be just the impetus your boss needs to take action; if it isn't, at least you've done your best to keep him involved in the process.

From here on, you MUST be absolutely professional in your presentation — stick to the facts, focus on the dilemma and the potential consequences to the company, not the personalities, turf wars, and the like. Again, document, document, document the date and substance of every conversation.

Step 5: Talk to a division head, ombudsman, human resource representative, or other formal "listening post" within the company. By this time, the formal damage control and public relations machinery of the company should begin to work with you to resolve the problem. It is at this time you must decide if the company's approach is going to be effective. If you determine that it is not, you have to drop it or be prepared for an adversarial relationship. Expect to begin signing reports, official statements, and otherwise cooperating. You will find to your dismay that every new level of administration seems to require returning to the beginning point and re-examining the concern from the ground up, and from the inside out. And — you guessed it — keep documenting each step of the process and what does or does not happen. Keep copies of everything you sign, too.

Step 6: Secure legal representation for yourself. You are going into shark-infested waters, and the stakes are rapidly escalating. Be prepared to hire your own shark to look out for your interests. You may not want to formally engage an attorney — that may be an overreaction that will just compound the problem — but you may want to have a preliminary discussion with an attorney to help you assess your situation. During the next round of discussions (see Step 6), what you say and don't say may have profound consequences. For example, you may be asked to waive your rights or incriminate yourself — a little preparation with your own attorney will be time well spent.

Step 7: Tell your story to the media, relevant government agencies, and citizen groups. Presuming you did not find a satisfactory remedy within the company, you have to decide if you want an adversarial relationship with the company. You may attempt to remain anonymous in some venues, but not many. Few people or organizations are willing to stick their neck out for someone who is not prepared to share the heat. Do not lose sight of your objective: You want to create enough pressure on the company via public opinion, economic sanctions — whatever fits your case — to change its behavior. Fortunately, if your cause is deemed just in the fickle limelight of the public stage, surprising support from outsiders will begin to trickle in. Just in time, too — you'll probably be wondering by now why you ever grabbed this tiger's tail.

Step 8: Sue in a court of law. Short of resignation, this is the option of last resort. You will burn some bridges with former colleagues and certainly be no longer welcome at your former company. You may even attract some unwelcome notoriety as a whistleblower and become "unhireable." This process is not fast and not cheap. Most cases are taking years to get a day in court! Personally, I think this justice delayed is justice denied, but that's beside the point. The legal remedy has profound implications to your peace of mind and financial security.

Step 9: Finally, you always have the option to quit your job and walk away from the entire situation. This may be necessary if your mental health begins to suffer. Remember you HAVE to continue to take care of yourself. Personally, I find this option frustrating, and I don't like it very much — after all, why should we be the ones who have to start over in a new job? Nevertheless, you always have the option of quitting. There are good, practical reasons we may want to resign instead of fighting the good fight. For many of us, the reality is we don't want to rock the boat, brand ourselves with the stigma of "troublemaker," interrupt our careers for a "fight," worry about getting a reference for our next job, etc.

Pretty grim, hmmm? But it's reality. Obviously, you need to think through your complete situation carefully, and then act accordingly. You have to ask yourself: Am I willing to take the risks? If your answer is, "No" — or, "Not now, anyway" — then, make your decision to make the best of the situation and try to put the dilemma behind you.

One of your considerations will have to be that you have to live with your decision, whatever it is. Do NOT saddle yourself with negative feelings you can't get beyond. Unresolved guilt, remorse, shame, and anger will make you punish yourself every day. And do not let others second-guess your decision after the fact. No one has the power to judge you unless you surrender it to them. You have to make the decision that is best for you, all things considered.

Finally, don't feel you need to rationalize your unwillingness to take action by whitewashing or minimizing the original cause of your concern. It's okay to say to yourself, "This situation is wrong and unfair, but I've tried and I can't change it, so I'll have to try to live with it." In other words, be honest with yourself. Don't try to justify your unwillingness to act by painting a wrong as a right, or excusing the offending action as something it isn't. To do so would just erode your own ethical standards. You may have to choose NOT to act when you know you are in the right, but you'll compromise your personal integrity even further if you talk yourself into believing there is nothing really amiss.

Fighting for a more ethical office is difficult. I have been very close to several dozens of colleagues as they went down their personal trails of tears. I imagine many of us find these experiences unbearable. Tough ethical decisions have to be made one way or another, however, even though they may change you forever.

"I need a Plan C."

I want to suggest a third approach, too. Try this approach if the informal discussion approach explained in Chapter 9 doesn't work, and you don't want to risk the formal approach we discussed in the last few pages. (Perhaps a formal approach is too strong a response for the dilemma at hand, or you believe it will unnecessarily jeopardize your job and/or your relationship with your boss.) Use this "hybrid" approach if you want to try again to keep your discussions informal, but you want your talk to be tougher and more effective. This works when you still want to keep your job, but need to give your boss a stronger wake-up call. I've used this myself when I've had to go back to a manager a second time, after it became clear he just didn't take my first informal discussion seriously enough.

Situations change, too, so there may be some reason to hope that a second discussion that is more structured, yet still informal and friendly, will have the desired effect. Even if earlier attempts to "talk this thing through" yielded only unhappy consequences, perhaps a few of your arguments got through. Maybe your boss has rethought and tempered his position, or maybe there are sufficient incentives (like the threat of a lawsuit by another person because of a similar dilemma) to cause your boss to return to the discussion and try to work out some sort of an understanding. Whatever your reasons, I applaud your efforts to persist. I wish I could personally pin a medal on each and every one of you who continue to fight for what is right.

Basically, with this hybrid approach, you have to turn the clock back and try to rebuild or "reinvent" your relationship with your boss.

Remember the early days of your relationship with your boss, just after you were hired? They were the "honeymoon days." You both worked hard to be your best with each other — extra listening, extra communication, no presumptions, etc. — trying to figure out how to work with each other. Gradually, you settled into a routine that worked for both of you.

When your boss suddenly asked you to do something you considered unethical, you suddenly needed a new way to talk about ethical dilemmas. It was a real learning experience, wasn't it?

Did you comply or not comply with his request? Shut up and do it, divorcing yourself from the act with some rationalization like, "No one is getting hurt, so why not?" or, "I have to do it to keep my job"? Challenge him to get his act together and do the right thing? Close your eyes and let him rip off the company, knowing that if you challenge his actions it would cost you your job? Accommodate him, figuring that if he doesn't care, you don't care? Attempt to "fix" him, or save him from himself, or rehabilitate him? Turn him in to the ethics police in your company? Use your knowledge for leverage in the future?

What hurt, of course, is that he asked you to do the deed in the first place. The act of making the request communicates volumes, doesn't it? He apparently doesn't understand you, which means you've misjudged the relationship, or him, or both. Does he perceive you as a co-conspirator, a person willing to do these things without a second thought? Does he think you don't care, or won't notice? Does he think you're too stupid to catch on? Or, maybe he views your opinion and concerns as unimportant?

This is a big mistake on his part! When you think about it, your boss's request reveals a lot about him, what he thinks of you, and the kind of relationship you have with him. Your challenge is to update his thinking! The key is to move the relationship to some solid common ground you both recognize as "safe." Here's what to do:

Step 1. Give your boss a chance to retract his request. Rewind the videotape and play it back to him. Say something like, "Am I to understand you wish me to tape a telephone conversation this afternoon between you and a client, but without the client's knowledge?" In other words, clearly state your understanding of his unethical request "so there is no misunderstanding." Seeing his request through your eyes may be enough to cause him to withdraw his request ("No, I didn't mean that ... oh, never mind."). This enables him to think twice about what he's doing and change his mind without embarrassment.

Step 2. Begin by saying "NO" to the request you find objectionable. This puts the dilemma on hold and reopens the discussion. Remain firm. Your boss will probably get angry and uncomfortable, but you won't be asked again until this is resolved. Your objective is to use this opportunity to declare your position and negotiate a resolution to your dilemma, even if you have complied with his unethical request in the past.

Just saying "no" is not enough. You can be fired for insubordination, unless you clearly and credibly base your refusal to obey his instructions on the basis that to do otherwise would violate the law or your religious beliefs. Most situations will not be that clear-cut. So follow up immediately with the steps below that have a good probability of a win-win outcome.

Four things will probably happen when you suddenly say "no" to doing something unethical that you have been doing for some time: (1) The person who made the request will be upset with you for refusing; (2) The person will understand why you are saying "no"; (3) The person will respect you for saying "no"; (4) And the person will never ask you to do it again! For example: If you, as a Notary Public, have been routinely notarizing documents for which you are not personally witnessing signatures, what do you think would happen if you suddenly stopped this practice?

If you have to, do the distasteful deed "one last time" to avert a company crisis, provided your boss agrees to talk about your dilemma with it at the earliest opportunity. You are not saying "NO" just to be difficult — rather, you are using this incident to get his attention and begin a discussion. So when your boss asks you why you won't do what he's asked you to do, grab the chance to tell him. This is the time to start talking and redefining yourself in your boss's mind, starting by covering the basics again. Who knows? Maybe he simply didn't have time to listen when you said it the first time, or he didn't remember, or didn't take you seriously enough at your word, or didn't incorporate it into his management style.

Step 3. Pick a good time and place to talk about your disagreement. You wouldn't start talking to your spouse about buying a new family car at the exact moment your home's old water heater gave out, would you? You wouldn't start a discussion that would likely become, well, LOUD in an embarrassing place, would you? Pick a moment and pick a place that is conducive to rational, adult conversation.

Step 4. Thank your boss for meeting with you. Tell him how much you appreciate his willingness to continue your effective working relationship and how much you appreciate the "open" relationship you have established.

Step 5. Define your ethical expectations again. You did this once · when you were hired; now, do it again, clearly and simply. Remind him of your earlier agreement to tell each other when something is bothering you about your working relationship. You can acknowledge that his standards may be different. However, you wish to have his respect for your standards, too.

Step 6. Tell your boss you are concerned about this dilemma, and you wish to protect his reputation and that of the company. Keep your conversation on a positive note.

Step 7. State your problem clearly and briefly, specifically pointing out your boss's behavior that is causing you to have the problem. This is the behavior your boss can do something about. Keep it simple, and try not to be accusatory.

Step 8. Ask questions. Acknowledge you may have misunderstood the situation, and give him ample opportunity to provide an explanation or clarify the details. Remember: It is possible you don't have all the information or even the correct information. For example, you may think your boss is padding her expense account report, but perhaps her boss has instructed her to handle certain expenses in a certain way.

Step 9. Suggest a solution that is agreeable to both of you. Don't just whine — make yourself a part of the solution. Louis Gerstner says, "There will be no more prizes for producing rain. Prizes will only be given for building arks."

Step 10. Be sure to ask for a commitment to action. You don't want to walk away from your meeting wondering where you stand.

Step 11. Always thank your boss for listening and making an effort to work together on this matter of mutual concern.

Now, a few tips about your style — you can make this discussion tougher, stronger, and more effective if you:

- Avoid becoming defensive or emotional. If you find this happening, you may have to take a "time out" and arrange another time to meet. Emotions can hinder an objective discussion.
- Be careful not to get sidetracked. It would be easy for you and your boss to spend a lot of time talking about other aspects of the business, but now is not the time. Stay focused on the issue.

- Be careful not to put your boss down. The Native Americans put it this way: "You cannot know another man until you walk a mile in his moccasins." You may not know the private horrors with which your boss is struggling.
- Never give the impression that you do not care or that ethical compromises can be made. You now are personally involved in the building of your company's reputation for ethics. You DO care!
- Avoid using the word "you" in an accusatory way. You are not the judge and jury. Frame your statements in neutral terms when you can. Example: Instead of saying, "You are handling the client poorly," it would be more constructive to say, "Would it help if we handled the client differently?"
- Avoid using judgmental words, such as "should" — "have to"— "wrong" — "always" — "never" — etc.
- Avoid using emotionally charged words, such as "hate" — "furious" — "fed up" — etc.
- When you've finished, STOP TALKING. The story goes that U.S. Senator Bob Dole once stood up on the Senate floor while a fellow Senator was delivering a lengthy oratory on why his bill deserved support; Dole said, "Would the respected Senator please sit down — while some of us are still FOR your bill!"
- Remember — your aim is to build trust and continued teamwork. Lead by example. Demonstrate that you can discuss and resolve tough dilemmas in a professional way with no lingering hard feelings.

Finally, if you have to dissolve the relationship with your boss, do it fairly by stating your reasons. As we've already discussed, resigning is the last resort.

Here's another true story of how this approach works in the real world: An administrative assistant to the president/CEO of a medium-sized paper company once told me her boss asked her if she would take over the payroll supervisor's responsibilities while the payroll supervisor was on vacation for two weeks. She accepted the responsibilities. When the day arrived for her to handle the payroll tasks, she observed that several of the officers of the firm (including the President) had listed their home addresses as being in a neighboring state. She knew these individuals resided year-round in the town near the paper plant. She questioned her boss the next day about the bogus addresses, but he just brushed it off as a trivial matter, not even worth discussing. She thought about it some more and soon returned to press the issue with a "hybrid" informal discussion. She was ready to get to the bottom of this, no matter what. Her boss sheepishly replied, "Well, you know the tax situation in [the neighboring state] is much more lenient than it is here."

Her ethics alarm sounded loud and clear. She was now privy to something her officers were doing that is probably illegal. She did not want to get involved but, like it or not, she now knew about the illegal tax evasion. She said she went home and worried all night about the situation. She also told me she was a single mom, raising two kids, and could not afford to get fired. I hesitate to even make a point of this, because I believe whether we are single, married, have 12 kids, or 10 pussycats, the reality is, we all need our jobs!

Nevertheless, she bit the bullet and did the right thing for her. She went into the office the next day and tactfully, but firmly, forced her boss to discuss this dilemma. Her boss bristled and huffed and puffed but, in the end, he said there was nothing she could say or do that would cause the officers to change their practice. To do so would cost them huge sums in back taxes and penalties, to say nothing of the humiliation and expense of admitting and correcting their scheme. She did not blow the whistle on them (hurting the company would have had a direct, negative impact on her personal livelihood), but she said that because she was aware of this illegal practice, she didn't want to be involved in any of the payroll responsibilities.

Her boss didn't fire her; instead, he relieved her of those responsibilities (she thinks he took them over for those two weeks himself). In a perfect world, she could have taken an active role in bringing her bosses to justice, but it isn't, and she didn't. But, she lost all respect for her boss (and the other officers involved). Eventually, she left the company on her own volition.

Summary

The trouble with the boss is that he (or she) is the boss! Like it or not, this person has a lot more power than you do. Your job satisfaction, quality of worklife, advancement opportunities, job security, compensation, and benefits depend upon how satisfied your supervisor is with your performance. This relationship is the centerpiece of your job.

For the obvious reasons of authority, access to information, contact with others, etc., the manager is the only one in the office who can raise or lower the ethical standards of an office by himself.

But consider this: You are not without influence. You and your boss still have the power to affect each other. Your boss communicates his feelings about company rules, courtesy, fairness, honesty, respect, and integrity by his example. So do you. You also communicate your feelings by how you respond to his directions. Acknowledging this is a good starting place.

Sometimes, an informal discussion about the ethics of a situation will not be sufficient to resolve it. The situation will escalate until your employer-employee relationship is at risk. In this chapter, we looked at formal and informal-hybrid approaches you can use that may lead to a satisfactory remedy to your dilemma. Each step in each of these processes comes with a price, however — each one extracts a greater and greater price from you, and there is no certainty that it will all be worth it in the end. A moral victory is sweet, but you can't put it in the bank and you probably don't want to put "troublemaker" or "ethics enforcer" on your resume.

This is the empowerment message: You have some power in this situation, probably more power than you believe right now. Be bold! You are not as powerful as your boss, but you are not completely powerless, either. You can choose to move toward, or away from, a more ethical office simply by deciding how you are going to act and react. You have the choice, so you have the power to change the ethics of your office. The trick will be to do it in a way that's professional and not self-destructive.

One final word:

This fight is usually worth it! In almost every case where I saw an otherwise confident and competent colleague back away from an ethics fight, she came to regret it. I've concluded that the words of Goethe are absolutely true, "We become that which we tolerate," hence the fight is never as simple as a tussle over a single principle. It always affects your overall relationship with your company, your boss and co-workers, and your self-esteem. Take heart! And feel free to call me at the number in the front of the book (see the Introduction) if you need specific advice or just a few words of encouragement.

"The boss is always right."

— Russian proverb

11

The limits of loyalty

Think about it: *"If I should ever die, take this key, open this drawer, and destroy this file," said Jill Fenton, Roger's supervisor of 12 years. His boss was about to travel to Europe to open a new manufacturing plant. Roger tried to laugh it off, but Ms. Fenton was serious. "I mean it, Roger. I want to know this will be taken care of if I'm ever incapacitated. You're my assistant, but I also think of you as my friend and colleague, too. You're someone I can really trust." If your boss said this to you, would you comply? How far would your loyalty go?*

I can't count high enough to tell you how many times assistants have told me they had the same request made of them.

We all know what the original "secretaries" — the first scribes — would have done. If they did not agree to do as they were told, they swiftly lost their jobs — and probably their heads!

During Medieval times, lords had two simple rules for the knights they sponsored:

Rule One: Do what I tell you to do, without questioning my reasons

Rule Two: Protect my best interests as you understand them, no matter what the personal costs to yourself

King Arthur had it made! Many of you will recognize these as the rules that summarize the relationship between some modern managers and their office professionals, too!

In this chapter, I want to spend a little time thinking out loud with you about loyalty.

Remember Rose Mary Woods, secretary to President Richard Nixon, who testified at the investigative hearings into the Watergate scandal? With the slip of a foot she "accidentally" erased about 18 minutes of audio tape recording that appeared relevant to her boss's guilt or innocence. In fact, she even demonstrated in the hearings how it actually occurred (by reaching for a file and stretching too far, causing her foot to slip on the "erase" pedal of her machine).

Whether you believed her story or not, the critical information on the tape was lost. Her predicament, however, helps us think about our personal limits of loyalty. No one ever said our jobs were easy, right?

Traditionally, loyalty has been an important aspect of who we are and what we do. But this is a new day, and loyalty is much more conditional than it was in the past. What are the new expectations and limits to your loyalty? And just how much loyalty does your paycheck buy?

Loyalty dilemmas usually arise when you promote or protect someone for the wrong reasons. Some examples of loyalty dilemmas are:

- Changing or concealing incriminating documentation
- Lying
- Creating a false impression or allowing a false impression to persist
- Choosing to do nothing or remain silent while some wrongdoing occurs
- Choosing between favorites — say, choosing between your boss and a co-worker or your boss and the company

New limits to our loyalty

Think of how many of our ethical dilemmas would just go away if we subscribed to a 100 percent loyalty oath, all the time, no matter what. Then, we would only have to make one decision — to let someone else make all of our decisions for us! Our lives would be simpler, that's for sure.

Unfortunately, we would have no power, because we would have no choices. That's wrong. Today, we are empowered to choose to do what we think is right.

Think about how many of the troubles we've discussed in the previous chapters are caused by your boss's actions or inactions. Unfair decisions, corruption, harassment, self-serving actions — how many of these troubles would simply go away if your loyalty was blind?

If I had only one sentence to sum up the most important changes in our profession in the past 10 years, it would be this: *Loyalty today is different from the blind allegiance of yesteryear!* We are learning there are limits to loyalty.

We can thank an executive secretary named Fawn Hall for making this a point of national discussion. Her unfortunate situation became a lightning rod for many discussions about supervisor-subordinate loyalty. She was called to testify against her former boss, then-Lt. Colonel Oliver North, about his involvement in the three-way munitions brokerage deal commonly called the Iran-Contra scandal that rocked the National Security Council and the presidency of Ronald Reagan. Briefly, in return for immunity, Ms. Hall testified she had gone to extraordinary lengths to help her boss in his schemes, including shredding evidence, deleting computer files, creating fictitious documents, altering records, and even smuggling files out of the office in her clothing to keep them beyond the reach of investigators.

Ms. Hall explained she acted out of a blind loyalty to Mr. North which, coincidentally, was the same defense her boss was using in relation to his bosses, including President Reagan. In the end, we were left asking ourselves what the new definition of loyalty to the boss was — and could it ever be confused with patriotism?

I believe a lot of executives were squirming while Ms. Hall was testifying under oath in front of the Senate's investigating committee. Many were envious, wishing they had a bright, supportive assistant who would go to such lengths for them if the need arose. Others, the ones with foresight, saw the excuse of blind loyalty beginning to unravel.

While watching the televised hearings, I recalled a group of executives I met in a seminar in St. Louis a few years before. I asked them this question from the podium: "If you had to name the single most-important trait you would want your assistant to have, what would it be?" I asked them to write their answers down so as not to be influenced by what someone else said. I expected them to use words like these: professionalism — organizational skills — positive attitude, etc. Was I surprised! The word that appeared the most in their responses was: *Loyalty.*

After the Iran-Contra hearings, I've often asked my seminar attendees what they would have done in Ms. Hall's circumstances. The question always generates lively conversation and controversy. I recall asking the question in Washington, DC where most of my audience worked on "The Hill." Although most of them said they would not have acted as Ms. Hall did, they were quick to point out that, although she was a civilian herself, she was still working for the military and thereby used to following orders.

I know a lot of secretaries, assistants, and other office professionals were uncomfortable with Ms. Hall's testimony. They said they could easily imagine themselves up there on the stand, facing the glare of a national television audience, trying to explain why they did what they did. No one talking to me imagined their actions affected national security in the same way, of course, but in their own worlds their actions were just as dramatic. How did they excuse themselves for throwing themselves into situations so they could "save" their bosses? Old-fashioned, blind loyalty.

Ms. Hall's public attempt to justify her actions was a wake-up call for many. Judging from what I heard in my seminars during and after Ms. Hall's testimony, many, many office professionals were rethinking the presumptions of loyalty held by their supervisors. In a matter of days, Ms. Hall managed to have everyone take a fresh look at office loyalties.

Looking back, how many of us have unwisely exposed ourselves to grievous consequences in the name of loyalty? Taken the blame for our boss's mistakes, larceny, unshipped packages, unreturned messages, and late reports? Bit our tongues when we were portrayed as the bottleneck, mistake-maker, low-level drone who could not be held accountable? What's sad is that so many of us have allowed ourselves to be characterized this way.

A paycheck doesn't buy blind loyalty anymore. *You are an eyes-open professional, with your own set of responsibilities and, as such, you will remain personally accountable for your actions until you leave your job.*

You can no longer use those old-fashioned "cop-out" words, "My boss told me to do it!" YOU are accountable. And, no one else will be in that courtroom with you to defend you or take the blame for your actions. I am sure my mother, when she was a secretary, felt she could have gotten herself off the hook safely by defending an unethical act on her part with the words, "Well, my boss told me to do it!" Today — that defense holds no water.

Conversely, however, just as office professionals should no longer feign unaccountability, *managers should no longer blame their mistakes on their office assistants!!* I am always telling managers in seminars that the days of "Me Tarzan, you Jane" are over. Their assistants do not have to take blame for that late report when it was late because the manager was late getting it to them! This has to be a two-way street of respect.

We all know a part of our job is to cover for our bosses and, again, serve as their protectorate. Furthermore, we all know all professionals at times have to "take the bullet" for their supervisors. This is simply being a team player and recognizing that we are all working together to accomplish our shared goals.

Today, however, no office professional has to be the whipping post or scapegoat for his or her supervisor. There IS a difference between protecting and supporting your supervisor, and continually taking the rap for him or her.

Blind allegiance no longer has a place in business today. "I was just doing what the boss told me to do" is no longer an excuse. An unfortunate example of this was the "Phonegate" scandal in my home state of Minnesota. One of our state legislators inadvertently gave his telephone access code to his teen-age son, who then provided the number to an entire college network system. These kids ran up over $100,000 worth of telephone charges by placing calls around the world before it was discovered. The legislator, needless to say, resigned; and, he has been court-ordered to reimburse the state of Minnesota.

In the wake of this discovery, our attorney general decided to investigate all legislative telephone access codes to see if any other improprieties had occurred. Guess what—there were many. All of a sudden, a number of other state legislators had to account for their improper uses of state credit card phone calls. As a result, several legislators lost their re-election bids and others did not even try to run again because of their exposure.

The one person I felt bad for was a secretary to one of our state senators. Her mother was ill in Florida and, as she tells the story, her sympathetic boss had given her permission to call her mother any time she wished by using his credit card number. She did so, and ran up over $1,000 in telephone bills in the process. When the investigation took place and this was discovered, she was fired, ordered to reimburse the state, and is being charged with a felony. I was irate when I read this account in the newspaper. Her boss told her she could do this—why should she be penalized?

My husband, Lou, however, brought me up short! He served for years on the Minneapolis City Council, several as president. He reminded me that every time he picked up the phone and made a toll call, he made certain it was only for legitimate Minneapolis City Council business, as he was aware he was using taxpayers' money. Every time that poor secretary for the state of Minnesota called her mother in Florida, she had to know she was using taxpayers' money, too! Have phone calls ever been free? She should be held account-able — no matter what permission or authorization she had from her boss. She, ultimately, is responsible — just like everyone else who made the same error in judgment. What a difficult lesson to learn!

Loyalty dilemmas and the office team

Harvey Mackay, author of the classic business books *Swim with the Sharks* and *Sharkproof*, says, "Teamwork comes from diverse people respecting each other and being committed to each other's successes."

Your greatest loyalty dilemmas arise when "the team" is in jeopardy and you respond by trying to protect or promote the wrong person or cause for the wrong reason. In this context, "the team" could be just you and your boss, or you and the rest of your office mates. In either case, the dynamics are similar, although your loyalty to your boss often tends to be stronger because of the close one-on-one relation-ship you have with your boss.

I've heard from some office professionals at the executive level who became totally captivated by their charismatic bosses. This often hap-pens when you work for a highly visible and popular politician, enter-tainer, salesperson, etc. However exciting it is, though, this is rarely a happy or healthy situation for the assistant. Working closely with a high-energy, charming, wealthy, and powerful person for a long time can take its toll. I've heard women describe themselves as "head cheerleaders" and "recruiters for a personality cult." This almost always leads to a loss of objectivity, blind allegiance bordering on compulsiveness, and trouble with other relationships — because no one else can compare to the boss whom you worship! Fortunately, most of us learn there is a real person behind the mask and learn to relate to that personality in a way that promotes trust and honesty.

One such boss took charge of this kind of a situation herself. Ms. Sally Howard was an active, well-respected, and visible member of the Minneapolis City Council for several years. Sally told me she was fortunate to have inherited an excellent assistant, Elsie Mosell, when first elected. This is commonly the case — elected officials move on, while staff members remain and work with their successors. A person like Elsie is always an asset to a new council member. As Sally said, "Elsie really taught me how to do my job!"

Sally said she right away had what she calls her "puffed with importance" conversation with Elsie. She told Elsie she would look upon her as her right arm support, her alter-ego and, perhaps most importantly, as someone who would help Sally keep her conscience clear. As Sally put it, who would be in a better position to know you better than you know yourself than your office assistant! Your assistant sees you from so many different angles that he or she is in the best position to help you see yourself clearly.

"If Elsie *ever* saw me getting too big for my britches," Sally said, "I considered it Elsie's responsibility to say something like, 'Watch out. You are heading for big trouble if you don't stop,' or, 'Just look at what you are doing and rethink it.'"

Sally gave me a great example. She said she once went to Elsie and asked her, "Can we pay this freelancer this way?" Elsie looked at her and firmly said "no," and then explained the way it should be handled according to the system. Elsie followed up with the words, "And, don't ask me to do this any other way because it will be ME they are going to come after!" She was absolutely right on all points!

In situations where your office mates and you are struggling to meet a goal or solve a problem, you have multiple pressures to bend the rules and cut corners. You are committed to the outcome because this is your battle, too. You are emotionally involved with your teammates who are your friends. You genuinely want to be helpful. You have a natural desire to remain bonded to your group and to be accepted as a "good team player." Under these circumstances, it is difficult to be the one who puts the brakes on a plan because it is unethical. Who wants to be the wet blanket? Who wants to be the one to squelch the team's opportunity to meet the goal or solve the problem? You may find it difficult to make the right decision because you feel you are hurting others' incentive pay, chances for promotion, and so on.

Resolving loyalty dilemmas

Is it really in your best interests—or any other team member's best interests—to cut corners when negotiating the copier contract? Shopping the printing bids? Evaluating the performance of the temporary staff? Reorganizing the order-entry system? If you think about it — and raise the tough questions about what is the right thing to do — I think you'll usually find that most people support you and respect you for being a moral leader. *Being able to persuade your office teammates to look at the larger picture and the longer view will speed the process of building an ethical office environment.*

This is true even when your boss is your only teammate, too. The pressures to yield to the path of least resistance is greater here. After all, your boss controls your career in many respects, so you have to be more diplomatic and tactful when you argue to take the moral high road. This should not deter you, though. You are doing your boss a favor when you "remind" him to stop trying to make short-term solutions work for long-term results.

I think it is important to note here that if you do call an unethical situation to your boss's attention, be prepared to provide a solution.

My boss, Judd Ringer, always used to say: "Don't ever come into my office with a problem unless you have the solution!" He was right. Bosses are impressed only with positives — not negatives. If you raise the ethical issue, you should be the one to first suggest a way to resolve it.

A likely dilemma

Here's a likely scenario: Your five-person team is frantic to get the report done on new leasing options, and everyone is staying after work to finish the report so it can be presented at a meeting the following morning. At about 6 p.m., the group realizes one of the leading vendors, Acme Leasing, misunderstood the bid specification, so you need some clarification regarding its final quote. You try calling Acme's office, but no one answers. This vendor has a high profile, so if it's left out of the report, the omission will have to be explained. Still, you and your teammates want to have a tight, complete, and comprehensive report tomorrow morning because it will make all of you look like the capable decision-makers you know you are.

Peter and Pauline are eager-beaver types, and they say, "Let's just plug in a reasonable number so we can include this vendor in the report. Based on the rest of the bid, Acme will be a second or third choice anyway. This way, the project can move forward, and that's important."

Julie and Jeff are more cautious. "What if the numbers we plug in are wrong, and we have to explain them later? It will make the entire report, and all the rest of our work, suspicious. There is a 50-50 chance Acme will get the contract because Acme has some political friends here, and they've had this contract before. Maybe this decision is going to be made by taking other factors like that into consideration. And what if Acme misunderstood the other part of the bid, too? That means they could be selected based on totally insupportable numbers. That puts us back at square one, looking like idiots."

Your opinion will lead the group. What would your ethical compass tell you to do? How would you persuade them? And do you have their respect, trust, and confidence to be a moral decision leader? Challenging someone else's plans or activities on ethical grounds is potentially explosive. You are, in a sense, questioning his or her "goodness" as a person.

As the King of Siam ranted, "'Tis a puzzlement!"

Here's the reality: Just like we have to demonstrate our skills and talents in order to gain recognition, promotions, raises, etc., we have to demonstrate that our ethical compass is in place and functioning before we will be trusted to make ethical judgment calls. We have to demonstrate we know what we are talking about. We have to share some rough-water experiences with our teammates before they develop some confidence in our ability to navigate ethical dilemmas.

Here are some practical suggestions that may help you breech the delicate subject of doing the right thing. Remember, it is your loyalty to your personal values and accountability, your loyalty to the long-term interests of the company and, finally, your loyalty to your boss and/or teammate that motivates you to speak up.

To your boss: "Jennifer, can we talk about this report? I think it's in our best interests to consider the long-term consequences of inputting this questionable data. I'd like to explore a couple of other ways to do it. Here are my suggestions..."

To your teammates: "Look, guys—I want to win the Luther Prize as much as you do. But this just doesn't seem like the way. I feel very uncomfortable about how we evaluated this situation. The Luther Prize is supposed to bring out the best in us, so what do you say we try it a different way? I have some ideas..."

Again, keep your comments and suggestions positive so as to avoid putting anyone immediately on the defensive. You are not accusing anyone of any wrongdoing. Arguing the "high road" is actually easier than trying to defend cutting corners. How about saying something like: "This is too important a project to take a chance on having it blow up in our faces. And, I don't think any one of us wants to take that chance. What do you think about this idea...?"

Other dilemmas will arise that force you to choose loyalties between friends, boss versus co-workers, company versus coworkers, Vender A versus Vendor B, etc. Trust your ethical compass to guide you. As long as you keep your priorities in mind, you can take care of yourself first, take care of your company second, and take care of your boss third.

It is difficult to balance conflicting loyalties and to judge just how much loyalty is too much. The next situation is another illustration of the complications that may arise through blind allegiance.

You have assisted Mr. Jones for five years. He is the hardworking sales manager for your company, a frozen food processing plant owned by a large, multinational firm headquartered in another state. As your supervisor, Mr. Jones has impressed you with how effective he is at "bringing home the bacon." He is a star performer, boosting sales 20 percent or more every year. His sales keep the plant busy, and the plant is a large employer in your small town.

His job dictates that he be on the road most of the time and, because of his extended hours, he has not hesitated to take an occasional day off after a strenuous trip. You have been sympathetic to his need for time away from the job so, up until now, you have done what you can to make it possible for him to do so. You have assumed he has made some sort of arrangement with the plant manager regarding the amount of "face time" he spends in the office.

During the past two months, however, his unaccounted-for absences have reached alarming proportions. He did not come to the office at all during the previous week although, as far as you know, he was neither traveling for business nor on official vacation. He telephoned from home every day to dictate letters and report a few orders.

On Monday, Mr. Jones called and asked you to tell the president he was in San Francisco working on the Johnson order. You know Mr. Jones is at home because you are to call him there later in the morning. When the president checks in for an update, what should you say? What would you do about the entire situation that is developing? Would you respond differently if you suspected Mr. Jones was having an illicit affair, or if you suspected he was about to be recruited away from your company by a competitor?

This story is familiar to all of us, isn't it? Most office professionals recognize their value as the "protectorate" of their bosses' time and energy, and nearly every secretary has grappled with the issue of telling "little white lies," such as telling a telephone caller that the boss is not in when, in fact, she is.

For those uncomfortable with this deception, this common dilemma can be handled by simply stating that the boss is "unavailable," followed by your immediate offer to be of service or to take a message. It doesn't matter whether the boss is in the restroom or Boston—as far as the caller is concerned, the boss is unavailable and cannot be reached. Remember, all the caller requires is a clear statement about whether or not he is going to be able to talk to the boss now.

The professional way to handle most of these situations is by following this simple rule: *The less information you give, the better.* For example, if Mr. Jones is on the golf course for the day, it is no one's business. A caller needs to know only that he will be back in the office tomorrow and you're available to offer assistance and to take a message right now.

Executives complain to me often that they call another executive and the assistant gives them all kinds of unnecessary information about her boss's whereabouts, e.g. she's on the golf course, he went to the bank, he's in a meeting about the company picnic, and even that he's at a competitor's office! They tell me they doubt whether the executive knows his assistant is revealing all this information.

The situation with Mr. Jones is more complicated. It is not your responsibility to judge your boss (or anyone else, for that matter). Many times, executives work long hours at home and they often have special arrangements with their own superiors regarding their working hours that you may not be privy to. Because you may not know all the facts, giving your boss the benefit of the doubt is certainly the wiser course of action.

To think this situation through, start by checking for unusual behavior. Mr. Jones has been a top performer in the past. He always put the company first. Now, all of a sudden, his behavior is incongruous with his previous track record. Apparently, something quite serious is occurring in his life to cause him to make such an unprofessional request of his assistant.

Mr. Jones specifically asked you to lie to a person of authority who represents the company. In fact, the president of the company is "the" person of authority! True—there are times when we have to cover up for our bosses and "fudge" a little. It's a part of the job, and we are a part of the team.

However, *I draw the line at lying FOR the boss—in any regard.* I believe it is wrong and completely unethical for you to lie, say, to your boss's boss, about your boss's whereabouts.

This is more than a little white lie. You are being asked to help Mr. Jones mislead the boss into thinking something that is not true. It places you in the role of co-conspirator. You have no way of assessing the significance of Mr. Jones's apparent deception—he may be attempting to create the impression of activity, covering up or fabricating a tale for the purposes of company politics or his expense account or a romantic interlude, or even looking for another job on company time.

I have yet to hear a defensible reason to ask a secretary to lie for the boss. Likewise, I have never heard a secretary satisfactorily explain why she absolutely had to do so.

I used Mr. Jones's case in one of my columns and, as usual, I was proud of the responses from my readers. The consensus was overwhelming that they would *refuse* to lie for their bosses.

Here are a few of their responses:

Rhonda R. Strong, secretary at GTE Telecom Marketing Corporation in Carmel, IN notes: "Under no circumstances should the secretary be placed in the position of having to deceive the president and make excuses for the supervisor's absence from the office."

Lupe Shepherd CPS, Johnson & Johnson Medical, Inc., El Paso, TX reinforces this comment: "You can say that 'everyone lies,' but that also leaves you deciding when it's OK to lie. Lying is tempting, but it's also irresponsible and cowardly in facing the truth and consequences."

I also liked the response of Carolyn Hankins, administrative assistant at the Florida Poultry Federation in Tampa, FL. "When Mr. Jones told me to tell the president he was in San Francisco, when in fact he was not, I would have told Mr. Jones I would not lie for him. Recognizing that Mr. Jones is my boss and that it is not my responsibility to be reporting on him, I would not volunteer the information of his whereabouts to the president. However, if the president should ask me, I would definitely tell the truth and tell him where Mr. Jones could be reached."

An anonymous reader responded cleverly: "You can always say to the president, 'Mr. Jones told me to tell you he was in San Francisco working on the Johnson order'." You are certainly stating the truth. However, if the president persists and wishes to know exactly where Mr. Jones is, you then must respond according to your own ethical standards (*not* those of Mr. Jones).

Respond immediately

Nancy Reagan says, "Just say no!" It's not always that easy; but, on the other hand, *I believe it is always best to respond immediately to an unethical request.*

Tell Mr. Jones immediately you are "uncomfortable" (this is a great word for this situation — because it is the truth!) complying with his request. An excellent way to handle such a situation is to repeat the boss's request back to him: "Do I understand correctly you wish me to tell the president, if he asks, that you are in San Francisco instead of saying you are at home?" In other words, clearly and succinctly let him know you are aware he is asking you to lie on his behalf. You might even add, "In other words, you wish me to lie to the president?" This will give him the opportunity to alter or withdraw his request (and perhaps even save face).

Even though your boss may not like your refusal to follow through on his instructions, *he will respect your reasons.*

Sense of powerlessness

Sadly, many assistants feel powerless to tell their supervisors they will not lie for them. They believe the consequence of saying "no" is to be labeled insubordinate. They fear that taking a moral stand may result in the loss of one's job.

A sense of powerlessness is an unfortunate reality for some office professionals. If this is the case at your company, you must go to someone in the Human Resources Department and speak confidentially about the situation. Tell that person exactly what you have been asked to do, how you handled it, and ask for that person's counsel. Tell her also you are going to document each conversation, including the one with her as the human resources department representative. And, then do it — *document, document, document!*

Let's return to the case at the beginning of this chapter: Your boss, Ms. Fenton, asks you for a commitment that should she ever die, you are to destroy an envelope (contents unknown). This is a classic loyalty dilemma.

We have — and always will have — an unspoken loyalty obligation to our employer, just as attorneys have to their clients and physicians have to their patients. Traditional confidentiality expectations for professionals like assistants require that you not do certain things (e.g. mention names of clients, discuss cases, etc.).

However, Ms. Fenton's request is for you to take action. How much action you take to protect your boss or employer in the name of loyalty is the issue. Certainly, there are instances when you would be expected to take action, such as when you witness criminal behavior. The ethical judgment call here is: Just how much do you do after you're no longer working for a person? Where does your loyalty as an employee end and your loyalty as a friend begin?

I used this case in my magazine column also. My resulting mail ran 10 to one against making the agreement to destroy something you knew nothing about. Most said they wanted to know what was in the package before making such a commitment, and then, if they agreed that it should be destroyed, they would agree to participate.

Let's say you asked Ms. Fenton what was in the package, and she told you. Unfortunately, this leads you to another problem: Are you going to take her at her word? This approach gets you deeper and deeper into something you don't want to be in. What exactly qualifies as "destroyable"? How could you avoid forming an opinion as to whether she was doing the right thing by destroying the "time bomb" or "smoking gun" or whatever it is? Whether you judged her right or wrong, you would never really know. Are you ready to be the judge and jury of her decision?

There is only one circumstance where I would agree to help someone in this situation. If my best friend, Kathy, asked me on her deathbed to go home, go into her bedroom, and get some letters out from under the mattress and burn them, I'd do it. And, no, I wouldn't read the letters, either. But, that's my best friend I'm doing this for. Roger is not Ms. Fenton's best friend. Ms. Fenton is Roger's boss. Roger would be wise to decline to help her in this way, and instead suggest she see her attorney.

Frankly, there are too many "what if" questions to consider if you "blindly" agree to burn the file. What if you were destroying something illegal (e.g. blackmail material or embezzlement papers)? What if it was evidence incriminating or even exonerating someone? You could be destroying patent documentation, birth/adoption/custody papers, stock records, love letters, etc. What if you were destroying money?

Before you conclude I've been watching too many lawyer shows on television, consider this: You cannot put yourself into a position of agreeing or disagreeing to destroy something when you don't even know what it is! This amounts to a leap of faith reserved for very, very few people who are close to you. Some of you might consider honoring such a deathbed request from a best friend, but I think it's too much to expect from an acquaintance or workplace colleague. *No matter how close you are to your boss, you are still in a business relationship first, and a friendship second.*

If you are still not persuaded, consider these possibilities pointed out by two of my readers, Kay Harding of Mitchelville, IA and C. J. Maniatis, Administrative Assistant at the Gulf Coast Research Lab in Ocean Springs, MS: "You may not be available at the time of her death and someone else may find the envelope. Furthermore, someone else could discover the envelope before her death and discover your agreement to dispose of it!"

An executive stood up in one of my seminars and posed this possibility: What if you agreed to destroy the file and, six weeks later, Ms. Fenton confronts you with the fact that the file has disappeared? Your acceptance of this responsibility now places you in a position of suspicion because you knew about this file and now it is missing!

A regular respondent to my column, Tracy Heslop of Canadian Western Natural Gas Company Ltd. of Calgary, Canada suggested the best remedy. Her approach preserves the relationship with your boss/employer. It also preserves your integrity, your conscience, and your boss's confidentiality: "Thank Ms. Fenton for expressing such complete trust in you. Tell her removing the envelope from company premises would make you feel uncomfortable (there's that great word again). Suggest that she take the envelope to an attorney so her wishes could be carried out by an unbiased person in a non-compromising position."

In fact, one of my readers did just that! Rosie Laquerre CPS of Bethel, VT wrote she had this same request from a former boss and she handled it similarly. After making the above suggestion to him, he said: "Rosie — you're probably right." She typed an express mail envelope and sent it on its way five minutes later.

Loyalty to friends and coworkers

What about loyalty to friends versus the boss? How would you respond if your boss asks you to "spy" on a co-worker because he suspects this co-worker is abusing her time sheets, coming in late, leaving early, etc.? If your boss asks you to observe her behavior for a month and then report your findings, what would you do? You are being asked to play James Bond and "get the goods on her," and you know this will make you feel like a traitor to your friends. Is this kind of spying fair?

This kind of dirty work is not in anyone's job description, and I can't imagine anyone who would be eager to accept this responsibility (unless there were already bad feelings between you and this co-worker — in which case, you should NOT be asked to do this because you are no longer unbiased).

You must take all or none of the responsibility for the situation. If it were me, I would explain to the boss that, "Yes, I'm willing to take on the additional responsibility of getting this co-worker back on track and following the rules, *but only if* I also have the authority to rectify it." In other words, if it is going to be your responsibility to monitor an employee's behavior, then you need the authority to handle the situation yourself, in your own way that you judge is ethically right.

Instead of just "spying" and reporting on her, you could handle this in a more fair way that was less damaging to the morale of the team members, and quicker, too. I'd first probably call the entire department together to remind everyone about the rules and the importance of following specific procedures. This could be done in a way that was nonjudgmental, without pointing fingers.

If this didn't solve the problem, you could have a personal discussion with the problem employee so you were certain she got the message loud and clear. In other words, give your co-worker clear feedback about your expectations and a reasonable time to mend her ways before YOU take action. This avoids the inevitable discussion where the boss says something like, "I know you're guilty of coming in late, etc., because I'm getting my information from a very good source. I'm not going to tell you who it is, I'm just going to tell you that I believe her. Therefore, based on this information, I'm going to punish you in the following way…"

Not very ethical, is it? Certainly not the way we would want to be treated. It's not fair because the misbehaving employee is disciplined on the basis of secondhand information and without a chance to change or even explain her behavior.

Finally, the knowledge that secret spies are being recruited and whatever they say is apparently taken seriously will have even the innocent looking over their shoulders, wondering whom they can trust. This practice is not respectful or fair to anyone (even the boss—he'll be blamed, too!), and it's almost certain to undermine whatever sense of teamwork exists. True, something has to be done—you owe it to the rest of the team to maintain standards, share the work fairly, etc.—but there's no reason the problem cannot be solved in an ethical manner.

One more point: In this situation, your boss is asking you to monitor a fellow employee's behavior. Isn't this above and beyond your normal job responsibilities? What if you somehow do manage to handle this problem in an ethical manner? In essence, you are doing part of your boss's job when you communicate with someone with the intention of solving a performance problem. If this is a formal request from your boss, you should ask for appropriate compensation and/or recognition.

Let's return to an earlier case: You are a human resources representative for your firm. You learn that the company plans to lay off a long list of employees in three months. Your best friend, who is currently negotiating to buy a new home, is on the list of employees to be laid off. You know that, if she realized there was even a possibility she might lose her job, she would not consider the purchase of this home at this time. What should you do?

Those of you who work in the human resource area know that this is, unfortunately, not all that uncommon an occurrence. This case illustrates how people may respond to situations differently, depending upon their personal versus professional relationships. Can you keep the company's secret and still help your friend? Probably not—at least not officially. The company leadership may be sympathetic to your friend's situation, but there are probably many more similar hardship situations scattered throughout the employee roster.

The obvious professional answer is: You should not share the information about the layoff with your friend because it would breach the confidentiality of your position. If your friend is going to hear about her impending layoff, it will have to come from "unofficial" channels, quietly and confidentially. If you decide, however, that you have to divulge this knowledge to your friend—and that certainly is your personal option—understand your action will constitute grounds for dismissal with no recourse if it is discovered. Everyone has to do what they believe in; but, it's important to understand what is at stake.

Loyalty to the "Old" boss versus the "New" boss

Mary, executive assistant to the CEO of a Fortune 500 firm, called me one night with a splitting headache. She had worked for her boss for 10-plus years and, two weeks before, her boss was fired. It was an overnight "coup," all based on company politics, she said (as so often is the case). She had arrived at the office one morning and her new boss, the new CEO, was sitting at her boss's desk (he had flown in the night before). Since then, she had had to assist both her former boss (he has a one-month contract to remain to assist with the transition) and her new boss. She felt loyalties to her "old" boss and regretted he was leaving; and yet she wanted to assist her "new" boss, too, because he represented her future security. The two gentlemen did not like each other, and they barely spoke to each other.

Mary felt caught in the middle! Her "old" boss needed and depended upon her assistance, but he wasn't handling the situation in a professional manner—so she had to listen to him ask questions about the "new" boss ("What's he planning? What's he saying about me? What's he like to work for?"). Any help she provided to him was viewed somewhat suspiciously by her "new" boss, who was understandably uncertain about her loyalties at this point. She told me she went home each night with a headache that was worse than the one she had the day before.

I recommended she follow her Ethical Compass: Take care of herself first—her company second—and her bosses third, new boss first and old boss second. She called me a few weeks later and said this approach worked beautifully! From that day on, whenever a dilemma arose, she stayed centered and said to herself: "I work for XYZ Company—and, I'm going to do what I think is best for the company, period." She said she got through that difficult month without any more Tylenol.

Similar situation: Another executive assistant, Joan, told me she went into a board meeting with her boss, who was the president. Immediately, the CEO announced it was going to be an executive meeting. Joan picked up her papers to leave the room because she was never included in executive meetings. Then the CEO said to Joan's boss, "And, you can leave also." Unbeknownst to Joan and her boss, there had been a secret board meeting the night before, and her boss was voted out of her position. Joan immediately started assisting her boss's departure from the office (packing her belongings, etc.); and, her boss left the company that evening.

For the next few weeks, her former boss called frequently to ask Joan to gather information, additional files, books, etc., she said she had forgotten and to have them ready for her to pick up. Joan immediately went back to her Ethical Compass. Joan realized that she now reports to a new boss, the newly elected president. Thus, she sought permission and approval of her "new" boss for everything she gathered for her "old" boss. She said whenever she felt "torn" personally, she just returned to her Ethical Compass and took care of herself, her company, and her boss, in that order.

Loyalty in the family-owned business

Other secretaries have told me about situations where they worked in family-owned businesses for many years, then had to navigate a transfer of power. When the boss's son or daughter joins the company as the heir apparent, they report receiving conflicting directions between the "new" and "old" regimes. These assistants say the ONLY way they got through these difficult transition times is by staying focused on doing the best they could for the company first, and their boss-for-the-moment second.

It's only natural that we try to take care of our boss AND our company. I'll never forget the Salt Lake City secretary who told me her boss was continually using his private golf club for personal use, but charging the company for its expense. He played golf on weekends with his personal friends (his secretary knew this for certain because she made the tee times for him and called his cronies to set the schedule). Then, on Monday morning, he filled out an expense account report listing clients as the members of his foursome. This allowed him to be reimbursed for his expenses. In addition to this, she knew he bought golf clubs "as gifts for clients," but the clubs never left his own bag! She did try to talk to him a few times about the situation, but he just brushed aside her qualms.

Finally, because she was so worried about the company, she said she got "pushed over the ledge" — she walked into the CEO's office, sat down, and told him she wished to discuss something confidential. After she related her story about her boss, the CEO stood up, shook her hand, and congratulated her on her honesty. He said management had been suspicious of her boss's actions for some time and her confirming story was "the straw that broke the camel's back." Her boss was fired, and he never knew she was involved.

Are we our brother's (or sister's) keeper?

When SHOULD we get involved? The Salt Lake City secretary became involved because, as she told me, "I just couldn't stand to see my boss cheat the company any more!"

My Office Ethics Survey indicates many of us observe a lot of the misdeeds of our co-workers. Considering our positions, it's no surprise we often see the unethical behavior of employees around us. But, when do we get involved? We don't want to be labeled the company "busybody," nor do we wish to have the reputation of "ratting" on our co-workers, etc.

People often say, "Give 'em enough rope and they'll hang themselves." That's true, but sometimes it takes a lot of rope! On the other hand, you may not have to wait too long, because if you are observing outright unethical behavior (tardiness, leaving early, spending too much time on the telephone with personal calls, stealing, etc.), you can be certain others are observing the same things. You aren't really ever alone in this observance.

I counsel getting involved whenever I see repeated behaviors that have a negative effect on job or company performance. If a behavior is job-affecting, or if it affects the success or profitability of the company, then you have a problem and you should take action. The precise time and manner of your intervention is a judgment call only you can make. No matter how you choose to handle it, and no matter whom you end up trusting to help you, be certain your confidential information is protected and you document, document, document.

Loyalty is seductive

I once was presenting a seminar at an insurance company and we were discussing how the old-fashioned, blind loyalty compares with the realistic, conditional loyalty of today. Mary Ann, one of the attendees, raised her hand and told her story. About six years before, she had been secretary to one of the officers of a company in the automotive industry. She said she enjoyed working with her boss and also enjoyed the salary. She slowly realized, however, over a period of time, that her boss was falsifying sales report figures, altering figures, and, in general, shuffling the company records to show his department in a highly favorable light—that just happened to be completely bogus! She innocently assisted him in all these deceptions in her role of secretary.

Mary Ann said she never planned to be a co-conspirator in a scheme to rip off her company. She said that for her, it was a "seductive process," occurring gradually over several months as she was slowly drawn into the process. Eventually, it began to bother her more and more. She said she stopped eating right, got little sleep, and was, in her words, "en route to a mental breakdown." One day, she looked at herself in the bathroom mirror and "didn't like what I saw." She went in that morning and quit her job! Her boss was shocked, and he tried to talk her out of it. But, she walked off the job that day and never looked back.

When she got to this point in her story, Mary Ann started to cry. She explained she was crying because she realized right then that her circumstances were similar to those of an abused wife. She slowly got into the sick situation and, because she needed the salary, the security, and liked the company itself, she stayed in the situation much too long. She also realized how much she lost when she quit her job.

What frosts me was that SHE had to be the one to lose her excellent job because someone ELSE was behaving poorly. I was gratified to know that, had this all happened today, she could have taken action by going to someone in the company for help.

Later during the seminar, Mary Ann told us that two years after she quit her former boss was charged with embezzling company funds and fired. Maybe there is some justice, sometimes.

I was proud of my class that day. Many spoke up to reassure Mary Ann that they, too, understood how she could have been drawn into such a situation. They helped Mary Ann forgive herself , and they told her how proud they were of the fact that she got out.

Essentially, the lesson from the field appears to be: If you can keep yourself sane and take care of the company's best interests, you have the best chance of sorting out the details of a loyalty dilemma. Then, no matter what happens, you can explain your decisions in the context of what is good for the company. Try to stay happy, do good work that helps the organization—and hope you will eventually get some recognition for continuing to perform your duties in ways that genuinely make positive contributions. THAT's what professionalism and personal accountability are all about.

In the final analysis, loyalty dilemmas are inevitable because of our unique position "in-between" so many people. We are expected to be loyal to our bosses, our employers, our company's customers, our office mates, and everyone else from the first day on the job. Sadly, this is not a quid pro quo ("this for that") situation — it is just too much to expect that our bosses would be just as loyal to us from the first day on. I know in my heart that we each deserve this reciprocal loyalty. However, the reality is that we have to earn and re-earn this loyalty from our bosses over and over again. I do know it can be done, though, and it will give you a great sense of pride when you have accomplished it.

> *"If you want blind loyalty these days, buy a dog."*
>
> —Nan DeMars

12

Tell me no secrets

... the dilemmas of confidentiality

Think about it: *Dear Nan — I work for Mr. Newell, the CEO of a major corporation. By virtue of my position, I am privy to all kinds of information — most of which is confidential. Mr. Newell wishes me to be on a friendly basis with everyone, and also to be his "eyes and ears" to keep him apprised of anything I think he should know about. Also, I am constantly being "pumped" for confidential information by employees at all levels. I do want to continue to serve Mr. Newell's request for relevant information; but I don't want the information to flow both ways. I'm an information collector, not a gossip trafficker! What can I say to squelch the requests for confidential information from other coworkers?*

After reading the previous chapter, you know that loyalty is fertile ground for ethical dilemmas. Its twin is the focus of this chapter: Confidentiality. Just like loyalty, confidentiality is on the short list of professional job skills presumed to be simply "understood" by everyone, without benefit of a lot of discussion — and that, of course, is why the ethics of confidentiality get people into trouble so often.

Like loyalty, executives tell me they regard confidentiality as a must-do and must-have part of their assistant's job description, yet they rarely talk about it. One said it this way: "I'll fire you in a heartbeat if I discover you failed to keep confidential information confidential. You can make other kinds of mistakes, but confidentiality is one aspect of the job you can't screw up."

Whistle-blowing, revealing sales and salary information to the wrong people, gossiping, giving a company phone directory to an outside salesperson, and talking to the media without authorization are some common breaches of confidentiality. So is saying something—anything—in public that will embarrass the company. A secretary in Kansas City told me about overhearing a co-worker complaining about and belittling his manager to a friend while on an exercise bike at her health club. Everyone around this guy got a good laugh at the company's expense, and she said she was certain that story was repeated in a half dozen other offices the following morning.

Confidentiality dilemmas arise when someone decides you have mishandled information with which you have been entrusted. You may disagree with that judgment, or see your mistake after the fact—either way, the information genie is out of the bottle and the damage done. The objective of this chapter is preventative: Let's try to get some understandings about managing sensitive information BEFORE it gets loose and skitters away.

Loose lips sink careers

Let's begin by orienting ourselves. A certain test of your professionalism is your ability to keep a secret. Generally, an office professional is a de facto clearinghouse for all sorts of information. If you are paying attention at all, you probably know quite a bit about your company, your company's customers, and your co-workers. Common sense tells you that most of this information is no one else's business, and therefore is off limits.

But is it REALLY that simple? Think about your office. I'm sure you have experienced confidentiality dilemmas similar to these:

The boss: She wants you to be her "eyes and ears" on the plant floor and in the office. If you hear about a problem, she wants to hear about it. She also wants to know what other managers are saying about her to their secretaries. Or, what do you do when your boss asks you—or orders you—to keep a company secret about illegal or immoral acts? And how are you expected to handle secrets about your boss's personal problems, or secrets about his mistakes? How long, and under what circumstances, are you obligated to be a loyal team player who "knows how to keep your mouth shut"? If you transfer to another part of the company, or if your boss leaves the company, are you still bound by your implied or explicit oaths of confidentiality? Do you pretend you never knew, or you forgot, certain information, even if it affects the company's overall well-being?

Co-workers: At some companies, keeping mum about your co-workers' long breaks and bogus reports is the highest form of loyalty. Lying to protect each other is noble, even heroic, in some "it's-us-against-management" cultures.

Other managers: Who gets to see the budget? The creative ideas and the marketing plans? What do you do when you know about, or are drawn into, a dirty little turf war that amounts to petty, political gamesmanship? Do you sit on the sidelines, refusing to help your boss fight a silly turf war—and then feel bad when she loses and gets bumped down the corporate ladder? Or do you help her fight the battle, and fight to win? Or do you pretend you don't understand anything that is going on around you, and naively attempt to mediate more cooperation instead of competition?

Corporate officers: Imagine you are talking to an officer of the company, and she asks you directly for an honest answer: She smells a rat, or a cover-up, or a problem no one is fessing up to, and she wants to know what you know. Whose secrets will you keep, and whose will you give up? Do you say anything to anyone that is at variance with the "corporate line"?

Outsiders: Inquiring minds want to know how big the deal is, who's in and who's out, whether the company is planning to relocate or not, what new products are coming out and when they'll be ready, what the balance sheet will look like at the end of the quarter, who the company's biggest clients are, how many lawsuits have been filed and why—this is a long list.

The dilemmas above are common enough. Respondents to the Office Ethics Survey are no strangers to them, either.

Have you shared confidential information about:	*"I've sometimes/often done it myself"*	*"I've sometimes/often seen others do it"*
hiring, firing, or layoffs	26.8%	60.0%
salaries	22.9%	53.4%
company or business trade secrets	7.3%	27.5%
employee directories	29.2%	12.5%
information that would affect a vendor's bid	2.5%	14.7%
personal information about a co-worker's fitness to work	27.0%	46.5%

In addition, there are probably more issues of confidentiality that are unique to your company or industry, such as:

Law Firms: A corporate counsel once told me he believed the "second or third most common reason law firms are sued is the breach of confidentiality of a staff member." (I always wished I had asked him the first reason!) In that same conversation, he told me about a secretary who went out to dinner with a large group of people and ended up talking about a case his firm was handling. She named names of the families involved, and even revealed the serious accusations (child abuse). A woman at the table next to hers overheard the conversation and, the next day, the gossip mavens around town had a field day. Needless to say, the secretary was fired. The attorney reported that the law firm was sued and "almost wiped off the map!"

A different attorney told another story that made the same point about the hypersensitivity of client confidentiality: A few years earlier, while at a different law firm, he found himself pressed into the back of a crowded elevator going down for lunch. His secretary got on the elevator with a friend, but didn't see him. On the ride down in this crowded elevator, she dropped the name of a client. The lawyer said he "walked off the elevator and fired her on the spot!" I agreed with him — he was right to fire her because the secretary was hurting the client and her employer.

Another legal secretary bravely shared the following story in one of my seminars: She works for a high-profile divorce attorney in her city and says she never talks about any of her attorney's cases. However, one night she slipped up and "inadvertently" mentioned a case and the family's name at her family's dinner table. You guessed it — her 16-year-old daughter went off to a hockey game that night and related the story to her young friends, who happened to know the young people in the family. The story made the rounds at school the next day and, by the end of the afternoon, the legal secretary's office was in an uproar because of a call from the client's distraught wife. It seems her son had been confronted with the information and was extremely embarrassed. The legal secretary said, "It took a while — but the story eventually came around to me. When I realized what had happened, I admitted my mistake. I didn't, but I certainly could have, lost my job just because of an unguarded comment." These are difficult lessons to learn — and even more difficult to teach your family!

Health Care Providers: The administrative staff people within the medical industry have unique confidentiality problems, too. In a seminar workshop, one unlucky hospital secretary told us about her supervisor who caused her to violate data privacy laws. Here's how it happened: Her supervisor, calling from home, asked her to call up the patient information file on the computer for her supervisor's best friend, who happened to be in the hospital for surgery. The secretary could tell that her boss's concern was genuine and, after all, this was her boss making the request. The secretary did what she was asked — but a short time later, the secretary AND her supervisor were fired for violating the data privacy laws governing hospital patients' records.

These data privacy laws can be big trouble. Another medical administrative assistant told a story about when she worked for the OB-GYN department of her hospital: One of the women who came in for an examination learned she was pregnant and appeared elated with the news. The assistant accordingly helped the woman set up future appointments.

A few weeks later, the assistant encountered this woman in the grocery store where she was standing in line with her husband and another man. The assistant again congratulated her on her pregnancy. The woman's face went completely white. She apparently had told no one about her pregnancy. This assistant said this was a hard lesson for her to learn, and she almost got herself fired. Be aware that hospital administrative staffs have not only strict confidentiality rules pertaining to their patients, but to their patients' families and visitors, too.

Dr. Peter Ubel, a staff physician for the Veteran's Administration and a faculty member at the University of Pennsylvania's Center for Bioethics, sent researchers to ride elevators at Pittsburgh hospitals and later jot down remarks they found inappropriate or revealing. In 259 elevator rides, the researchers counted 41 remarks — one out of every six rides — that threatened patient privacy or raised questions about care. His survey is another wake-up call to hospital administrators about the importance of confidentiality.

Government Employees: I used to naively believe no government worker could ever be fired. Was I wrong! Now that I've presented many seminars to government employees, I've learned there are two reasons government employees will be fired on the spot: (1) falsifying time cards, and (2) revealing competitive bid information.

Educators: Knowledge is the currency of power in the information age, and academic and training credentials are the most common way this knowledge is documented. Educators are in a position to waffle on credentials, requirements, certifications, tests, and in other ways that fracture the integrity of the process. You, or your boss, may be tempted to become a part of this practice.

I recall one assistant who was told by her supervisor, a manager of training for a telecommunications conglomerate, to certify a senior manager as having attended a particular program. The assistant checked, and the senior manager had been registered, and he did sign in, but he almost immediately left and did not return.

"But he [the senior manager] did not participate," the assistant protested.

"Never mind about that," said her manager. "I'll give him the course materials, and I'm sure he'll study them . . . Look, I know this is pretty lame, but what do you think I can do?" The assistant fumed, but registered the new graduate anyway.

Now, I suppose this is one of those situations where no one would have been the wiser or affected in any way if this guy just quietly used this program to puff up his resume when he negotiated his next golden parachute. But his sleight of hand backfired. The missing senior manager's name was read at the evening "graduation" ceremony right off of his now-bogus "diploma" — and every participant in the room who had worked so hard all day, and who knew that this guy was absent all day, seemed to deflate. What should have been a jubilant get-together became a resentful and cynical gripe session.

The other sensitive trouble area for educators is in the area of records. Transcripts and registration information are part of a person's confidential personnel record and must be safeguarded accordingly.

Hotels, motels, and other parts of the hospitality industry: Personal privacy is sacred in the hospitality business. If any one of us wants to hide out in a posh suite with room service, it's no one's business but our own.

I know the catering manager of a major Minneapolis hotel. She related a story to me about how proud she was of the hotel's entire staff when it came to confidentiality. It seems the famous rock musician Michael Jackson stayed in the hotel for three weeks in a row, leaving every morning and returning every night, visiting a recording studio during the day in a distant suburb. Unbelievably, no reporter ever learned he was even in town until he had already left the city. To keep that kind of secret that long in the hotel business is most unusual. Yes, reporters did ask the hotel personnel about the celebrity because they had "heard something about it" on the local grapevine, but every one of them walked away believing the rumors were incorrect and there was no story. The hotel guest's privacy was protected throughout his visit. What a compliment for that hotel!   .

Celebrities: Many high-profile personalities (entertainers, politicians, etc.) request that their assistants sign a non-disclosure agreement. This is intended to prevent assistants from ever revealing confidential information following their departure from the job, e.g. writing a tell-all book or an exposé, selling an interview to tabloid TV, even. Wouldn't Queen Elizabeth have saved herself a lot of headaches if she had required such an agreement with all her staff people!

A good example of these kinds of problems is the actions of Rose Kennedy's secretary following the death of Mrs. Kennedy. You will recall Rose Kennedy was the mother of U.S. President John Kennedy and several other famous children. One of the children is mentally retarded and still resides in an institution. When she was in her late teens, Joe Kennedy, Rose's husband, authorized a lobotomy for the child. However, before that time, the young girl kept a diary. Shortly before Mrs. Kennedy's death, she and her secretary were clearing out her files and they ran across the child's diary. The secretary apparently asked Mrs. Kennedy what she should do with the diary, and Mrs. Kennedy (allegedly) said to "toss it." The secretary did not do so, however, and is now publishing the diary. This kind of a breach of confidentiality could have been prevented had the assistant signed a legally binding non-disclosure agreement upon taking the job.

I know many assistants to high-profile persons who have signed such agreements. All of them tell me they were happy to do so because they all felt their employers had the right to request such a commitment.

"Ex-Bad Guys": If your company has been publicly shamed with a large product liability settlement, or if your industry has been found to be violating environmental compliance laws, you can bet your pinstripes that someone is going to be hovering just out of sight, waiting to pounce on any hint of a repeat performance.

Keeping secrets is no fun

The ethics of confidentiality are slippery, subtle, and complex. Saying the wrong thing at the wrong time to the wrong person is rarely a dramatic event—no bells go off, no hidden cameras zoom in, no envelopes stuffed with cash are exchanged. You just speak the words and the information just . . . slips away. One moment you have a secret, and the next moment you don't. Maybe you feel a rush of panic if you suddenly realize you've let something slip. Maybe you scramble to talk your way out of the situation, blathering lies in a desperate, futile attempt to re-cover up the secret. Maybe you say, "Uh-oh, I shouldn't have told you that," and try to extract promises of secrecy from your listener. Maybe you lie awake at night, replaying the conversation in your mind, trying to figure out a way to take back the words and undue the deed. This is the nature of confidentiality dilemmas. They can drive you crazy—and make you wish you worked alone, far away from the responsibility of managing the information to which you are privy!

Incidentally, if you have the word *secretary* in your title, you may be interested in its origin. The word secretary, not surprisingly, is derived from the same root as the word "secret." In Latin, *secretarius* means "one entrusted with secrets," a "confidential officer," and a "protectoress." The Romans gave their assistants the name *secretariatus,* which meant "keeper of secrets." And in France from the 13th to the 16th centuries, the word, secretaire meant "a confidante." Thus, these concepts—secret-keeper, protectorate, confidante—have been a part of our profession's code of ethics since the beginning of the profession itself. (Incidentally, the very first secretaries of the world were the scribes of long ago. Back then, when blood sports were popular public entertainment, the punishment for breaking a confidence was much harsher!)

Let me share a few anecdotes from the group discussions at my seminars. They illustrate some of the difficult judgment calls that come your way when your job description includes "secret keeper." You'll recognize some of the common conflicts around the questions of WHAT information do we share with WHOM, and WHEN do we share it?

Barbara Ann (not her real name, of course) worked as a secretary for a church in Columbus, OH. Hers is an unfortunate story. She was hired by the minister, reported to the minister, and took direction only from him. She interacted with the board of directors, but did not attend board meetings (they had a separate board secretary). One day, the minister told her in confidence that he was going to walk away from his contract and leave the church within the next few months. He wanted her to know, but asked her not to tell anyone else. She appreciated his trust in her and said she would keep this information to herself.

A few months later, he not only left the church, but the clergy altogether! The day after her boss announced his plans, the board president called Barbara Ann into his office and asked her if she had known the minister was going to leave his position. She said yes, he had told her in confidence about his plan. The president fired her on the spot!

This hardly seems fair, yet the president believed her first responsibility was to the church (and therefore the board of directors) and not to the minister. He thought that when she received this information she should have immediately reported it to the board.

What a pickle! Barbara Ann didn't seek this information, it was just presented to her out of the blue. Also, she didn't break the minister's contract—HE did! Why should she be held accountable for the minister's behavior?

Well, hindsight is always 20/20. When her boss told Barbara Ann his plans, she should have told him he was placing her in an unfair position. She should have told him to tell the board about his intentions, and to keep her out of the middle of the situation. But what if he then didn't tell the board? She was already in possession of information directly affecting the well-being of her employer—shouldn't she have taken a more active role and initiated a discussion with the board that would have led to complete disclosure? But what if her boss was only *thinking* about leaving, and wasn't ready to "burn his bridges" with the board?

This is one of those unfortunate circumstances where the secretary is trapped by two poor choices, either one of which will have a negative splash-back to her. But Barbara Ann was wrong to become a de facto co-conspirator against the best interests of her employer. From the outside of this situation, she probably should have spoken up sooner, or at least negotiated an equitable compromise with her boss, e.g., "If you don't say something by the end of the month, I'll feel compelled to talk to the board myself." I'm not making a value judgment on Barbara Ann—I wasn't there, and she did what she thought was right for her—but there is nevertheless a lesson here for the rest of us. As a professional, Barbara Ann is bound to communicate any and all information that, without a doubt, will affect the organization. The penalty for her "sin of omission" was her job.

One extra note of caution. Has anyone ever said to you, "I'm going to tell you something, but don't tell your boss"? Jump out of your chair and say, "Stop!"

Sandy works with an executive who serves on several boards of directors. She often goes to these meetings with him to take notes. At one meeting, the board was discussing whether or not to buy a new insurance program from a new vendor. The board president, just before she called for the vote, asked the board members, "Does anyone here have any financial ties to this company?" The board president, obviously, was trying to avoid a conflict of interest. No one answered in the affirmative. Sandy was shocked. She knew not only that her boss's good friend owned the insurance company but, also, that her boss had a financial interest in the firm. However, her boss did not disclose that information in the board meeting. The new insurance company's program was approved and purchased.

Upon returning to the office, Sandy asked her boss why he did not reveal his interests in the insurance company. He shrugged off her question and avoided a direct answer.

What should she do? This situation had nothing to do with her job or her company. Her boss sat on the board as a volunteer. It was *his* ethical dilemma, not hers, strictly speaking. After much thought, Sandy decided to go and see the board president. She met with her confidentially and told her what had occurred. The president surprised Sandy by saying she was already aware of her boss's involvement with the insurance vendor and she, too, was disappointed that he didn't reveal it. An executive committee meeting of the board was called (minus Sandy's boss), and it was decided they must confront him with their knowledge of his conflict of interest. They did, and Sandy's boss resigned from the board. He *should* have revealed his conflict of interest by declaring his interest in the insurance company, his support for the proposal, and *then left the room while the rest of the board took its vote*. The same insurance company still might even have been approved.

Her boss never knew Sandy was involved, and Sandy still works for him because, "He's basically a pretty good guy," she says. Some of you may have chosen to do nothing, and you may believe Sandy stuck her nose into someone else's business where it didn't belong. Sandy, however, told me she "could not live with herself" if she just let the situation lie.

Cindy worked for a well-known and highly respected gentleman in the Twin Cities. (Are you getting the impression that all sorts of questionable behaviors are going on in my home town? Relax—there's no more and no less than anywhere else, based on what I hear at my seminars around the country.) Actually, Cindy's boss is highly respected by everyone else BUT her and me! She had worked with this charismatic, high-profile man for many years; she also knew his wife and children and planned activities for them over those years, too.

Here was her problem: She returned to the office about 10 o'clock one night to pick up a personal item she had forgotten to bring home. She noticed the light was still on in his office, so she walked in to turn the light off. There, on his office couch, Cindy found her boss in a most compromising position with a woman who was not his wife! To make matters worse, she knew the woman. She left immediately without a word, but there was no mystery about this "encounter." She saw them, and they saw her!

You may wonder, why didn't he choose to go a hotel for this liaison? Well, I know why he didn't. He is simply that well known.

I often ask my seminar attendees what they would do under similar circumstances. (Once, a woman stood up in the back of the room and yelled, "Ask for a raise!") It is certainly a classic dilemma of confidentiality. You could choose to do and say nothing, and to go about business as usual as if nothing happened. You may reason that it's his personal life, not yours, and therefore your best response is respectful silence. On the other hand, you may think you have to address the incident in some way just to clear the air.

Interestingly, when I ask supervisors what they think a secretary should do under these circumstances, most say, "She should do nothing. He's more embarrassed than she is. Just ignore the entire situation and never bring the subject up." However, these managers tend to change their tune when I reverse the roles and ask, What would they do if they walked in and found their secretary on the couch in a similar circumstance? I'll never forget one male executive who had, a few minutes earlier, adamantly stated a secretary should "do nothing" about the situation. When asked about what he would do if he came upon his secretary instead, he then replied, after some consternation, "Well, I think that would be a discipline problem. I would have to talk to her!" Let me tell you—the entire room jumped on this poor guy. He was visibly shocked at his own double standard. He actually ended up apologizing to the group.

Back to Cindy and what she should have done: The following morning, even before she could take off her coat, her boss immediately called her into his office and apologized profusely for his disappointing behavior and for placing her in such an awkward circumstance. He stated he would understand if Cindy wished to leave, although he did not want her to go, and he would support her decision, no matter what it was. If she decided to stay, he suggested they never speak of the incident again.

Cindy did decide to stay, and they never did speak of the matter again. She never forgot, however. Their relationship changed because she lost respect for him personally, and she ended up finding another job within six months.

Jeff works in the administration department of a large hospital in Washington, DC. While working out at his health club, he overheard two other employees of the hospital discussing, in detail, the cases of several patients. Other people working out in the vicinity heard the conversation, too. The patients' names were mentioned. Jeff felt embarrassed for the patients, and then his hospital. He wondered: Should he interrupt and remind the other employees that "telling tales out of school" was unprofessional behavior? Should he report it to his supervisor? Report it to the supervisor of the offending employees? Forget the whole incident?

This breach of patient confidentiality could be damaging to his department and to the hospital as a whole. As a professional, Jeff is honor-bound to do the responsible thing and try to stop future occurrences.

Interpersonal relationships may affect how you handle sticky ethical issues. If Jeff had overheard his best friend relaying this confidential information, he'd probably go to her and say, "Susan, knock it off!" And, he probably could talk frankly with Susan about how inappropriate she had just behaved. However, if the perpetrator is just an employee whom he recognizes from his hospital, but does not know personally, then he is probably better off going to his own supervisor and reporting the incident. When he does so, he should extract a promise of confidentiality from his boss and then document the conversation for his protection.

Lola is an administrative assistant in Tulsa with a professional demeanor—most of the time. Late one afternoon, after a tiring day and a difficult meeting, she "let loose" with a group of co-workers chatting near the copying machine. She complained bitterly about one of the client's representatives and her company's account executive, both of whom seemed to be the cause of problems with the project. One was a "fat control freak," she said, and the other was "just a dim bulb." She even went so far as to mimic the way they talked, giving everyone around the copier a good laugh.

Later, on her way home, she began to worry. She remembered she saw the look of mild surprise in the eyes of the others at the copier as she "unloaded," but she couldn't stop herself. Now, upon reflection, she knew she had said too much. Would her cruel comments get back to the client and the AE? She felt certain they would. Wouldn't it hurt her already-strained working relationship with these people if they knew how she really felt about them? By the time she reached home, Lola said she was in a worried frenzy. To make matters worse, she worried about being worried — her family needed *all* of her attention, and she felt guilty about bringing this problem home. She worried all night, didn't get the sleep she needed, and was stressed-out the next day.

Remarks that have the power to make someone else feel bad can make you feel bad, too. You would hate to have the target of your comment hear it, or have anyone else repeat it, or have anyone else talk about you in the same way. How do you take back words you wish you hadn't said? What would you do if you were in Lola's place?

In her case, Lola said she was so worried she had to take some action. The worry was getting to be worse than anything else. She said she attempted to explain herself directly to each person, and they appeared to take her comments in good humor for what they were, more or less — but she knew they would never, ever forget. By addressing her slip of the tongue quickly and directly, she probably managed to make the best of a situation that was otherwise hopeless.

Mary, the assistant to a company president, got a call from her boss's wife one day. She casually told his wife he was not in because he had "run over to the XYZ Bank to make a deposit." The president's wife replied: "I didn't know he had an account there." Mary, who at this point was in a bad spot, replied: "Oh, yes — he banks there all the time." The next day, the president reprimanded Mary for revealing this information to his wife. This situation points out all the more how careful assistants should be about revealing ANY information about their bosses. In Mary's defense, it was an innocent remark. However, Mary works for the president of a company, and, unless explicitly told otherwise, she should never reveal any potentially confidential information, even to his family. It was a tough lesson for her to learn.

John thought his boss was happily married, but he had begun to wonder one day after his boss asked him to clear his voice mail messages for him. Among the calls were several messages from a woman who talked as if she was his gambling companion, lover, or both. The woman was insistent about speaking with John's boss as soon as possible, and she left details about when to call and where to meet.

John had mixed feelings about being a "deaf and blind" messenger. At what point does his boss's personal business become company business? Should he just ignore the implications of these messages and simply pass them on with the others? Or should he express his true feelings, and say he is uncomfortable about being a silent partner in this tawdry affair at the racetrack? John went out of his way to tell me he wasn't a prude, but he noted that his boss would judge him guilty and terminate him without a second thought if the situation was reversed. His boss, John said, would conclude that this kind of extracurricular activity was certain to affect John's work performance, so that would be the end of John's job. John's boss obviously believed he was above that standard.

John had no power over his boss, so he felt trapped into implicitly supporting his boss's shenanigans. When he brought it up, his boss just leered at him and winked, as if to say, "Pretty cool, huh?" The last I'd heard, John was actively circulating his resume.

Frank told me about the following incident when we shared a flight out of Boston. We started talking about the topic of ethics in the office and he told me his story of how a secretary "betrayed" him. For years, he and his wife and five other couples would go to a coastal resort in the month of October, arriving on a Thursday evening and departing the following Monday morning. They would all enjoy dinner together that evening and then, Friday morning, the men would pack up for a sailing trip until Sunday evening. The women, in turn, would enjoy a relaxing weekend together shopping and sightseeing. They continued this routine for several years.

However, the men would not go sailing! Frank said they would say good-bye to their spouses, go to the airport, and fly to Las Vegas for a weekend of gambling and other fun. When they returned Sunday evening, their stories were about their exciting sailing trip and their wives never thought otherwise.

Then, Frank's long-time secretary became ill and a temporary secretary was brought in to replace her for a few months. It turned out that the "temp" knew Frank AND his wife. One of her responsibilities was to reconcile Frank's personal bank statement. While doing November's bookkeeping, she noticed several checks to Las Vegas establishments. When Frank's wife phoned one day, the temporary secretary casually said, "I didn't know you two went to Vegas last month!" The wife said, "We didn't!" You know what happened after that. There was a sudden end to the annual "sailing trips" and, unfortunately, one of the couples actually separated afterward.

Frank asked me the question, "Do you think that temporary secretary was right to reveal that information to my wife?" As much as I hated his deception, I had to agree with him. I said, "No, I do not think she should have. It sounds like an innocent mistake, made in a casual conversation between friends, but the secretary had a choice, and she made the wrong one." The secretary should have limited the conversation with Frank's wife to the aspects of the friendship that she would have normally talked about, just as if she were not working for Frank. Why? Because the temporary secretary does not sit in judgment of Frank, any more than Frank sits in judgment of her. At the time, she was working as an extension of Frank, and she would have served him much better if she followed the rule of keeping everything confidential unless told explicitly otherwise. If you err on the safe side, you'll always come out on top!

You get the idea. The possible breaches of confidentiality are almost without limit, and every one of them is a potential ethical dilemma. How about those incidental, unprotected conversations we all appreciate, for example? Don't even think about casually sharing confidences in the lunchroom, restaurant, or restroom. It is perfectly natural to use this personal time to catch up on the latest news, but voices carry and someone is always there to listen! Even the elevator has to be considered off limits. One employee learned in the elevator he was going to be laid off the next month when he overheard two people from a different department talking.

Salary information appears to be another category of leaky secrets.

One out of every four respondents to the Office Ethics Survey say they themselves have shared confidential salary information, and more than half have heard someone else doing it. I posed this case in one of my columns, and it drew a huge volume of responses — probably because it's such a familiar problem. I asked, If you and seven other employees are human resource assistants in a large company and you overhear one of your group revealing confidential salary information, what should you do? I remember reading some of the responses out loud to my husband (he's a great sounding board, and a pretty fair listener, too) while we were driving in California on vacation. He stopped me suddenly and said, "I can't believe all the responses saying 'do nothing — it's not my responsibility'...!" I agreed; many of my respondents were taking themselves totally out of the situation, and deciding a human resource assistant should *do nothing*.

This shocked him, but it saddened me. Reading into their responses, I knew they felt powerless. Logically, they felt it was not their concern, so they washed their hands of any responsibility. They reasoned: What possible good could come out of making an issue out of a co-worker's behavior? The human resource assistant I wrote about in my column was just starting her career, and she needed all the friends she could get. Haven't we each asked ourselves: Why make trouble for yourself when you cannot have any impact on the situation anyway? I know that's how I've felt in similar situations during my career.

Of course, leaks of confidential information of any kind are everyone's responsibility because they affect your department, your co-workers, and your company. The answer is not to look the other way, but to speak up. *Improving ethical decisions and ethical behavior is everyone's responsibility!* I love then-Vice President Hubert Humphrey's comment: "I was looking around for somebody to do something; then, I realized I was somebody!"

Surprise! Everyone is tempted to gossip

Gossip — the indiscriminate chatter about someone else's private affairs — is probably the most common case of breakdown of confidentiality, and it merits some special attention. We all recognize it for what it is because everyone is tempted to gossip. If the sins of the flesh are the world's oldest sins, the sins of the wagging tongue take second place.

Why do we do it? Mostly, I think, it is because of our natural desire to be accepted by others. Few among us are immune to the temptation to tell what someone else is eager to know, especially if we want to impress or please that person.

Being a source of "good gossip" can guarantee you a certain popularity—but certainly no respect. People learn early who contributes to gossip and who does not. I believe there is nothing true about office gossip except:

a) You NEVER hear the full story.
b) If it's easy to gossip about someone, it's even easier to have that gossip get right back to the person about whom you are gossiping.
c) If someone gossips WITH you, you better believe that person will someday gossip ABOUT you.

In any group, there will always be some people who gossip. These are individuals who do not take their profession or career seriously. And, again, people pay attention—they know who gossips and who does not! One client I was assisting in finding a new executive assistant told me he interviewed an otherwise fine candidate who shared all kinds of personal matters with him in the interview. He said they were only personal stories about herself—but, he said, he had just met her and he didn't think it was necessary to hear about her two broken marriages. What he was thinking while she was "sharing" all this personal information was, "If she talks so freely about these matters, what will she some day be saying about me?" End of interview, and end of consideration as far as this manager was concerned.

Loose lips DO sink ships—and stop careers! I once had a CEO of a major firm tell me that, when his secretary retired, he wanted to promote one of the vice presidents' secretaries to the position. There were six of them to choose from, and they all wanted and applied for the job. He said it was a tough choice because they were all equally qualified. Then, he recalled he had at one time or another overheard five of them sharing gossipy stories. (Apparently, all six secretaries worked at desks near his office and within earshot.) He said, "Although these stories were personal incidents and did not affect the company, I still did not like it." But, he said, one of those six secretaries never, to his knowledge, contributed to these wicked conversations—so he chose her for the promotion!

What can we do? How can we be sure to protect confidential information?

Let's return to the first ethical dilemma we looked at in this chapter. Remember Mr. Newell? He wanted his secretary to be his "eyes and ears" and serve as another forward listening post for problems in the company. This was a role with which his secretary was apparently comfortable. In her situation, it was a logical part of her job duties to look out for the best interests of the company. To her, that included being a reporter of problems that she, in her judgment, believed serious enough to merit the attention of her boss. Her problem was the pressure she was receiving from other employees to tell *them* confidential information, too.

Put yourself in this secretary's position. On one hand, your boss has asked you to be his "eyes and ears" and report everything you judge to be important to the well-being of the organization. Generally, this is a reasonable expectation for a person in your position. "It is almost your non-official role . . . probably because your boss does not have the intricate communication network a secretary usually maintains," writes Angelique Berg, Administrative Assistant of Mallinckrodt Specialty Chemicals in Mississauga, Ontario. You have agreed to this request, at least in concept — but do you and your boss both share the same idea about what is "important to the well-being of the organization"?

On the other hand, your colleagues and coworkers expect you to be everything from a confidante, a communication channel to the boss, a teller of secrets, an early-warning system for bad news, a tabloid reporter of senior management's shenanigans, and maybe even a friend.

No wonder you feel like a pin cushion! Everyone is disappointed and upset with you when you don't meet their expectations.

The situation boils down to this: **Who** expects you to share **what** information with them, and what should you do about it?

These dilemmas (like so many others) are rooted in misplaced and misunderstood expectations. People are expecting certain types of information from you that they have no business expecting. You can remedy this situation — IF you take some decisive steps to control those expectations.

You must communicate in advance to your boss and coworkers what kinds of information they can expect from you. As long as you are clear and consistent in your approach to what information you will and will not pass on, you can satisfy most of the people around you, most of the time, without becoming trapped in an ethical dilemma. If you don't "draw the line," so to speak, don't be surprised if they keep badgering you for more information.

Let's start with what your boss expects of you. OK, you're another set of eyes and ears for the company—that's reasonable. But are you and your boss in agreement about precisely what types of information are important enough to merit reporting back to him or her? If you observe a safety violation, or an illegal act, or sloppy quality control, you are honor-bound to speak up. But if you're quizzed about who is sleeping with whom, or what people are saying about someone's new shoes or new toupee, you'd better make it clear you will not pass on that type of information. You can be counted on to report all the information that you judge to be important to the well-being of the company, but that's all.

My boss used to say to me, "Tell me what's going on in the office and tell me what's going on in the factory—IF it's something really significant." I didn't want to bother him with the trivial stuff, or become a tattletale, yet I feared something horrible might happen and I would be blamed because I knew about it, but failed to speak up. So I kept in mind the two guiding words from the Ethical Compass (see Chapter 8): *Job affecting.* If something affected someone's ability to do his job, or affected the company's overall well-being, I concluded that my boss should know about it, and so then I would tell him. I kept mum about everything else.

I know, I know—occasionally, you hear gossip that could soon be something more than that, like someone is thinking about leaving the company, or someone is furious about something, or someone is seriously distraught, or everyone in the copying center is so peeved they are ready to start a revolt. Some of this kind of information is really just plain gossip, but it may be important. I suggest you err on the side of caution, and tell your boss about it. Please protect yourself, though. Preface the information you are passing on with some contextual comment so your boss has some idea about what kind of information this is. For example, you might say something like, "This is strictly hearsay at this point," or, "It was my impression that . . ." It will serve no one's best interests if you pass on information to your boss and he misuses it out of ignorance. Little scraps of information, out of context, are like firecrackers going off when you don't expect them!

You probably are an important link in the informal communication system that flows through your office. This is commonly called the grapevine. The grapevine carries lots of gossip, which cannot be trusted, but it also carries early warnings of a problem, the truth about who should get credit for that big project, etc. — and this information is usually dead-on accurate. The good news about the grapevine, or the informal communication system, is that it empowers people to communicate. Your co-workers probably depend upon you to have a special kind of relationship with your boss — so don't be too surprised when you are told things your boss is expected to know. Sometimes, you will be chosen as the messenger for important information that needs to be delivered anonymously.

Make no mistake about it: You can over-report to your boss. It feels good to bring information to your boss because information is power; so, you may use information to elevate yourself in the eyes of your boss. But it can be overdone.

Bonny Fitch is a reformed reporter. An administrative assistant for 13 years with the Campbell County Parks and Recreation Department in Gillette, Wy, she writes that she was willingly the "eyes and ears" of a former supervisor. When he resigned, her new boss told her she was regarded as a "tattletale" by the rest of the staff because she was "always telling (her supervisor) what was going on." Interestingly, her new supervisor still wanted her to be his "eyes and ears," too!

"I was in shock," Bonny writes. "I had discovered that fellow co-workers had no respect for me. It was a tough thing to swallow, but I learned a very good lesson: Be careful about what is said to your supervisor. Unless (a) situation concerns the well-being of your company, mum's the word. . . . Gaining back the trust of co-workers is not easy. Sometimes I feel I am left out of many fun things because of what happened."

This brings us to what your co-workers expect of you. If they tell you things in confidence, it is because they believe they can trust you to keep those secrets to yourself. On the other hand, if they "pump" you for information, they are doing so because they believe — for some reason — that they can get the information from you. Why do they think that about you? Have you given them some reason? Is it time to update people's expectations?

What you have to do is communicate your rules regarding confidential information ahead of time. Debbie Schaefer, CPS, was administrative secretary to the Chief of Police in Palm Bay, FL when she wrote me. Clearly, by virtue of her position, she was privy to highly sensitive information. She wrote, "From the day I began my job, I made it politely clear that unless the item was discussed in a staff meeting (for which minutes are available to all employees) or reviewed in a memorandum, I was unable to answer any questions." Her standard response then became: "I hope you can understand I'm not able to share any information about that."

This is precisely the professional-type response that will earn you the respect and trust of everyone with whom you work, although you may be viewed as a bit standoffish. Even though some of your co-workers may not like the fact that you extricate yourself from gossip sessions, and even though your boss may not get all the "dirt" he'd like to get on everyone in the office, they will all respect you for minding your tongue.

Still, you may receive prying questions that test you, questions like: Who's on the layoff list? What's the budget? What does he think of me? How much does so-and-so make? What really happened?

Some of the office professionals who have written me suggest the standard reply should be, "I don't know." Tracy Heslop of Canadian Western Natural Gas Company, Ltd., in Calgary suggests an ironic and unique twist if you wish to use "ignorance" as a way to put off an inquisitor; just say: "I haven't heard anything about that. You must be privy to matters I know nothing about. Why don't you tell me all about it?" What a great question-stopper!

Personally, I'm uncomfortable pretending to be ignorant when I'm not. It doesn't work for me! I think feigning ignorance reflects poorly on your professional status because you are implying that you do not have a position of confidence, and this diminishes you. Besides, is anyone really fooled? The questioner knows you know the information — and you know that he knows that you know! Burdening yourself with a lie sends the wrong message — namely, that you will lie under some circumstances. Suddenly, your integrity seems negotiable.

I prefer a firm, even blunt answer that says, essentially, without apology, "I can't tell you that because it's confidential information." Another one that works is, "Do you need this information to do your job?" You must give yourself permission to be rude, if necessary, in order to stick to what you know is the proper course. As Elizabeth Van Blarcom, member of the Beacon Hill Chapter of PSI in Boston, MA states: "Anyone who asks you to divulge confidential information is out of line."

Kelly Adams, property manager and legal assistant at Lariat Companies in Eden Prairie, MN says her most effective way of handling the persistent, rude questioner is simply the silent treatment. "If they ask the off-base question in person, I stare at them silently and expressionlessly. If they ask it over the telephone, I simply say nothing. In both cases, it works beautifully. The questioner becomes most uncomfortable and usually retracts the question or changes the subject."

Your style may be to use a little charm and humor to turn down inappropriate requests. Try expressing shock and amazement ("I can't believe you're asking me that!") or strike an exaggerated pose ("Why, Bubba, are you trying to pry some little 'ol information out of 'lil old me?").

At least, be firm in your resolve and communicate it clearly and professionally: "Please don't take this personally, but, professionally, I cannot divulge that information." Appeals to their professionalism will help, too — they cannot risk pushing too hard without making themselves vulnerable, e.g., "But you're a professional, too — so you KNOW I can't divulge that information." They DO know they are asking for something they shouldn't be asking for, too — and don't think for a moment they aren't aware of exactly what they are doing.

In short, preempt prying questions before they are asked. Become a person known as a good secret-keeper. Build a reputation for tight lips. Find a way to tell people as often as they ask that you put the company's welfare above everything else, and there is nothing anyone can say or do that will change your mind when it comes to confidential information.

Need some more ideas? I've heard a lot of great ways to say "no" that are polite, firm, professional, and consistent. Thank you, colleagues, for the following suggestions:

"Smile — and reply, 'That's confidential information and I do not have the authority to discuss it.'" — *Susan Wilbanks, CPS/CLA, Clinton, MS*

"'I'm sorry, I'm not at liberty to give out that kind of information.' If the questioner persists, repeat this response over and over again." — *Peggy L. Sanders, CPS of Akron, OH*

"I am unable to divulge the information you are looking for and I thank you for understanding." — *Angelique Berg, admin-*

istrative assistant of Mallinckrodt Specialty Chemicals in Mississauga, Ontario.

A few more: "Would you like me to ask my boss that question and get back to you?" (This usually backs them off in a hurry.) Or how about: "I can't believe you asked me that!" Or, quash an outlandish request by simply repeating it in an incredulous tone of voice: "Just a minute, let me get this straight — you want me to tell you about _____?"

One of the most humorous responses I ever heard was from an office assistant at Pacific Gas & Electric in San Francisco. She said she is frequently asked for confidential information because she works for a top officer. She always says, "I can't tell you that information, because, if I did . . . I'd have to kill you!"

Skip the regrets by agreeing ahead of time about what is and is not confidential information

After a seminar in Oklahoma City at a huge manufacturing firm, I spent about a half hour with the director of human resources relating some of the group's takeaway lessons. Six months later, the gentleman phoned me. He said, "Nan, you are the first person I wanted to call. Tell me — Can you fire a secretary for a breach of confidentiality?" I replied, "Yes . . . but tell me more about why you are asking." I was afraid he was going to hang up and fire someone immediately. He was so angry, his voice was quavering.

This is the story he told: Three months hence, there were to be some major layoffs in the firm. One of their top officers was on the list of people to lose their jobs. Just before he called me, the director of human resources had been in a meeting with this particular officer. This officer was seated next to the director of human resources' secretary, and they whispered throughout the meeting. The director said he suspected the officer was pumping his secretary for information about the impending layoffs. He got nervous, so he walked behind them to get a cup of coffee during a break and noticed that on the top of the papers in front of his secretary was the list of employees who would soon be relieved of their jobs. The director told me, "The cat's out of the bag now — I just know this officer now knows he will be losing his job. Nan — my secretary is only 22 years old and she has only worked for me for three months.

But shouldn't she be held accountable for this slip of confidential information?"

Age has no bearing on a person's judgment. And, length of service is no guarantee either. I firmly believe a 22-year-old can be extremely professional and behave responsibly with confidential information, and likewise, a 52-year-old experienced employee may not be able to handle it!

I asked my caller if he had ever had a conversation with his secretary about the importance of confidentiality on the job — after all, he was the director of human resources. He replied sadly, "No, Nan, I never have. I assumed she would know!"

I never forgot his words. I believe there are many executives who assume their assistants know their expectations regarding confidentiality, but their assistants are really only guessing.

CAUTION: Don't be one of those who are playing guessing games when it comes to confidentiality issues!

Perhaps you have tried to pinpoint exactly what types of information are to be considered confidential. If you've tried to categorize every scrap of information, or if you've tried to imagine every contingency, you've probably been frustrated. This aspect of your job defies prediction and standardization. What is required is your common sense, good judgment, and conviction to follow through on what you know is right, regardless of the temptations to do otherwise.

It's critical that you sit down with your supervisor and establish explicit guidelines to whatever degree it's possible. Chances are, there are a handful of "hot" or sensitive issues in your office that are what I call "career breakers" or "career stoppers" because transgressions of confidentiality on these issues will not be overlooked and they are likely to cost you your job. These may be topics that your industry holds sacred, such as patient records in the healthcare industry, settlement offers in the legal profession, or credit information in the banking business. These may be customs in your company, such as strict rules about client billings. Or, they may be sensitive or pet peeves of your boss. In any case, it's your job to find out about them and strictly adhere to them. There will be no excuse for not knowing these unwritten rules. Your boss may be willing to overlook, forgive, and forget a casual slip of the tongue regarding competitive pricing or his actual age, but what about the amount of his advertising budget? His salary? Your salary? The date of the new product launch? Plan to periodically review these guidelines because circumstances change, especially as you move on to new projects or are trusted with more responsibility and more information. By discussing it ahead of time, you have a reasonable chance of protecting your company's confidential information.

Sample questions to clarify with your boss

To help you and your boss clarify the confidentiality questions in your office, discuss these questions:

- What documents are strictly confidential — i.e., for your eyes and your boss's eyes only? Are there any exceptions, such as his or her spouse, other managers, project leaders, etc.? What documents are for your boss's eyes only?
- Do you have the authority to open any type of package or mail, including those items marked "Personal" or "Confidential"?
- Besides you and your boss, who else has access to particular information? Under what circumstances?
- With whom, besides your boss, can you share materials relating to current projects? Any specific limitations or exceptions? Here, be sensitive to the political environment and turf wars. Your boss may say, "No problem." However, just to be sure you're both reading off the same page, challenge him with a hypothetical like, "So it's okay if Mr. Smith comes in and looks at your sketches?"
- Does your boss prefer to personally approve all requests for access to restricted materials?
- Under what circumstances are you authorized to use your own judgment regarding requests for access?
- When your boss is unavailable, how are you to handle requests from your boss's supervisor for information, documents, computer files, etc.?
- Who else has the right to access your boss's office and files, and under what circumstances? Is anyone else allowed to use his computer? Are his computer files protected with a password? Should you know his password, "just in case?"
- Who has your boss's permission to look for things in his office or remove items from his office? We all know this happens. Clarify with your supervisor how he or she would like this handled. For example, should you accompany them, stand right beside

them, and ask if you can help them find something? Document
what is taken? What if it is your boss's boss who does this? In any
case, always report to your boss when he or she returns that
such actions have occurred and how you handled the situation.

- Under what circumstances, if ever, are you allowed to talk to the
media?

- Finally, what are your boss's most confidential materials, the
ones that he or she values the most? Probe a little bit here.
Whenever I ask this question, I am always surprised — the
answers are those I never would have guessed in a hundred
years, ranging from one-of-a-kind videotapes, irreplaceable
designs and artwork, a loose-leaf binder of personal notes and
plans, a key research report, photos, computer disks, etc. Ask
your boss, "If there was a fire in the office, and I had time to
grab only one or two things, what would you want me to save?"
(A side benefit of this discussion is some additional security,
such as a backup copy, of his or her most precious materials.)

These things may not be exactly national security secrets, but they
may be very, very expensive to recreate, such as advertising art,
research, videos, photos. How many times has this happened: Someone rushes in, looking for that one-of-a-kind design or report or photo
so he can use it for a presentation? He whisks it away, promising to
bring it right back, but then it proves nearly impossible to retrieve it
after the crisis passes. Beware the corporate pack rats who like to collect corporate treasures!

Perhaps the most confidential work products of your boss will be
his or her personal notes. These may be computer files, a notebook,
a set of legal pads — whatever it is, they are probably always close by,
and probably not backed up regularly. Become familiar with these.
Watch out for them. I know a conductor-musician who had a personal collection of sheet music in a tattered leather briefcase, each
page of which was heavily marked with all his personal crib notes.
He literally kept this briefcase with him every day, all the time. When
he slept, it was next to his bed. He told me the only time it had ever
been beyond his immediate control was for a period of about 15 minutes after a concert in New York City. He somehow forgot it in a cab,
and he was panicked. He raced into a store and demanded to use the
phone, whereupon he called the cab company dispatcher. Then he

returned to the curb. A minute later, the cab drove by. Without even slowing down, the cabby flung his precious briefcase from the window of the cab, straight into his waiting arms. When he returned to his office, the first thing he had his secretary do was copy every page, twice. He said he was certain he was the luckiest man alive that day.

Be sure you have an understanding with your boss about how these records and documents should be protected:

- names and status of clients
- contracts (even the fact that a contract exists may communicate too much information)
- performance evaluations (even general, seemingly casual characterizations of performance reviews, like, "Oh, it went very well," may be too much)
- employee records of all kinds
- salary information (people seem to not care as much if their benefits are discussed because it is more likely to be a standard benefit package that will surprise no one)
- personnel changes (proposed and/or under discussion)
- advertising and publicity campaigns (you may know a lot about these — haven't we all been pulled into a meeting for an informal "what d'ya think about this?" poll?)
- the company's plans to expand or downsize
- labor negotiations
- pending and filed lawsuits
- financial records and forecasts
- research data
- new product ideas

Even when you and your manager establish guidelines for the most sensitive situations you can imagine, there will still be circumstances when you must make an on-the-spot decision about whether a document or other information can be shared.

When in doubt, zip your lips. Unless otherwise instructed by your boss, treat all information received, written, or spoken as strictly confidential. You will always come out ahead. You can release the information later with an apology and explanation; but once the information genie is out of the bottle, you'll never retrieve it.

We mentioned the unwritten rules of confidentiality earlier. These are the rules of conduct you are assumed to know that are so general and so basic that they will not be discussed with your manager. Lest you be caught unaware, let's write down the unwritten rules:

1. Be discreet in all conversations, in all locations.

Cultivate self-restraint as a part of your personal code of ethics. Listen to yourself — then ask, "Would my boss approve of this conversation if he or she overheard it?" It is surprisingly easy to make a slip during a conversation and divulge confidential information without even realizing you're doing so. We've all experienced those times when we wish we could take back a comment we'd made and pretend it was never said.

The CEO of a huge Minnesota firm told me about the time he was on one of his small company planes returning from a factory. His guest on the plane was a potential investor from New York. The only other people on the plane were two company engineers whom the CEO introduced his guest to upon boarding. The plane only had one seat on each side of the aisle. The two engineers sat directly in front of the CEO and his guest for the hour-long flight. All during the flight, the engineers talked with each other, passed papers across the aisle to each other, and shared other information on the company's new product line that had not yet been introduced. The CEO told me he was extremely uncomfortable because he KNEW his guest could hear the conversation. The CEO was also wondering how many other employees were being equally as loose with this kind of information. He said that, upon his return to the office, he immediately made plans to give a company-wide presentation on the importance of confidentiality.

2. Discuss company business only with your boss and other authorized individuals.

Be particularly wary of casual conversations involving information you don't consider important. Seminar attendees complain often of their co-workers' loose lips in elevator and restaurant conversations. I know of one employee who was overheard on the elevator that her entire department was being laid off the following month! Was it true? It really doesn't matter, does it? The damage was done, and the whole department was thrown into turmoil.

3. Speak softly.

Be sure your conversation is low-pitched enough not to be overheard when you accompany your boss or colleagues outside the office. In these conversations, work is bound to be discussed. You cannot assume that the person in the next seat on the plane, in line at the lunchroom, or in the next stall in the restroom doesn't care what you are saying. That person you don't recognize could be a prospective client, a gossipy vendor, even a competitor — or their best friend.

Help your boss and co-workers keep their voices down, too. Example: An assistant to the marketing manager accompanied the sales team to a trade show. After a long day on the show floor, she spoke freely about their sales, their prospects, their impressions of competitors — in short, she talked way, way too much. And where did she choose to do this? On the escalator, on the shuttle bus, and in the hotel elevator — every one of which was packed with people in the trade who were also attending the show. Boy, did they get an earful! She slipped up simply because of the excitement of being at the show for the first time and fatigue after working the booth all day. It was understandable, but not forgivable.

4. Minimize your socializing with co-workers.

This is necessary if you find the "no shoptalk" restriction difficult to observe. If you participate in coffee or lunch breaks with your colleagues, don't initiate or respond to discussions of company business. Be especially wary of the seemingly innocent efforts to "pump" you for information. Some of that casual chitchat has very serious motives just underneath the patter.

5. Be especially on guard when you attend a work-related party.

Doesn't it stand to reason that the other people attending this kind of an affair are going to be people interested in your business, your market, your suppliers? Sometimes the casual party atmosphere relaxes you, your defenses slip, and you end up sharing information. I know one office professional who hinted to another guest "confidentially" about a pending lawsuit against the company. The guest turned out to be a reporter! Fortunately, in this case, the reporter had the ethical good sense to identify herself immediately and thereby avoid a potentially damaging "off the record" discussion.

6. Do not mix your professional life with your private life.

Do not, do not, do not divulge company matters to your spouse, other family members, or friends. I wince every time I hear a new, young employee say, "Well, I just got married, and I tell my husband everything." One of those husbands turned out to be a real gossip hound — and he sold copiers, so he trafficked heavily in whatever information he could glean from whatever source available. He learned early that the more stories he told, the longer people listened to him — and the more copiers he sold!

Your spouse may not intentionally wish to divulge confidential information you have told him, but he may inadvertently do so in a casual conversation when you are not around to kick him in the ankle. Then, the damage is done. Most infractions are unintentional by people who are just not thinking. How can they possibly know and appreciate the confidential nature of the information you have? You are really just protecting your spouse and family from disaster by not revealing anything to him or her.

7. Don't release information based on unfounded assumptions.

A secretary told about discussing some budget information about a project with a colleague simply because she assumed he already "was in the loop." In fact, he wasn't — he was specifically excluded from this information at the direction of the project manager. The recipient of the information was smart enough to just stand there for several minutes, encouraging her to say more by being attentive and saying things like "uh-huh" and "what do you think about that?" at all the right times, all the while she was spilling out this new information, complete with her analysis! The best actors are not in Hollywood, folks — you're probably working with a few of them!

8. Be realistic about and alert to the determined efforts of others to gain information.

Some people are not above lying, stealing, or acting in devious ways to obtain information from you. In a very real sense, information is what I call "portable power," so it is a commodity well-worth the effort to go after. What you know may be just enough to make or break someone's career. So, develop a healthy skepticism and cynicism about why you're getting all the attention, the free tickets, and the compliments. Why is this guy hovering around your desk? Why is he trying to read your computer screen, or the file on your desk? See Chapter 16 for some insights into how you can be entrapped into divulging information.

9. Be good-natured but forthright about your gatekeeping role.

When people pump you for information, do not become defensive or apologetic. Ann Landers has a common and effective answer to nosy, prying personal questions. Just say, "Why do you ask?" Or — better yet — "Why would you ask that question?" We looked at some other great responses earlier in this chapter.

10. Lie when you have to.

In some instances, you may regard lying as your most ethical response. Many office professionals tell me they consider it acceptable to tell a lie to someone who is lying to them in order to get information because "lying to a liar doesn't count." For example, lying to someone who works under your supervisor may be perfectly proper because it may be none of that employee's business where your supervisor is, or, if you were truthful about your boss's whereabouts, it might cause unnecessary talk and speculation. However, as I explained earlier, I draw the line at lying to my boss's boss just to conceal my boss's whereabouts. For me, that is always wrong and completely unethical.

Telling "little white lies" or "fibettes" is sometimes necessary to save one from embarrassment — in other words, to be polite. This happens all the time, like when someone asks, "Do you like my new haircut?" and you say "Yes," even though you mean "No." Using a lie to spare someone's feelings, or extricate yourself from an awkward situation, is not nice, but it can be expedient and justifiable. See Chapter 16 for a complete discussion about lies and lying.

11. Know your company's code of ethics.

We've discussed this before — if your company has one, read it, understand it, and follow the spirit and the letter of the code.

Summary

Safeguarding information — both written and oral — is one of the greatest challenges facing office professionals today. Information leaks, even if unintentional, have the potential to cause significant damage on several fronts. An instinct for confidentiality is essential to protect your company, your boss(es) and yourself.

Romantic peccadilloes are not the most common ethical dilemmas — that distinction goes to breaches of confidentiality. In fact, questions of confidentiality are one of the most interesting lenses through which many ethical dilemmas can be viewed. Who has what kinds of information? Who can information be shared with? What safeguards are in place to protect information? What are the consequences of violating implicit or explicit confidentiality agreements?

If information is power — and it is — then, we have a lot of it. But keeping secrets secret is difficult. There are many opportunities and temptations to share what you know. It takes a wise professional to appreciate the power and value of the information you are privy to, and to guard that information accordingly.

We've discussed situations where the judgment for a breach of confidentiality was termination. Some may regard this punishment as a bit harsh, but I disagree. These bosses were not being mean, just careful. The consequences and penalties for violating data privacy laws, confidential marketing agreements, client and patient confidentiality, and so on are severe. As soon as you cross that line of divulging confidential information, you have become a liability to the organization and you can expect — and deserve — to be cut loose. As your manager will tell you, business is tough enough without making more trouble for ourselves with stupid mistakes regarding how we handle the information entrusted to us.

Once you and your manager have established the guidelines for what information should be kept confidential, stick to them. Don't share this information with anyone, including co-workers, friends, or even spouses.

Lest you think the rules of confidentiality are turning you into a prisoner in your own office, be clear about this: It can be done. A little common sense, a lot of self-restraint and self-management, and an ever-vigilant appreciation for the power of the information you hold will keep your ethical compass pointed in the right direction.

Some of the highest praise I ever heard about an executive assistant came from the husband of one. Eileen Preksto was executive assistant to Irwin Jacobs, CEO of Jacobs Management in Minneapolis. Mr. Jacobs is a highly respected developer in the Midwest; Eileen had worked for him for many years. Eileen's husband and I were having a conversation about the topic of confidentiality in these positions. He said, "Nan, in all the years Eileen worked for Irwin, the only things I ever learned about Jacobs Management were what I read in the newspaper!" What a compliment for a true professional!

> *"Gossip is the art of saying nothing in a way*
> *that leaves practically nothing unsaid."*
>
> —Walter Winchell

13

Closing the barn door

...and other security dilemmas

Think about it: *Dear Nan — I know how to keep my boss's secrets, and I fully understand my role as a gatekeeper for the information in my office. But do I have to be the company's police force, too? I've witnessed theft of supplies, harassment, software piracy, bogus reimbursement vouchers, and worse. And these are just the obvious rip-offs. There's a whole separate category of "casual crime," too — you know, the padded-expense-account kind of thing. (Around here, expense accounts are a highly creative art form. If the sales people and officers would only spend as much energy doing the rest of their jobs as they do trying to weasel a couple of extra bucks out of the company, we'd all be rich by now.) Where does my responsibility begin and end concerning overall corporate security? And whom do I tell when the corporate culture is a bit on the sleazy side?*

Your commitment to protecting the company extends beyond the loyalty and confidentiality dilemmas we looked at in the past two chapters. As a professional, your code of ethics cannot automatically turn off when you walk beyond your desk or leave your office. Your values and standards of behavior travel with you into meetings, onto the plant floor, and off to lunch with suppliers. You are a representative of the company and, if you are working hard to create an ethical office environment, your effort needs to extend to wherever the company has a presence.

Protecting the company's assets

The simplest way to think about corporate security is in terms of the company's assets. The company has *intangible assets*, like information, employees' time, and the company's image; *tangible assets,* like facilities, equipment, and money; and *human assets,* which include you and the other employees. The company has made investments of time, money, and other resources in order to obtain and develop these assets, and it correctly expects everyone who works for the company to exercise their common sense to protect them.

Some threats to company assets are so clear-cut they pose no ethical dilemmas. Stealing inventory is a crime; so is any action or condition that endangers an employee's health or safety. For example, if you're walking through the plant to deliver a report to a quality assurance manager, and you witness bullying, horseplay, liquid on the floor, or a drug transaction, you'll of course speak up and report it to the appropriate supervisor. Likewise, if you see someone loading supplies, stock, or tools into his van after hours, or if you see someone placing a piece of equipment into her briefcase, you know what to do with your suspicions. Do you get involved in these situations? Of course you do — because you are a professional and your concerns about doing the right things right extend far beyond your office.

For most of us, ethical dilemmas relating to corporate security crop up around the company's intangible assets of information, employees' time, and company image. The U.S. Chamber of Commerce labels any individual behavior, management style, or perceived expectations that prevent company assets from being used properly to the fullest extent of their intended purpose as "intangible crimes." Have you witnessed any of the following common breaches of security?

- Theft of information (the documents, plans, files, etc., actually leave the premises). Information that is circulated beyond the company's protective walls could embarrass the company or your boss, diminish the company's image, cost the company money, compromise employee morale, grant an unfair and unearned advantage to a competitor, etc.
- Misappropriation of information (the information physically stays in its proper place, but a physical copy or mental picture of it is taken by someone who misuses it). This happens when the wrong people get a look at plans, budgets, etc., and then use that information against the company.
- Indiscriminate circulation of notes and minutes from meetings that include who participated in the meeting, what was discussed, etc.

- Violation of data privacy, such as retelling the details about a client's or employee's situation, needs, objectives, financial condition, etc.
- Tape recording phone calls without both of the parties' knowledge.
- Premature "leaking" or distribution of financial information, product information, etc., prior to the authorized date and time (this would be easy for us to do because we probably made the copies!).
- Talking to the media without authorization or supervision.
- Participating in a protest demonstration while wearing the company logo on a shirt or cap.
- Writing a letter to the editor on company letterhead.
- Lying to a supervisor in a report (this is a common ethical problem in any case — but in some circumstances, it compromises security, too).
- "Stealing" time by arriving late, leaving early, or taking long lunches.
- Use of company equipment for personal gain.
- Conducting personal business on company time.
- Faking sick days.

In my 1995 survey, many respondents admitted skating on the edge of tough ethical choices. Let's look at the numbers:

- 60.8 percent said they had sometimes or often taken company property for personal use; 73 percent said they witnessed others doing it.
- 9 percent said they falsified time sheets themselves, and more than 32 percent said they saw others doing it.
- Only about 5 percent said they falsified expense or travel/lodging vouchers, but more than 25 percent reported seeing others do it.
- More than a quarter of all respondents admitted sharing confidential information about hiring-firing-layoffs, salaries, and personal information about a co-worker's fitness to work, and the number who said they saw others doing it ranged from 46 to 60 percent.

Tangible or intangible, the company assets are the targets of many people with malicious intent, usually for personal gain. Perhaps it is for power or status. Perhaps it is for a recognition or reward they believe the company owes them. Perhaps it is simply greed. Regardless of their motivation or form, unethical acts compromise security and result in a loss of productivity, job satisfaction, and quality.

Bottom line here: You are a part of the company's security system. Your eyes and ears are often early-warning detectors of security problems. If you subscribe to values and codes of behavior that protect the company, you have the ethical standards of the true professional. The professional's response to a breach of security is to try to stop it. If you see a compromise in your company's security, or know about it, or are asked to assist in a remedy, you are ethically bound to do your best to help solve the problem.

My best security tips

After talking to many office professionals about the security problems they've encountered, I've developed the following eight guidelines that will keep you out of most kinds of trouble, most of the time.

1. Do not disclose your boss's whereabouts, or the whereabouts of anyone else in your office, unless you know the person to whom you're speaking. We touched on this as a privacy issue in Chapter 11, but it bears repeating. A secretary once told me she got a phone call one morning from someone whose voice she did not recognize. He asked for her boss and she replied he was out of town until the next week. Her boss's home was burglarized that same day! NEVER divulge that anyone is out of town. Instead, say only that he or she is unavailable, but you will be talking to him or her soon and you can deliver a message!

2. Protect written documents. "Don't lead others into temptation" is your best guide to protecting written documents. Recognize that some people are naturally curious and they will be tempted at times to at least glance at papers if you leave them in plain view. A visitor from a rival firm, a journalist looking for story material, an insecure employee feeling threatened by a new hire—all may have a strong interest in what is on your desk.

The value of information depends proportionately on who does not have it. The more people who know a secret, the less valuable the secret. Once the wrong people have the information, the value of that information is diminished. Your job is to protect the value of information by keeping it secret.

Here are a few suggestions for protecting confidential written documents entrusted to you:

a) Keep your desk clear of any papers you consider confidential. This is crucial if there is a lot of traffic in and out of your work area. Most secretaries tell me they have to struggle to get periods of uninterrupted time — they are always being asked to catch the phone, respond to this or that crisis, etc. It's easy to forget that what you have in front of you cannot be left unattended, even for a short bathroom break or a few minutes at the copier. How many people do you know who can read upside down? Plenty! Flip your papers over even if you are just leaving your desk for coffee. Remember that snoops and thieves are clever and persistent! If someone wants to find something, a trusting and helpful nature places you at a great disadvantage. It's prudent to be a little suspicious of everyone.

b) If you're going to be away from your desk during the day, even for a short time, double check to make sure all important documents are either placed inside your desk or locked in a file cabinet.

c) If you are working on a sensitive document that requires you to have a lot of sensitive materials on your desk for several hours at a time, you can avoid the traffic around your desk by scheduling to work on the project during off-peak times, or to set up camp at another work station.

d) Always clear your desk before you leave at the end of the day and lock up anything you don't want others to see. This includes checkbooks, deposit books, plans, schedules, correspondence — even your shorthand books can be read by people who are familiar with your form of manual note-taking.

e) Neutralize or "sanitize" documents when you remove them from your office. Conceal them inside a folder or envelope, even if you are just hand delivering them to someone on the next floor. Someone standing behind you in the elevator, or next to you in the hallway, may be able to see just enough to get the rumor mill cranked up. You really can't be too careful when handling confidential information.

f) If you carry confidential documents to and from work, or on business trips, keep them in a locked briefcase. Then, don't leave the briefcase unattended in public places, such as air-ports, waiting rooms, restaurants, or even restrooms.

g) When attending meetings, conferences, or briefing sessions, don't leave confidential papers exposed where people nearby can see them. If you want to keep the papers handy on the table in front of you, make sure they are face down or are in a protective folder except when you are referring to them directly. Never leave documents behind when you leave the room, even if it is for just a short time.

h) When mailing confidential documents, seal them in an envelope and mark it "confidential." Then seal that envelope inside another envelope and mark that "confidential," too.

i) Shred confidential documents, rough drafts, photocopies, and notes. Never dispose of these papers in a regular waste-basket or recycling box from which they can be recovered by the curious or dishonest.

3. Protect your electronic documents. New rules here, folks. Computer-generated documents must be protected from prying eyes and tampering. This is particularly important if your computer is linked to other computers via a LAN (local area network). Deleted files can be recovered, other nodes on your network may be able to peer into your files without your permission or knowledge, and there may be an automatic backup component of your office protocol that puts a complete copy of your work for the day within easy reach of many people. Here are some suggestions to keep you from getting the "byte" put on you:

a) Know the limitations of your system. The computer is just another tool, not a "black box" that assures secrecy. Learn who in your company knows how to use your computer bet-ter than you do, and use them as a resource. The network supervisor (a.k.a. systems manager) can help you devise secure systems. It is your responsibility to understand the realistic limitations of your system.

b) Develop a sound system of backing up files and archiving files, and then stick with it. You may be your own worst enemy if you do not follow consistent procedures. You should be able to retrieve important files quickly, ensure they will be safe, and remove files you no longer want in ways that render them unrecoverable.

c) Store floppy disks in a locked area so they cannot be accessed or altered.
d) Use a password sign-on procedure to prevent anyone from accessing your hard drive without your permission. This is not unbeatable, but it slows down the casual interloper. Best system: Use two passwords known only to you and to your boss.
e) Position your terminal screen in a way that prevents people from reading it. Be prepared for a quick sign-off, or use a "hot key" to engage your screen saver if potentially prying eyes approach your desk when you are entering confidential material. Another technological solution from the boys and girls in the lab: Screen covers are available that make it impossible for anyone to view the screen unless they are positioned exactly in front of the screen.
f) Sign-off whenever you leave your terminal if you are working with confidential information, even if it is just for a quick break.
g) Remove your printouts as quickly as possible from the printer. Community printers are common when several computers are networked together, and they are logically placed in a location that everyone has easy access to. Don't leave your confidential material unattended, or else you risk it being read by your office mates. They may read it unintentionally, just to determine whether it is their document or not — is that going to be OK with you?
h) Put your original program disks under lock and key. These are rarely used after the software is loaded onto the hard drive, so they may be "borrowed" and never returned, yet they will not be missed for months. Each should be registered, so when the copy with your serial number turns up on a bootleg copy, there could be trouble. Software piracy is a smoking fuse in corporate America. Many people have developed bad habits, like making numerous copies of proprietary software. Unauthorized copying of software may violate your company's purchase agreement and the copyright laws. The software industry is responding, so be warned: Abusers are being found (many companies are being turned in by ex-employees) and significant penalties are being levied.

Here's an ethical dilemma for you to talk about at dinner tonight with your spouse: He is starting a business. You

make copies of your software at work to load onto his computer, thereby saving him significant startup costs. You
know this isn't quite ethical, but tell yourself that the only
one who loses in this incident is a multi-billion dollar software company who would not have made a sale to this
poor entrepreneur anyway. Besides, now your husband is
"hooked" on a set of software, and he will buy more when
he gets successful, so isn't this "freeware" really a good pro-
motional investment on the part of the software company?
What's the right thing to do?

**4. Don't post highly confidential information on the company's
e-mail system.** They are not secure, despite what the techies tell you.
I've never met an e-mail system supervisor who did not tout the security of the system but, when pressed, admitted that it was less secure
than an envelope and a stamp. Forget about trusting your password—
it's no defense against someone who is "hacking" and wants to read
your mail. I love e-mail, but don't confuse efficiency with security.

A few other interesting ethical wrinkles have surfaced relative to
e-mail. Some companies report being plagued by broadcast messages ranging from jokes to recipes to offensive materials to political
or social slogans. Sometimes these are innocent messages that seem
to cheer people up and add a human dimension to the super-tech
offices that have less and less personal interaction. But sometimes
they are an abuse of the system, wasting everyone's time with unwanted and unnecessary mail.

A more insidious dilemma seems motivated by old-fashioned
greed. People are sending the electronic equivalent of chain letters to
solicit sports bets, charitable contributions, or business cards. These
are scams and should be squelched.

It's interesting, isn't it? Every new generation of technology comes
with its own updated variations of age-old ethical dilemmas. What
does this say about people working together? I hope the social
researchers are keeping up with these changes so they can explain
them to us someday!

5. Report thefts of all kinds. I hear these complaints often. Bogus
expense account claims are probably the most common. Travel, supplies, gifts—you can fill in the blanks based on your own experience. Report your concerns following the guidelines in Chapter 9.

Two new examples that are becoming a problem in some offices:

First, what should be your response when your boss uses his accumulated frequent flyer coupons for personal use? And what if your boss appears to be arranging his travel schedules not to save the company money but, instead, to increase his mileage coupons? Again — use your Ethical Compass. Think about what is good for your company, not your boss. It is easy to slide into looking the other way and, consequently, an unethical situation builds and builds. Most companies now have policies that speak to the use of these coupons. Make sure you know your company's policy.

Another situation: You work in a department with six other support staff personnel. One day, you notice Susan, one of your co-workers, slip several small office supply items into her purse. You don't say anything at the time, but you begin watching her. You soon observe a pattern of petty larceny, but you never see Susan take anything larger than a stapler or a package of computer disks. Susan is not aware you have observed her actions.

Now that you are paying attention to this, it seems like other people are beginning to comment on the shortage of supplies. You think it is just a matter of time until someone speaks up about the apparently serious theft problem. You know what you need to do — you need to stop this behavior — but perhaps in this case you want to start by talking with Susan and give her an opportunity to come up with her own solution. Be careful of becoming her one-person reform team, though — you're in a position of power that may be misinterpreted as bullying or extortion by Susan, and you may be viewed as a co-conspirator later when all of this comes to light.

You need to talk to Susan during a quiet moment. You need to say something like, "I know you're doing this, and I want you to stop it." If you prefer a less confrontive style, suggest a cooperative effort among several coworkers to "get to the bottom of this problem of the missing supplies." Whether you choose a direct or indirect approach, the result should be satisfactory. In 99 out of 100 cases, Susan will immediately stop. Any hint of public disgrace, or the possibility of compromising her job security, because she has been discovered to be a thief, will be enough to reassert the reasonable standards of conduct she is expected to follow. (Of course, if it is commonplace for employees to steal, you have a different problem altogether, and Susan is likely to respond by asking, "Why are you picking on me? Everyone else is stealing a lot more....") Look again at Chapter 7 for more discussion about standards of ethical conduct and how they are established.

If Susan did not respond to your direct or indirect message, back off. You MUST talk to your supervisor now. If her petty larceny is more important to her than what you think of her, you may be dealing with someone with a bigger problem. Do NOT let this become a point of personal conflict between the two of you by pushing further. If you say something like, "If you don't turn yourself in by Friday, then I will," you are creating an extremely personal conflict. It's risky, maybe even dangerous, to force someone to change her behavior just because you know something that can hurt her. The push you try to give her in the right direction may be a push over the edge of reasonableness. She may retaliate if she feels threatened by you. Your health, wellness, and peace of mind are certainly more valuable than a boxcar full of office supplies.

What would you do if your boss asked you to spy for him? This question came up earlier in our discussion about loyalty to the boss in Chapter 11. The simple answer stands: Don't do it. This is especially true if you sense your boss is on a generalized "fishing trip," just trying to cast a wide net to catch someone doing something wrong for who-knows-what reason.

Like most ethical rules, this one has flexibility. Consider this case:

> *I am an executive assistant to the vice president of our human resources department. My boss has recently expressed his concern that one of the other assistants in the department may be abusing some privileges, such as taking a longer lunch hour, arriving late, and leaving early. I have noticed these transgressions by my coworker also. My boss has asked me to keep a close watch on the activities of this employee to see if his suspicions are correct. I do not wish to be a spy for my boss. Any advice?*

Karolyn Sharp, CPS of Topeka, KS describes this dilemma best: "Such a request is probably a veiled order that cannot be declined. In that case, it will be a challenge to maintain a balance between personal integrity while complying with an organizational expectation."

I hate spying, too. But in this case, I would comply, even though I would be unhappy about doing anything that brought trouble to a co-worker. Three aspects of this case make it different: One, the boss is the human resources director. That means a big part of his job is to protect the intangible assets of the company. My job is to support his job, so his problem is my problem. Also, his request is more specific than the "fishing trip" described above. He wants me to observe some specific behaviors that I can see, but he can't. Finally, he is asking for confirmation of something he already suspects, not new sins. This is actually to his credit — he wants to get corroboration before he initiates any remedy. If I were to not see any of the abuses he suspected, how he handled the situation would likely be different.

Unless this boss was asking the letter writer to lurk around corners, ask questions of others (thereby getting them involved and shaking the office grapevine), or putting her in other very uncomfortable situations, simply asking her to observe someone's professional behavior in his absence appears to be a reasonable request.

My readers were generally inclined to agree. Jacqueline M. Scepaniak, CPS, District Office Assistant, Nationwide Insurance Enterprise of Baltimore, MD writes: "This is an assignment no different than being asked to monitor spending on office supplies with the idea of cutting costs. Abuse of privileges is a form of theft from the company. She would have no qualms about reporting it if she saw the co-worker walk out with a computer under her arm; she should have no qualms about monitoring minor abuses of time if it can be done in a nondiscriminatory way."

Linda Fedryk-Harui of the Boiler Inspection and Insurance Company of Canada in Toronto and Margaret H. Caddell, CPS, past president of the Alabama Division of PSI, wrote to remind us that respect, cooperation, and productivity — the essence of the ethical office — depend on the fair application of standards and rules. To allow one person to continue an abuse of privileges undermines the trust that binds co-workers together as a team.

6. Don't talk to any representative of the media without the knowledge and guidance of your supervisor and/or the company's public relations representative. The president of a major accounting firm once told me about an incident with his secretary that made him furious. His side of the story went like this: A newspaper reporter called his secretary and asked her if the Governor's office had recently contacted her boss soliciting a political contribution. She said, "Yes." Had her law firm contributed? the reporter asked. Again, she replied, "Yes." And, the reporter finally asked her, Just how much did your boss contribute? Without a trace of hesitation, she told the reporter the figure. Well, guess what — the front-page story the next day was about companies making political contributions (this was when it was still acceptable). She — and her boss — figured prominently in the story because the reporter could "hang his hat" on the news hook she provided. The president, his secretary, and the accounting firm were embarrassed to the bone.

I asked the president if he had ever had a conversation with his secretary about when she could and could not talk to the press, and what subjects were off limits. He had not.

ALL employees of a firm should be made aware of the risks of talking with the media. I'm a member of the working business press, and the wife of a successful politician, so I can say from first-hand experience that my quill and keyboard colleagues are generally behaving in a shameful and irresponsible manner these days. In my opinion, they take too many shortcuts, look only as far as they need to for a quote instead of the facts, and engage in ambush interview tactics that diminish the message and the messenger. I'm sorry to say it, but THEY CANNOT BE TRUSTED to keep their promises of confidentiality or to even get the facts straight.

My advice is to throw up a firewall around the company and insist that every reporter talk to the company's press relations or public relations person. If the company has no such person, insist it be the president or a designated officer. Reporters hate this, but they've brought the trouble on themselves. "Sticking to channels" does little to further the truth but, sadly, media relations these days is not about the truth — it's about who controls the "spin" on the message. You have much to lose, and virtually nothing to gain, by getting your picture on the evening news. Run, don't walk, away from reporters who say they have been frustrated by the people in your public relations department, and now he or she wants to "get the real story" from an insider like you, on a strictly "off the record" basis, of course. Don't believe it. NOTHING you ever say to a reporter is "off the record" — no matter what the reporter promises.

Some of the reporter's sleaziest ploys are to flatter you ("What is your job? You must be a very important part of the vice president's team") or befriend you ("Does the company really appreciate all your contributions?"). In my experience, a reporter will say whatever he or she thinks they need to say in order to get you to open up and start talking. Do not think you can beat them at their own game and manipulate *them* — they'll get you every time. Finally, don't underrate the value of that seemingly innocent background information they want. If you can't or won't fill in all the details of the story, the seemingly innocent information you provide will be used in the next con-versation with another employee, i.e. "The way Julie (that's you) explained it, it sounds like . . ." This cynical and crass exploitation should not be tolerated.

Let me tell you one more horror story. During a recent Professional Secretaries Week®, a newspaper reporter phoned the president of the local Professional Secretaries International chapter and invited her and six other chapter officers to lunch to discuss "the secretarial world." They had a delightful time discussing the many changes in the profession, trends, etc. Then, the reporter asked the group, "What do you dislike most about working for your bosses?" The most com-mon answer was "keeping track of him (or her)." The secretaries expressed their frustrations about how important it was to know where to find their bosses at all times. One secretary said she wished she could "put a beeper on him." Another secretary added jokingly, "I wish I could put him on a leash!" Everyone laughed. Guess what? The article came out the next day in the newspaper with the headline: *"Secretaries Think Their Bosses Should Be Put On Leashes."* The sec-retaries were mortified. The comment, of course, was taken com-pletely out of context. They tried to explain to their bosses; but, the damage was done and they just ended up looking foolish and petty. You HAVE to be careful when talking to a reporter!

7. *Do not say anything confidential on a cellular phone or a speaker phone.* Most cellular phone conversations can be easily pirated. Attor-neys and developers tell me they talk on their car phones to their offices about schedules, assignments, and other mundane matters, but they never name client names and/or financial figures for fear of having their conversations picked up. Who scans for these conversa-tions? Mostly flakes, I think. These people need a real life — but they are not above calling the information in to their stock broker, a news reporter, or their friends in order to puff up their feeling of impor-tance (remember, some people believe any information is power, regardless of the source).

Do you use speaker phones in your office? These are convenient for obvious reasons, but they can compromise privacy. For example, when you talk to your attorney, it's like talking to your physician. It's doubtful you want anyone else to hear your conversation. I know a man who fired his attorney because, every time he called, his attor-ney put him on a speaker phone. This gentleman told me, "Nan, probably every time I was talking to that attorney and I was on the speaker phone, there was no one else in the office — but I didn't know that." Your confidence in your conversation being a private affair certainly goes down when you are put on a speaker phone. Heaven forbid that someone walks in at the wrong time. If you're going to put someone on the speaker phone, the best thing to do is use it only when there is a good reason to do so. Explain your reason, and then ask the other party's permission: "I'd like to put you on the speaker phone. My door is closed, and there's no one (or only the agreed upon people) in my office. Would you mind?" That's fair.

8. Presume others will read your faxes. If there is any question about whether a document or information will be compromised when it's sent over a fax, don't send it. Imagine three or four people at the receiving fax standing around, passing your transmission among them, saying things like, "Gee, this is interesting — look at this..." and "Hey, did you know that..." and "Wow, listen to this..." Be smart. Send it by courier or overnight delivery if you have to or, if you absolutely must transmit something confidential on the fax, call ahead to let the receiver know that he or she should expect it within the next few minutes so he or she can watch for it. Or send only the minimum amount, such as just the page with the revision.

Be aware that reading someone else's facsimile message is exactly the same as reading someone else's mail. Not everyone treats faxes with this respect. I suggest you incorporate the following notice, or something like it, onto your cover page. It's not much, but it may deter the casual reader.

⌇⌇ Confidentiality Notice ⌇⌇

The information contained in this facsimile transmission is legally privileged and confidential information intended only for the use of the individual or entity named above. If the reader of this transmission is not the intended recipient, you are hereby notified that any dissemination, distribution, or copying of this facsimile transmission is strictly prohibited. If you have received this transmission in error, please notify _____ .

Thank you.

Summary

The office professional is a frontline gatekeeper against all sorts of rascals inside and outside the company who place their personal interests above the company's interests. You are a target for those who want to steal or misuse your company's tangible and intangible assets. You are the "side door" through which they will try to creep because you are in possession of so much of the company's information.

You must adopt a somewhat skeptical view of others' motivations to talk with you and "hang out" around your desk. You must develop a sixth sense about protecting written and electronic documents, and plan your work and delivery of those documents based on the expectation that someone wants a look at them and is attempting to compromise your security measures.

Why is the company's security a part of your job description? Because you are a professional, committed to upholding high standards of behavior wherever you are. Office professionals are not required to have professional liability insurance yet, but it's possible that it is on the horizon. This is logical when you consider that you are the hub of so much information.

Security is an ongoing challenge. The office professional is now relied upon more than ever to "bar the door" against all types of threats to compromise the company's information and property. It isn't simple anymore, either—it requires technical expertise and a lot of psychological moxie. The challenge is to do your job with a healthy skepticism of others, while still expecting others to trust you. Who said our jobs were easy . . . ?

> *"Three may keep a secret if two of them are dead."*
>
> —Benjamin Franklin, 1735

14

Harassment dilemmas

Think about it: *Overheard at a management meeting — "How can a woman be suing us for sex discrimination? We've never even had one work here."*

Here are four short stories of harassment — Gail's boss yells at her every day, much of it profane and directed at her personal looks and abilities. He claims it is his "sailor's style" and he cannot change. Renee experiences sexual innuendo, explicit remarks, off-color humor, and "accidental" fondling and bumping at work by her boss and co-workers. They say "she asks for it" because she wears attractive clothes and "she doesn't really mind it" because she does not object. John is physically intimidated by his supervisor who yells at him, touches him, pokes him, and stands uncomfortably close. Carmela endures demeaning and belittling comments in most exchanges with her boss, such as: "What else could I expect from a dimwit like you?" and "I hope you take better care of your kids than you take care of me!"

They are each victims of one or more types of harassment. Between the time a person decides, "This has got to stop. I cannot work in this environment. I must take some positive action," and the time she or he quits or files a lawsuit, there are positive actions that can help remedy the problem. What can a person in situations like these do to introduce and enforce a more ethical code of conduct in the office?

The first employment sexual harassment case I ever heard was related to me, at an early age, by my mother. Before she married my father, she was secretary to a Minneapolis food broker named Harry. Although married, Harry had a reputation as a womanizer, and my mother wanted no part of his antics.

Harry invited her to accompany him to a three-day grocery convention in Chicago. Although my mother realized her presence at the convention would be an asset, she was wary of Harry's ulterior motive behind his invitation.

Therefore, she announced she would attend the convention with him only if her mother (my grandmother) could accompany her as her chaperone. Harry reluctantly agreed. My grandmother was a stately, no-nonsense Swedish woman, six foot tall and large-boned — a most formidable presence next to Harry, who was barely five feet tall. My mother always delighted in relating the infamous train ride to Chicago. She sat next to my stoic-looking grandmother (who knitted the entire trip), directly facing a very uncomfortable-looking Harry.

My grandmother, of course, roomed in the hotel with my mother, thus thwarting any shenanigans Harry may have had planned. All went well until the final day when Harry asked mom to come up to his room after the day's session to "pick up some materials." Mom's suspicions were immediately confirmed. Upon entering Harry's hotel room, he made an advance. My mother hauled off and whacked Harry across the face, causing his false teeth to fly out of his mouth and under the bed! The lasting scene my mother delightedly remembered forever was Harry on his hands and knees trying desperately to retrieve his choppers! Amazingly, she never experienced another problem with Harry.

Have we made progress since the 1940's?

Incredibly, harassment at work persists. Even at this late date in the movement to fairness and equality between genders, I hear the firsthand details of hundreds of shocking reports from participants in my seminars. These reports are all from women and men who have been harassed by male or female supervisors or co-workers. I have listened to their anger. I have seen their tears of frustration and humiliation. These victims are real people to me, not faceless statistics. I regard each of them as a corporate hero who has persevered in spite of offensive and demeaning behavior on the part of those they work with.

Happily, the number of people who tell me they have been harassed within the past 12 months seems to be declining. Ten years ago, you could get five office professionals together and hear horror stories from four of them that were as fresh as the daily newspaper. Today, only one or two in that group would tell similar stories.

What keeps surprising me is the persistence of these abusive behavior patterns that have been proven to be counterproductive and risky to the perpetrator. Either the message has just not gotten through to these abusers, or their short-term needs (fear, insecurity, emotional gratification, or whatever) master their long-term common sense.

Harassment is an up-close problem of interpersonal relations, so office professionals are frequently victims or witnesses. They are, therefore, in an excellent position to modify the inappropriate or abusive behavior of others. They may be the best soldiers in this fight. They must be savvy to the risks, however, or they lose their jobs, friends, or advancement opportunities.

What is harassment? How serious is the problem?

Harassment is never just about sex. It's about power.
A behavior is generally considered harassment if it is:

a) not welcome, not asked for, not mutual, and not returned, and

b) affecting the terms or conditions of employment, including the work environment and the capacity of the employee to perform his or her duties. This has become a touchstone for virtually all discussions about harassment because it is short, simple, and easy to apply: *If the behavior of another has a negative affect on your ability to do your job, it's harassment.*

Harassing behaviors tend to be combinations of the following:

- *verbal harassment* — yelling, profanity, public humiliation, and all other forms of demeaning or disrespectful comments and conversation
- *sexual harassment* — unwelcome sexual advances, requests for sexual favors, and other verbal or physical conduct of asexual nature
- *physical harassment* — pushing, shoving, touching, horseplay or other conduct that intimidates and/or threatens safety
- *emotional harassment* — abusive or disrespectful conduct that manipulates, coerces, and/or intimidates

When I talk about harassment in the office as an ethical dilemma, I group all types of harassment together. They are all wrong, hurtful, and disrespectful. They each have a profound, negative affect on the ethical climate in the office and the job performance of the victims. Two or more types frequently overlap in an incident, such as verbal harassment accompanying emotional and/or sexual harassment. In the following pages, we'll look at what simple, effective, and inexpensive actions you can take to stop harassment on the job.

Let's start with the numbers. How serious a problem is harassment? In a word, very. My survey respondents have "sometimes or often" experienced the following types of harassment:

- verbal harassment   56.9%
- sexual harassment that includes
  physical contact   33.0%
- physical harassment   8.5%
- emotional harassment   55.8%

In addition, my survey respondents say they have witnessed others being victimized "sometimes or often" in the following ways:

- verbal harassment   65.3%
- sexual harassment that includes physical
  contact   39.4%
- physical harassment   14.3%
- emotional harassment   58.8%

(I want to reiterate my confidence in these numbers. The 1,458 office professionals who completed the survey represent a cross section of the country. They include numerous seminar groups from many industries in every part of the country. In most groups, I insisted everyone complete the survey, even if they were normally reluctant to complete surveys. Finally, I stressed the need for them to be absolutely honest in their responses, and I guaranteed them complete confidentiality. In short, I believe these survey results are among the best indicators available regarding what is actually going on in offices around the country.)

Who is doing all this harassing? Sorry, boys—it's mostly men harassing women. Roy Ginsburg, a partner in the Employment Litigation Practice Group of Dorsey & Whitney in Minneapolis was willing to go on the record: "Although we want to believe otherwise, most harassment cases involve women as the victim. 92 percent of all sexual harassment cases are men harassing women, 5 percent are women harassing men, 2 percent are same sex harassment and 1 percent are unknown."

I think harassment at work is one of the most complex of human behaviors. The motivations for it are not easily identified or understood, and it defies generalization. It begs for more serious scientific study. As I said earlier, I am mystified as to why it persists among otherwise smart co-workers and colleagues who know very well its high indirect and direct costs.

What are those costs? Low morale, absenteeism, illness and accidents, high rates of employee turnover and corresponding training costs, mistakes, sabotage, and stress are some of the side effects of harassment that squarely hit bottom-line productivity and profit numbers. Tolerating harassment is not a part of any employee's employment agreement. No one argues that harassment has anything other than a negative impact on an employee's performance.

Large settlements to end lawsuits against a company, and the corresponding publicity and "sister suits," are upping the ante in obvious ways, too. A 1988 survey of Fortune 500 companies by *Working Woman* magazine revealed that 90 percent have received sexual harassment complaints, more than one-third have been sued at least once, and nearly one-fourth have been sued repeatedly. A typical large firm will lose more than $6 million per year from lost productivity, absenteeism, and turnover due to harassment.

While on a consulting contract with a construction company, I had an opportunity to make the point about the high costs of settling harassment complaints. It was no surprise to find the company's managers a bit chauvinistic, but I was shocked at their naiveté. This is a multi-million dollar concern with projects that span the globe, yet they ignored their exposure based on a small amount of experience and a large amount of fictional information. Here's what the president said to me:

"We don't do any training for harassment because we simply don't need it." I asked him why he thought that way. He said, "Well, we have only one woman who ever walks into the plant and interfaces with plant personnel. 'Shirley,' the plant manager's secretary, always wears short skirts, seductive clothing, and LOVES the attention she gets from the plant employees." This "attention," the president explained, was in the form of whistles, catcalls, off-color remarks, etc. So, he said, "As long as we have Shirley — we won't have a problem."

I couldn't believe my ears. "You know, you're sitting on a tinderbox," I replied. "One day, this young woman is going to find a nice boyfriend or nice girlfriend or somebody else who will help her, or maybe she just grows up one weekend. She'll come in Monday morning and she'll look professional, she'll be dressed like a professional, she'll act professional, and she'll clean your clock for harassment! It will make no difference whether you think your catcalls and such were appreciated. The environment here is hostile, and you cannot deny it. Your company could be seriously hurt financially because she would be absolutely right." To make a long story short, he did some rethinking and asking around to other companies, and he initiated a program of sexual harassment training for the entire company within the next few weeks.

The forced resignation of U.S. Senator Bob Packwood, a Republican from Oregon, stands as another reminder of the costly consequences that may await harassers. Among the other high-profile cases: The president of W. R. Grace Company was fired for harassment claims. A veteran partner at the San Francisco-based Baker & McKenzie law firm resigned when his firm was found liable in the amount of $7 million because of his behavior toward a secretary. And Dell Laboratories in New York City had to swallow a $1 million settlement because of its chief executive's sexual misconduct.

There are many sexual harassment court cases currently being tried, and many of these cases are being quietly settled out of court on the side of the plaintiff. These cases are costing corporate America millions of dollars! It will take a while; but, as we all know — it is the depletion of the pocketbook that is the wake-up call for companies.

The unique status of sexual harassment

Only sexual harassment has achieved the status of an actionable legal offense according to the regulations of the U.S. Equal Employment Opportunities Commission (EEOC), which determined sexual harassment to be a form of discrimination prohibited by the Civil Rights Act of 1964. Consequently, there are many resource materials available that address legal remedies to sexual harassment, e.g. when and how to file a complaint. (As for the other three types of harassment, we'll look at some effective informal strategies shortly.)

Does sexual harassment still occur? You bet your buttons it does. The many forms it takes will astonish you. Here's a sampling — again, these are all true stories:

A secretary in her early 20s was at her desk one day when her manager buzzed her on the intercom. "Becky, would you please come in here and make me happy?" She was stunned. This was only her first "real" job out of school, and she was unprepared for such a proposition. She waited a few minutes to try to collect her thoughts, then walked back to his office, closed the door, and did it.

Whatever feelings Becky had to set aside, her relationship with her boss grew into a full-fledged affair. "I was young and stupid," she says now. "I felt very sophisticated at the time, and he found ways to pay me a lot more money, which I really liked." The affair lasted six months. It ended one night when her boss asked her to take the place of a call girl he had arranged for a client when she canceled at the last minute. Would she please take care of this guy and his friend? She was shocked he asked her and said no, absolutely not. He fired her the next morning.

Cathy was the "Trophy Secretary" for the owner of a Midwestern sports team. She was a highly skilled and motivated professional, hired with the promise of lots of responsibility and career development. But it turned out her boss hired her just to "look pretty," sitting at his beck and call all day. Her boss insisted on telling her how to dress, how to fix her makeup, what to eat, and so on. "I don't believe he ever wanted to get in bed with me—he just wanted to show me off like a piece of property," she said. That kind of chauvinistic behavior resulted in a lawsuit and an out-of-court settlement of $2.6 million!

Hazel was blocked in her career by the old-fashioned (and illegal) custom called "rug ranking," a practice that links a secretary's career to that of her boss. She literally is treated like a piece of her boss's furniture or carpet—where he goes, she goes. Hazel was an executive assistant to the company president, but she was underpaid and underutilized. After months of discussion, she concluded that her situation was not going to improve, so she began looking around. She soon received a wonderful offer—more money, more responsibility, everything she wanted. But just before the official offer was made, she was told by the human resources director of the new company that her new boss would have to talk to her old boss "to see if it was okay that he hire her." You see, apparently the two men belonged to the same club, and her new boss didn't want to hurt the feelings of the old boss by "stealing" his secretary. Hazel, of course, was incensed—which was why the human resources director was chastised for telling her the truth!

What, exactly, is the legal definition of harassment? Courts and employers generally use the definition of sexual harassment contained in the guidelines of the EEOC. This language has also been used as the basis for most state laws prohibiting sexual harassment. Here's what the EEOC guidelines say:

Harassment on the basis of sex is a violation of Title VII, the employment-discrimination section, of the 1964 Civil Rights Bill. Unwelcome sexual advances, requests for sexual favors, and other verbal or physical conduct of a sexual nature constitute sexual harassment when:

1. Submission to such conduct is made either explicitly or implicitly a term or condition of an individual's employment, or
2. Submission to or rejection of such conduct by an individual is used as the basis for employment decisions affecting such individuals, or
3. Such conduct has the purpose or effect of unreasonably interfering with an individual's work performance or creating an intimidating, hostile, or offensive working environment.

Points one and two are commonly referred to as the "quid pro quo" standard. From Latin, it translates to "this for that" — in other words, it describes a situation where an employee is confronted with sexual demands to keep a job or obtain a promotion. This is a classic jobs-for-sex dilemma.

Point three frequently describes other types of cases in which the threat — or trade-off — is not as explicit. This typically involves sexually offensive conduct that makes it difficult for an employee to do the job.

Now, I want to expand this description to further clarify "the line" between acceptable behavior and sexual harassment. These are among the most useful, common-sense criteria I've found. Most of these additional thoughts apply to the other three types of harassment, too.

Behavior can also be considered harassment when:

4. The behavior is deliberate. Accidental bumps, jostles, remarks, and curses don't count.
5. The behavior is repeated, even after an explicit request has been made to stop it. Persisting with behavior that is known to annoy or frighten an employee is malicious in intent and

effect. And repeated "accidents" must be viewed with suspicion. The more offensive or severe the behavior, the fewer times it needs to be repeated before it is considered harassment; the less severe it is, the more times it needs to be repeated.

6. The behavior would be considered annoying, offensive, inappropriate, or hurtful by a reasonable person. This is what I call the "gut feeling" test. A reasonable person knows where the line is between objectionable and appropriate behavior, at least as far as he/she is concerned. For example, you know when you have been offended, hurt, abused, or insulted, based on your values, experiences, expectations, etc. There will be differences between what individuals find reasonable, of course — one person may object to a nude centerfold, and another may not. That's not the point. The important thing is that you know what you find to be objectionable for yourself so you can make your feelings known.

7. The behavior is unwelcome, not asked for, and not returned. There must be no question that the victim is unhappy with the behavior.

Before we move on, I want to share a part of the story behind the Civil Rights Act of 1964. This story drips with irony, and it provides a revealing look into the social attitudes that prevailed just a generation ago.

The virtually all-male Congress never had any real intention to pass a law against sexual harassment or sex discrimination. As it was originally introduced, the Civil Rights Act of 1964 only prohibited discrimination in employment based on race, color, religion, or national origin. Discrimination on the basis of sex was not included. But in the eleventh hour, conservative opponents to the bill attached an amendment prohibiting discrimination on the basis of sex. They thought that this addition of sexual equality was so obviously preposterous that it would undermine and defeat the entire bill when it came to a vote.

The very idea of prohibiting sex-based discrimination was laughed at on the floor of Congress, and it was derided without mercy on the editorial pages of major newspapers. A popular question mocked: Could men now sue to become Playboy bunnies? The Lyndon Johnson administration, however, wanted the bill passed badly enough that it decided not to oppose the amendment. So the Civil Rights Act, which now included the ban on sex discrimination, was voted into law. On paper, at least, it was now illegal to discriminate in matters of employment on the basis of sex.

As the wife of a former politician, I have seen many instances where the law-making process lags behind the public consensus. Here, the reverse occurred. In their attempt to scuttle the legislation with a far-out, crazy, futuristic, never-in-a-thousand years notion like gender equity, they managed to catapult the anti-sex discrimination cause ahead of public opinion. In short, they did the right thing for the wrong reason—and this time, they accelerated the process of social progress.

Still, it took several more years before the law was taken seriously. The first head of the EEOC—the agency assigned to enforce the statute—said he viewed the provisions disallowing sex discrimination as a joke and "conceived out of wedlock."

Constituents eventually insisted that the statute be enforced. The time was the late 1960s–early 1970s, and other ideas and trends in society were converging to make sex discrimination a rallying point:

- More women were entering—and staying in—the work force in large numbers. In 1959, there were 22 million women working, and they made up about 33 percent of the American work force. By 1991, 57 million women were working, comprising 45.5 percent of the work force.
- The birth control pill, the women's movement, and the sexual revolution became high-profile ideas and began changing society's views of gender roles, work, and family.

It would be about 10 years after the Civil Rights Act passed, well into the 1970s, before the federal courts would hear the first cases in which sexual discrimination was the primary complaint.

The trouble was—even when the Civil Rights Act was used to argue successfully for open-door, non-discriminatory employment practices, and thereby allow women the opportunity to compete for jobs, they still got sexually harassed when they showed up for work!

Women began to argue that sexual harassment was a form of sex discrimination. If the link between harassment and discrimination could be established, the Civil Rights Act that prohibited discrimination could be used to outlaw harassment as well.

But most courts initially rejected this line of reasoning. For example, in 1976, a federal court judge ruled that the Civil Rights Act was not intended to prevent a "physical attack motivated by sexual desire on the part of a supervisor" just because it "happened to occur in a corporate corridor rather than a back alley." The case was brought by Adrienne Tompkins against her employer, New Jersey's Public Service Electric and Gas Company, because her boss physically detained, assaulted, and then fired her for refusing to have sex with him.

Women's groups kept pressing the issue. They argued that sexual harassment is a form of sexual discrimination because harassment makes it impossible for women to work in certain types of situations. If harassment keeps a woman out of a job, it discriminates against them as much as a Men Only employment policy. Finally, in 1980, under the leadership of Eleanor Holmes Norton, the EEOC issued rules defining sexual harassment and declaring it a form of sexual discrimination prohibited under the Civil Rights Act. It wasn't until 1986 — 22 years after the Civil Rights Act was passed — that the U.S. Supreme Court acknowledged this. The Court said sexual harassment on the job is a form of illegal sex discrimination because it creates a "hostile or offensive work environment" for members of one sex that is every bit as demeaning and disconcerting as the harshest racial barriers. Since then, other courts have continued to refine the definition of what constitutes sexual harassment. Generally speaking, the courts now define sexual harassment along guidelines and standards that are parallel to those applied to racial harassment.

Adding a bit more irony to the zigzag history of the sexual harassment issue were the charges of sexual harassment made during the Supreme Court confirmation hearings for Clarence Thomas by Anita Hill. We owe a huge debt of thanks to Ms. Hill, who has had the courage to speak publicly about her experiences and thoughts about harassment in the workplace and, in the process, made them the topic of discussion in many offices throughout the country.

From October 12 through 15, 1991, Ms. Hill explained to the nation just what some men try to get away with when they have more power than a woman in the workplace. Many men were incredulous that anyone would make an issue of the incidents Ms. Hill related; to their credit, many men also admitted that she had gotten it exactly right. A lot of men reflected on their behavior and honestly appraised their actions; some, I'm told, actually conducted themselves differently when they returned to work on the Monday morning following the hearings. A lot of daughters asked their fathers, "You would never do something like that, would you, Daddy?" A lot of wives listened carefully for what was not said when their husbands talked about the Hill/Thomas hearings with eyes averted. A lot of men retreated to clean their basements that weekend.

The women listening to Ms. Hill knew they were listening to the truth. Ms. Hill was telling their stories. They were proud of Anita, for she did not break down and cry, refused to become shrill with outrage and met direct questions with direct answers. She responded to the baiting, demeaning, suspicious, and accusatory tone of the questioners with intelligence, wit, grace, and dignity. She did not give her detractors an opportunity to pin a caricature or stereotype on her, which would have provided them with the excuse they needed to minimize or trivialize the impact of her story.

Anita Hill was a reluctant witness, but her testimony has become a part of the national dialogue. She broke the silence surrounding harassment at work, and for this we will always be grateful.

While I am forever frustrated at the slow pace of change in our office cultures, I remain convinced this country and this time offers the best opportunities ever for professional women. We're not perfect, but it is to our credit as a free society that the Civil Rights Act eventually *did* have an impact, and Ms. Hill *could* tell her story, and that many others are trying to do the right thing. Like so many others, though, I am impatient for more change!

When I conduct seminars in foreign countries, I can compare firsthand how far we've come. We're fortunate in the U.S. to have a law that requires us to view sexual harassment as an illegal act. Not everyone does. I recently gave an office ethics seminar in Singapore and my hosts wanted me to include sexual harassment advice in the session. I replied, "But, we have a law prohibiting sexual harassment in our workplace; and, you do not." He replied, "Talk about it anyway. We do not condone sexual harassment in our country and all employees need to be aware of that fact." We had a wonderfully interactive session and freely discussed the topic. Whereas everyone in the seminar agreed sexual harassment was not acceptable in their workplace and that both management and support staff strive hard to eliminate it from the workplace, I returned home somewhat frustrated because I felt those office professionals were operating without a 'safety net.' As imperfect as they are, it is much better by far to have federal and state laws prohibiting sexual harassment so offenders can be legally prosecuted as a last resort.

From the Now I've Heard It All Department: One of the most bizarre situations I've ever heard was the company president who sought prior acceptance of his harassing behavior. My assignment was to help him recruit a new assistant. He must have been a good planner, because the first candidate I sent to him for an interview reported back that he asked her to sign a waiver protecting him from any harassment suits in the future. In the interview, the president told her he was "quite loose" with off-color language, etc., and that if she was to work for him, she would be asked to sign a waiver that this kind of language would not bother her and that she would never file a sexual harassment law suit against him or the company. She asked me what to do. I told her she should never sign any such document, and I was embarrassed I sent her on an interview with someone who would make such a request. I then confronted the president and told him I would not work with him if he continued to make such requests of my candidates. That was one client I've never been sorry I lost!

The first step to stopping harassment

The first step to stopping harassment is to call it by its correct name. Say after me: "This behavior is deliberate, inappropriate, unprofessional, unwelcome, never asked for, not deserved, and will not be tolerated. This behavior is harassment, and I want it stopped."

I believe that many of us experience one or more types of harassment, but few of us report it. I understand this. Whom would we tell? What would we say? Why would we knowingly bring down additional grief upon ourselves? How would we make our point, and get the harassment to stop, without alienating our co-workers?

In a 1991 poll by the National Association of Female Executives:

- 77% of those polled said that sexual harassment was a problem in the workplace
- 53% said they had been sexually harassed at work
- 64% of those who experienced sexual harassment did not report it, and
- of the 36% who did report it, most felt the problem was not addressed satisfactorily because they were made to resign, quit, or transfer to a position they didn't want.

I admit it — when I was just getting started in my career, I kept my mouth shut on more than one occasion when I should have been kicking butt and taking names. Why didn't I speak up? I was uncertain, inexperienced, intimidated, fearful of rejection and isolation, conditioned to avoid conflict — there were lots of overlapping reasons.

I've said this before, and it's true here, too — when you decide to do something to remedy an ethical dilemma, you have to be prepared to get roughed up by the process. Harassment dilemmas are as rough as they come. Can you zip on the thick skin you'll need to make your point and see it through to get some changes made? Is it worth it to make a "big deal" out of a harassment incident, considering that you may be jeopardizing your job, your friendships with co-workers, your relationship with loved ones, your advancement opportunities, your financial health, and your mental well-being?

It's common to feel powerless. We may feel like we are working under an "unwritten job description" that says, "this is the way things are here, period — if you don't like the way we do things here, leave." At times we may feel like victims of our success, telling ourselves we just have to tolerate harassment because of whom we work for, e.g. "He's the advertising manager, and people who work for him get treated like this, period."

A recent seminar attendee reminded me of the feeling of being hopelessly trapped by a harassment dilemma. I saw "the look" when she approached me at the coffee break and knew she was jammed up and struggling with a serious dilemma. She told me a horrendous story:

Her company's biggest client was aggressively harassing her — calling her at home, asking her out on dates, waiting in his car outside her office when she went home, etc. Her job was that of administrative assistant to the president of a large advertising firm. I replied as you might have: "Susan, you must go to your boss immediately and relate all of this to him." I thought, of course, that because he was the president, there would be a swift end to the situation.

Susan looked at me incredulously. "But, Nan, I can't go to my boss. This is our biggest client! If this client pulls out, our company will fold! Furthermore, if my boss learns about this, he will simply blame me for creating this problem!" Talk about feeling trapped and powerless!

We all know she wasn't creating the problem. She believed it, too. But the level of trust and communication with her boss was such that she felt she could not talk to him. (See Chapter 10: *The trouble with the boss* for more about how to have discussions regarding ethical dilemmas with the boss.)

Susan and I sat down and we had a long discussion. I, of course, told her she was NOT creating the problem and that she had to take care of herself by taking action and ending the situation. We explored her options. In her company, she said, all employees were encouraged to take anything like a sexual harassment complaint to the human resource director. She had little confidence in this guy, but reluctantly agreed to do it because it was the logical place to start. Then she called me about a week later with good news: She finally chose to talk directly with her boss about the situation and, guess what, he was as appalled as I was over the situation. He told her it would be immediately corrected. She said she didn't know what happened, only that the client immediately stopped harassing her — and he also remained a client!

About 60 percent of women in the American work force have experienced sexual harassment, according to conservative studies. However, only about 3 percent of them report the harassment, fearing they will not be believed, the company will not be responsive, or the victim or harasser will be harmed as a result.

My friend Gloria Steinem says, "Sexual harassment has the same ambiguous status that rape had in the 1970's." I believe she is absolutely correct. Years ago, if you were raped, you might not have even reported the crime. The reason? "The System" — the reporting, prosecuting, and enforcement process — was biased against the victim, set up to almost "rape" you all over again. You would have had to be pretty strong-willed to take action, knowing you would experience hostile interrogations, the stress and humiliation of having your personal life dragged through the judicial process several times and, finally, the almost certain countercharge that you were a voluntary participant and/or had "asked to be raped."

Today, our process is much better and the rape victim feels more protected. Rape, apparently, is still the most unreported crime; but, it is better than years ago. I believe the same will be true about sexual harassment in the office in the near future.

There is a parallel here to child abuse situations. About 10 years ago, a terrible child abuse case in my state surfaced and stayed on the front pages for months. As a result, Minnesota started to change its child abuse laws. For example: Today, if you see a child being physically abused, you can be held accountable if you do not report it, particularly if you are in the health care, law enforcement, teaching, or child care professions.

I believe, as a direct result of the Hill/Thomas hearings, new pro cedures were drafted in offices all over the country with regard to sexual harassment. Today, if you observe someone being harassed in any way in your office, you should report it to the proper authorities within your company. Some day, if a harassment suit arises due to the situation, you may be named in the suit as having observed the behavior, and you will be held accountable for knowing about it, but doing nothing.

Am I being harassed? If I am, what can I do about it?

Are you being harassed? If you think you are, the answer is yes. I say this because I believe it is possible to be harassed in many ways, yet not meet the strict legal definition of sexual harassment. Furthermore, I believe you have a professional responsibility to do something about it. I do *not* advise you to go immediately to the courthouse and file a lawsuit. I do believe you owe it to your employer and co-workers to speak up, make your concerns known, and take some responsibility for trying to resolve all dilemmas in a constructive way with an attitude of teamwork and mutual respect. If this is not possible, well, you can still exercise your legal options.

Because I view the ethical office as *a way of working together,* my definition of harassment needs to pass only a few common-sense tests. Let's face it—in the real world, if you are being hurt in some way by the behavior of someone you work with, you have a classic ethical dilemma. There's no need to quibble about categorizing the type of harassment, or whether it is considered sexual harassment in a legal sense. You just want the behavior to STOP!

Answer the following questions. Your objective is to define and describe the behavior that is bothering you, and to think through the degree of severity. After you answer the questions, we'll talk about some of the constructive steps you can take to remedy the problem.

Ethical Office Discussion #4:
〰️ Nan DeMars's Harassment Audit™ 〰️

*Use these questions to help you decide if you are being harassed.
Then, use the answers to your questions as a guide
to your follow-up discussions to resolve this ethical dilemma.*

1. What is a brief description of the person's behavior that you find objectionable?

2. How does the behavior make you feel?

3. Is the behavior affecting your job performance? In what ways?

4. Is the behavior welcomed, encouraged, asked for, returned, or reciprocated? Does the person think it is?

5. Does the person behave in the same way toward others? Do the others who receive this same behavior feel the same as you do?

6. Would a reasonable person find the behavior objectionable, offensive, or otherwise not socially acceptable?

7. Have you told the person you find his/her behavior bothersome?

8. Have you asked the person to stop?

9. Has the person repeated and continued the behavior? Is the behavior deliberate?

10. Has the person explained his/her behavior to your satisfaction? Would he/she be able to explain the behavior to his spouse? Daughter? Son? Mother-in-law? Boss? The company attorney? A reporter? A jury?

Again, do not focus on the legal dimensions of the dilemma first—instead, focus on the ethical aspects of the behavior. The objective here is to stop the behavior in the most constructive way possible.

How do we respond? What can we do to stop a co-worker's objectionable behavior? And how can we do it in a way that does not cause us to break up the team, leave our jobs, or make working together in the future painfully awkward?

I have some simple, practical suggestions for ending a harassment dilemma:

Step 1: Prepare yourself to discuss the problem behavior by (a) answering the 10 questions on the Harassment Audit, and (b) re-reading Chapter 9: *The ground rules for discussions about ethics*. The discussion process is informal (one-to-one, confidential) and *incremental* (if you can't get satisfaction doing it the "nice" way, you raise the stakes with more public disclosure, more severe consequences, etc.). Also, talk to others and read whatever resource materials you feel you need to read to affirm your perspective. You need to minimize your self-doubt (e.g. "Am I crazy to feel this way?" and "Am I the only one?") and familiarize yourself with your options. If a polite, respectful request to stop the behavior is not going to be successful, you must be prepared to immediately take the next incremental step. You're not bluffing or kidding around — and the person has to get that message loud and clear. ALSO: Don't delay. In many jurisdictions, the statute of limitations on sexual harassment charges is 90 days.

Step 2: Document in writing the history of the objectionable incidents, e.g. "at least twice a week for the past month, you've raised your voice and cursed at me in a staff meeting." This written record may take the form of a journal (date and incident description) or a letter summarizing your recollections. Do not skip this step — starting a paper trail communicates all the right messages about your commitment to getting this resolved, and it helps remove any differences in power between you.

Step 3: Have an informal ethics discussion with the co-worker whose behavior is objectionable. Use the outline for the discussion to RESOLVE an ethical dilemma in Chapter 9, plus your written documentation. If you are offended by someone's comments or behavior, you need to tell them so directly. If they still don't "get it," add these words, "Do you know how that comment made me feel?" In other words, hold them accountable for their behavior — don't let them push it back on you by saying something like, "Are you serious? How could anyone in their right mind think that?"

In more than 90 percent of the cases, this single discussion will be sufficient to change the offending behavior, particularly if you are well prepared. Do NOT use this conversation to start another problem by "rubbing it in" or by gleefully saying "gotcha" or by making the person feel foolish or vulnerable. If he/she offers some excuse for the behavior, however lame, fine (e.g. "I was temporarily under the influence of space aliens, but they've gone now and I'm my old self again."). Nothing positive can come out of arguing about the excuse. Let the person believe you believe him/her, if necessary. You don't care why the person did it in the past — you just care about stopping it in the future. In most cases, the dilemma ends here.

Step 4: Watch and wait. Has the behavior changed? Maintain your professionalism and give the person the benefit of the doubt; give him/her a chance to behave like he/she should. Your attitude is one of *expecting* the person to do the right thing and change the behavior, and if he/she doesn't, you will be sorely disappointed.

Step 5: If the behavior doesn't change, start escalating the consequences incrementally. Follow your office's procedure, if you have one, or just start talking with the person's boss or the human resources director. Document all conversations, especially those with promises to "look into it," "have a talk with him," and "follow up on this." The best company policies name two individuals, typically a supervisor or some other person in the organization, as the conduit for sexual harassment complaints. The reason for this, of course, is that the supervisor may be the harasser.

Step 6: No change? Now, it's time to get your attorney involved — and update your resume.

If you are a supervisor, you can prevent harassment-like dilemmas from undermining the effectiveness of your office team if you:

a) Keep your eyes and ears open.
b) Treat every complaint seriously.
c) Don't assume you know all the facts.
d) Handle problems when they are small and manageable.
e) Know and follow up on your company policies.
f) Keep good notes of incidents, statements of participants, and resolutions. Document, document, document.
g) Follow through to completion.

Are we going too far?

Some people dismiss harassment issues as an overreaction, a power grab, a feminist bias, hypersensitivity — we've heard 'em all, haven't we? Well, I've got a simple rule: The only opinion that really matters at the end of the day is that of the person being harassed. We cannot judge the merit of someone else's dilemma until we've walked a mile in their boots!

I gave a seminar once at a company where a secretary complained that the secretary seated next to her had posted, on the inside of the side of her desk, a magazine centerfold of Burt Reynolds (his famous picture of yesteryear)! She said no one walking up to the secretary's desk could ever see the poster. However, whenever she turned to talk to the secretary during the course of the day, she saw the poster. It offended her and bothered her to the point of distraction and stress. She asked in the class, "Is this sexual harassment?" Before I could even reply, the human resources manager, who happened to be in the class, immediately stood up and answered, "It most definitely is sexual harassment; and, that poster will go down tomorrow!" I'm not sure this one pin-up meets the legal definition of harassment, but it doesn't have to. It is enough for another person to say that she finds it offensive and a negative impact on her performance.

Here are some more examples of harassing behavior. From an outsider's perspective, these may seem so silly or trivial as to make us wonder if all our concern about harassment isn't a bit overblown. But believe me, there is real pain, stress, and hurt inside each of these situations. The people being harassed consider themselves true victims. Their "gut feeling" perspectives tell them these incidents are harassment, and who are we to say otherwise?

- a waitress is required to wear an ill-fitting and embarrassing costume
- a secretary comes to work every morning to find her boss has broken all her pencil points; this requires her to take several minutes to resharpen them under his leering gaze
- an assistant must respond to or ignore comments like,
  "Don't even try to talk to her. She's got a whopping case of PMS."
  "It would be a waste to give her that promotion because her husband has a great job."

"Don't ask her to negotiate. She's not hard-nosed enough."
- a secretary's boss avoids almost all eye contact
- a group member is excluded from social invitations offered to everyone else

"I don't know where to draw the line!"

Men sometimes complain they "don't know where the line is," and hence feel put upon about saying anything of a remotely personal nature, e.g. "Nice dress" or "I like your new hair style."

This is absolute nonsense. Men know what a bully is, and bullies know they make people hurt, angry, and miserable. They know the difference, and I don't allow anyone to plead ignorance anymore. If complimenting a woman on what she wears is perceived as a sexual jibe and it makes the woman feel badly, the man knows it. Just challenge these jerks pleading ignorance with a few of the following questions:

"Would you say that in front of your spouse or parents?"
"Would you say or do that in front of a colleague of the same sex?"
"How would you feel if your mother, wife, sister, or daughter were subjected to the same words or behavior?"
"How would you feel if another man said the same things to you?"
"Does it need to be said or done at all?"

On a Friday night, a week after the Anita Hill/Clarence Thomas hearings, my husband and I went out to dinner with five other couples. We took a long table at the restaurant. I ended up sitting in the middle seat facing a man who is the owner and CEO of a major Minneapolis-based company. He has a reputation as a womanizer; and, to my knowledge, his company has lost at least two sexual harassment law suits naming him as the offender.

All night long, he was pontificating and whining, "I just don't know where the line is anymore. I can't tell my secretary she has a pretty suit on because she'll sue me. I can't tell my female accountant she looks nice because she'll sue me." He carried on about this all evening, much to the irritation of everyone at the table. I thought I should curb my reaction because he had been a contributor to one of my husband's political campaigns. Fortunately, Lou doesn't give a rip.

Finally, over dessert, he made the comment once too often. I reached over the table and put my hand on his shoulder. The table went immediately silent—no one moved. The waiter even stopped waitering! I said, "George (not his name), you know where the line is. You have always known where the line is. Now, for the first time, you are going to have to pay attention to that line."

He stared in astonishment at me—then relaxed and sat back—and sheepishly replied, "You're right, Nan. I know where the line is." People who make a comment like that know exactly where the line is—they just choose not to behave.

Right after that, I had the *Today* show on my television while dressing for the office. Bryant Gumbel was interviewing a sexual harassment attorney. Gumbel asked my question. He said, "Tell me—I'm an employee here at the station. And, I don't know where the line is. Tell me how to determine that!"

I loved the attorney's answer, which I quickly took down in shorthand. He replied, "Bryant—I'll tell you three things. Number One—If you don't want your behavior to be replayed tomorrow morning on the *Today* show before your audience—don't do it! Number Two—If you don't want your behavior to be reenacted tomorrow morning in front of all your peers here at the station—don't do it! And, Number Three—if you don't want your behavior to be documented and in the hands of your spouse's divorce attorney—don't do it!" Great advice, I thought…

It's a two-way street, though. If we want the rest of the office world to behave—we must behave ourselves, also. I've had male employees tell me they are most uncomfortable when they are standing in the middle of several women and the women are sharing an off-color joke. If we don't want to be placed in uncomfortable positions, we have to be sure we don't place our male counterparts in the same.

A human resources director at a huge accounting firm once told me she had to discipline the female receptionist who asked a client out on a date one time when he visited the company. He apparently reported this to the CPA he was visiting, who then told the human resources director. The client did not appreciate this "unprofessional" behavior.

Here's a similar story: One day, Paul Newman, the actor, was changing planes at a major airport, on his way to an auto race. He had scheduled a press interview in a meeting room at the airport designed for the purpose. A female employee of the airline had the job of managing and "hostessing" the meeting room. The hostess welcomed everyone to the room (about 10 people), served them coffee, and made them feel comfortable. Then, she returned to her desk at the back of the room to observe the proceedings. Her boss also appeared in the room to assist and meet Newman.

After about an hour, everyone took a break. The hostess served everyone coffee again and chatted informally with the group. Incidentally, Newman apparently wore sunglasses the entire time. When the hostess served Newman another cup of coffee, she said, "Excuse me, Mr. Newman, but would you please take off your sunglasses so I can see your beautiful, blue eyes?"

That remark caused her to lose her job! Up until she made the comment, Newman had been chatting with her in a friendly manner, but her request got the opposite effect. He immediately turned away from her and stopped talking (he also kept the glasses on). The hostess returned to her desk where her boss told her they had to "talk" as soon as the interviews were over. When everyone departed, her boss fired her!

I was quite appalled when I heard the story. I agreed — that was a silly and inappropriate request to make of a client in an office setting. However, dismissal seemed to me to be a harsh discipline. I asked the human resources director (who told me the story) if this was a first offense or a "10th" offense. She told me the hostess previously had made four inappropriate remarks to clients who were in the same interview room on four different occasions. This was not a lounge, restaurant, or hallway in the airport — it was an office setting, and everyone in it was either a client, guest, or employee of the airline. She had been disciplined by her supervisor after each prior incident and told to curb her overly casual, inappropriate behavior. Apparently, the hostess did not heed the warnings. This fifth incident was the final straw.

About company policies

I applaud companies developing harassment policies, instead of just sexual harassment policies. This is more useful to employees and promotes the broader principles of the ethical office.

Please note: A sexual harassment policy is no place for corporate-speak. There should be no misunderstandings or slippage about what is and is not allowed. The policy against sexual harassment must describe the prohibited conduct in an understandable way.

Employment attorneys tell me that when a charge of sex discrimination or sexual harassment is lodged against a company, the first question asked is whether the company has a sexual harassment policy and if every employee is certain to be aware of it. The second question asked is whether all employees have been trained accordingly. (And, they mean ALL — throughout the organization.)

Let me share two incidents: At a seminar in St. Louis, the secretary to the CEO told me her boss had returned to the office after a sexual harassment course and made the comment to her: "Isn't it nice we don't have any of that terrible behavior here at _____!"

This secretary said the CEO was an excellent business executive who would never condone such misbehavior himself. And, as so often happens, he just could not even conceive of anyone else doing so — especially in "his" company. After this secretary overcame her shock, she said: "Would you do me a favor? Every time over the next few weeks that you are in town, would you please sit down for lunch in the lunchroom with a different group of people and ask them the question: 'Have you ever experienced sexual harassment while working here?'" He agreed to do so (and, he did!). Several of the employees in the seminar said, yes, he did sit with them and talk about their experiences. After each lunch, the CEO returned to his office in amazement and reported several more incidents he had heard from his employees regarding their sexual harassment experiences in "his" workplace.

As a result, the CEO stepped up the sexual harassment training courses for all employees. Isn't it true that people sometimes assume no one does something because they wouldn't do it, and they can't imagine anyone else doing it? If you see a similar opportunity to give your CEO a dose of the same medicine, do it!

The courage to change

Speaking up against harassment is one of the most difficult things you'll ever do. As we've discussed earlier, trying to remedy any ethical dilemma is a risky challenge and usually requires us to endure personal sacrifices — but harassment is the toughest. But, we must. If we remain silent and tolerate harassment, it will continue. It doesn't matter that we don't fully understand its root causes — outmoded social rules, primitive gender roles, economic discrimination, or whatever—the time has come to end our silence of compliance.

I urge all of you to confront your harassers, document every suspect incident and follow-up conversation, and generally let it be known that you are taking this inappropriate and unprofessional behavior seriously. Then, as soon as you can, try to stop the objectionable behavior through the use of informal, one-to-one discussions and incrementally stiffer consequences. When all else fails, resort to formal avenues of protest inside and outside your company, including educating yourself about other victims' experiences, meeting with other similarly situated people and, finally, exploring the feasibility of legal action.

A final note of optimism: We have, indeed, come a long way toward ending sexual discrimination. Yes, there remains much to be done—the battles against sexism are not yet over. But we should take some pride and hope, I think, from how much we have accomplished. In 1964, when the Civil Rights Act was passed, racial discrimination made it impossible for some blacks to vote or eat at the same lunch counter as whites. The fight against sexism, sexual discrimination, and sexual harassment is on a parallel path, just a few years behind. I am hopeful and confident we can continue to make steps forward every day so our daughters and sons perform their jobs in work environments free of harassment.

> *"How we enlighten people who are currently
> in the workplace about behavior
> that is beneath our (and their) dignity
> is the challenge of the future."*
>
> —Anita Hill

> *"Changing attitudes is wonderful if you've got 40, 50,
> maybe 1,000 years. But if you want to see improvements
> before you die, you have to change* behavior.*"*
>
> —Lynn Martin, former labor secretary to George Bush,
> commenting about 34-point reform program
> at Mitsubishi auto plant in Normal, IL

15

Let the games begin

Think about it: *You have worked in your current position for about six months. During that time, one of the supplier's sales people has become a good friend. She frequently invites you to lunch, and she always shows a genuine interest in your children and pets. From your discussions, you realize how hard she is trying to get more of your company's business. One day over lunch, she asks if you would give her a "ballpark" figure on what your company pays another supplier for a particular product so she has some idea what her company should charge. What, if anything, should you do?*

Not everyone is as nice as you are!

Some of our co-workers go out of their way to knowingly initiate actions that are unethical. This is hard to accept. We like to think we work with people who are basically honest and trustworthy. We like to think we can always trust our co-workers to be fair and to do the right thing. We like to think our colleagues would be unanimously committed to resolving any kind of ethical dilemma.

The fact is, they are not.

Most of our discussion up to this point has presumed: (1) your co-workers generally share the same ethical standards that you do, and (2) ethical dilemmas are exceptions to the normally pleasant and acceptable office behavior. In the real world, this isn't always true.

In this chapter, I want to speak plainly about situations where you find yourself literally under attack by malicious co-workers. These co-workers view office politics as a competitive sport, and they intend to do whatever they have to do to win.

When is a behavior a game?

Office games are conscious, explicit behaviors intended to benefit a selfish interest. They are competitive, and they can be ruthless and unrelenting.

These are not mere spectator events — they affect everyone in the office. Office games cause real stress and pain. They cost real dollars in lost productivity. Even a garden variety "game" can damage working relationships, team effectiveness, deadlines, schedules, budgets, trust, and employee morale.

Game-playing is clearly unethical behavior, disconnected from the normal morals and values in your office. Gamesmanship is any conduct that is self-serving, exploitive, and dishonest. Game-players are cynical, selfish, and manipulative when the game is afoot. It has been my experience that game-players almost always know exactly what they are doing, and they almost always know they "win" what they want at the expense of someone else. But, they don't care.

Why do some people play games?

Why do some people choose to play games to advance their self-interests? Are they lazy, looking for a shortcut to more status, more money, more power, more control? Do they feel insecure unless they tip the playing field in their favor? Do they lack morals or values, and see tampering with the scoreboard as a legitimate strategy for getting ahead? Are they simply evil, deriving perverse pleasure from the misery of others?

Only a therapist, behavioral psychologist, or talk show host would dare to hazard a guess. Whatever dark part of the human personality that drives an otherwise competent and intelligent co-worker to engage in malicious gamesmanship may be beyond what you and I can know. We cannot read a person's mind or heart to discern his true motivations.

But the question "Why?" is beside the point, anyway. All we need to know is that we have to deal with the consequences of games because gamesmanship sabotages the important characteristics of the ethical office: Trust, fairness, honesty, collaboration, and personal accountability.

My personal view is that people behave in these negative and destructive ways because of either fear or greed, or both. Fear of losing control, turf, status, or any other personal advantage is a primal emotion. Greed is the other side of the same mirror.

I think the thrill of "getting away with it" has something to do with some people's motivation, too. A boring, dead-end job that has become too easy breeds frustration and desperation. Running a game on your co-workers — and seeing if you can get away with it — might manufacture just the right amount of adventure to make the day go faster.

Revenge also comes up as a reason in my seminar discussions. Some people dwell on their lost opportunities and real or imagined sleights, and guess what? Their instinct is to blame someone else for their assorted misfortunes. This is the "stalker" personality — a normally ethical person who rationalizes his explicit decision to set aside all previous moral training and to live without limits on his conduct. Once a person has convinced himself that the company "owes" him something, watch out.

Do women play more games than men? Are they the "sneakier sex," just because they know a thing or two about carrying on a conversation? No way. I don't believe for a moment that one gender has an advantage in any of these games. In my experience, I have found men to be skilled social animals, and equally ruthless. They also have the advantage of usually being more focused on their needs. They may not have as many opportunities or options when it comes to deciding how to get what they want, but they've got more than enough arrows in their quiver. (I have female legal secretaries tell me all the time that they are often blamed for spreading rumors in the office, when, all along, it is the male attorneys who are the worst gossips!)

There's only one rule

There seems to be only one rule to these games: *Don't get caught playing.* To be discovered to be a game-player is to lose the high stakes. The game-player is branded untrustworthy, unreliable, a sometimes-friend, and worse. Stretching the sports metaphor a bit further, serious offenses (e.g., lying to the boss, spreading rumors, etc.) get the player kicked off the team. Technical fouls and other minor offenses (e.g., selectively distributing information to embarrass the other guy, taking undeserved credit, intentionally misdirecting messages and files, etc.) merit a penalty like demotion, reassignment, or new limitations to information.

Checking the sports pages

The following list is a brief program to office games. It will clue you in to some of the most common players and the games they play. I offer this list somewhat tongue-in-cheek; but, believe me, there's nothing funny about what's going on when these games are being played. These games can cause insidious and costly damage to an office team, even reaching into other parts of the organization. And these game-players play for keeps!

THE BLAME GAME

Pity the poor scapegoat. He or she is held accountable for the mistakes and poor performance of others. The successful players—those doing the blaming and excuse-making—are sure-fire winners only if the "goat" remains unaware of the blame. Scapegoats can become very vocal and belligerent if they feel they have been wrongly accused. The accuser manipulates the situation to minimize the possibility the scapegoat will confront him and, heaven forbid, demand an explanation, evidence, or an apology.

Three interesting moves can be observed among the more skilled players of the Blame Game: The Wink—"He was incapacitated, if you know what I mean . . ." (wink, wink); The Whisper—"Now, just between us gals—this conspiracy is soooo deliciously melodramatic..."; and The Weasel (a.k.a. Corporatespeak)—"You heard that I said *what?* Oh, no—I didn't mean that at all. I merely said you seemed to be having a problem with..." With colleagues like these, who needs the competition to tear you down, right?

THE STUPID FOX

The object of this game is to collect many bits of seemingly innocent information, then knit those pieces of information into a larger picture that will benefit the player or injure the player's competition. A common camouflage is the, "Gee, I'm just a stupid guy" act or the "I'm just the new gal here" act.

The game moves from small conversation to small conversation, none of which appear to have a specific focus or direction. Actually, this is strategic chitchat. The innocuous questions usually are a feigned interest in a person, process, or machine, like, "How does this work?" and "Can you tell me again how Mr. Bruster and Ms. Covington share responsibilities? Why do they do it that way?" Typical questions like these are open-ended nets, catching every morsel of innuendo, trivia, and office history for later use.

HANGMAN

This game is won by the person who does nothing. Give the boss (or colleague) enough rope, and he will hang himself, right? When a person fails to support another person by withholding information or remaining silent about risks, he's playing Hangman.

CHICKEN

Is avoiding risk your first reflex? Do you fear the consequences of failure more than you value the rewards of success? Trying too hard to be "safe" at all times is as unhealthy as taking foolish risks. Your office team needs everyone to share in the heavy lifting of solving problems, reinventing procedures, continually improving the way things get done — and these are not risk-free undertakings. Chicken is a funny, circular game — because those who win in the short term end up losing.

LET'S PRETEND

Here's a game of verbal skill the whole office can enjoy. It's maddeningly simple — just tell the other person what they want to hear. Again and again. Say whatever you sense they want to hear about the schedule, the budget, the problem they want to solve. And when they come back and ask, "What went wrong?" just give them another dose of what they want to hear. People who play this game cannot stomach confrontation. They believe the messenger with the bad news gets sacrificed, and they don't want to be that victim. Rather than experience the consequences of delivering the bad news, they pretend to believe in the most convenient reality. Interestingly, it takes at least two to play this game. While Player A is saying, "(Let's pretend) everything's just fine," Player B is saying, "(Let's pretend) I believe you."

HANDS OFF

We're all familiar with this game—it's the grown-up version of turf-guarding we learned in the sandbox as a child. When a person feels like he's losing control or power or status or influence, he'll react in surprising (and often embarrassing) ways to hang on to what he perceives is his.

The following comes from the good people at the YMCA. Substitute "it" for the task, responsibility, project, assignment, relationship, office supplies, desk by the window, or whatever else people tussle over in your office. Do you see anyone you know?

Property Laws of the Toddler (or Co-Worker!)

1. If I like it, it's mine.
2. If it's in my hand, it's mine.
3. If I can take it from you, it's mine.
4. If I had it a little while ago, it's mine.
5. If it's mine, it must never appear to be yours in any way.
6. If I'm doing or building something, all the pieces are mine.
7. If it just looks like mine, it's mine.

M & M

The M & M stand for meetings and memos—and both are far more common these days than when I started in this profession (come on, it wasn't that long ago!). So many people are well-trained at "doing meetings" and "memoing" (isn't that just a perfectly horrible verb?), they use them to double- and triple-cover their sorry behinds from accountability. Talk something to death, or document something to death, and you can distance yourself and insulate yourself from any tough decision or controversial program. The game of M & M is frequently played by those who have lost at the game of Chicken.

STROKING

This game is among the most seductive because it make you feel so good to play. Here's how it works: Player A uses a little bit of information—a name, a date, anything—to start a conversation with Player B (that's you). He draws you into the conversation by asking an open-ended question that implies that he knows more than he does. (Actually, all he knows is that he doesn't know.) You, being a trusting and nurturing person by nature, make a sincere effort to answer the question. He responds by voicing an opinion, which you agree with or disagree with. The game has now begun in earnest, and you're losing, but don't know it yet. He flatters you with your keen insights ("Gee, I never looked at it just that way before.").

You take the bait and give him even more of your pearls of wisdom. He keeps you going as long as he can by continuing to be impressed ("No kidding," and "Is that really true?") and/or confused ("Boy, I just don't get it! Why would they do it that way?" and "I don't understand how this connects to that."). This slimy guy is getting you to tell all you know by appealing to your sense of self-esteem.

What is amazing is that he can have you voluntarily share all kinds of information, and leave you feeling good about being the smartest person in the company. Expert players know just how far to push this before tipping you off by sounding false. Players at the Grand Master level gather innocent details from several people, immediately using the information they just learned in the next conversation. The more they know, the better prepared they are to get even more information from the next conversation.

FUDGING

This game isn't as sweet as it sounds—it is the "rounding up" or generalizing or outright fabrication of results. Let's face it—this is easily done in a busy office that runs largely on trust. Since you control a lot of the records in the office, you can, if you want to, put a positive spin on customer complaints, vendor bids, word processing output, project time logs, even the repair rate of the copier. This game is often confused with Let's Pretend.

SABOTAGE

Do you know anyone who gets really angry, then gets even? Stress, anger, frustration, blame, hurt—many kinds of negative emotions will come and go when smart, busy people work together. If the team does not have the capacity to effectively deal with these emotions when they come up, they linger and fester. Eventually, they grow out of proportion and affect relationships and productivity, and then, watch out. Spreading rumors and tampering with another person's work are two familiar forms of sabotage. They rarely have the desired effect, however — revenge is almost always a lose-lose proposition.

SMOKEY BEAR

Action is not necessarily productivity. We've all known people who work very, very hard at looking busy, or talking about being busy, yet accomplish little of consequence. When challenged, the common response is indignation — as if to say, "Haven't you been listening and paying attention to all my stories about my busy-ness?" If there's smoke, but never any fire — or light, but no heat — you have one of the most serious performance problems an office team can experience.

EMERGENCY

One of my favorite desk plaques reads, "Lack of planning on your part does not create an emergency on my part." Oh, that this were true! The fact is, some managers routinely shovel their crises downhill to our desks. That's our job, right — to bail them out of the "Mess du Jour"? In a perverse way, we sometimes like to play this game because it makes us feel good to be the boss's savior, but if we're too good at it, management by crisis (meaning "management without planning") becomes standard operating procedure. Be careful. The adrenaline rush of Emergency is narcotic, and the stress will wear you down and use you up. Take care of yourself before this happens.

FIREBUG

Haven't we all heard this: "Sorry, but I have to put out these grass fires, so I have to get crazy, change all the rules, and generally make everyone's lives revolve around me . . ." This is the advanced version of the game of Emergency. The effect is the same, but the motives are more sinister. In fact, these "firemen" who spend so much time and energy putting out fires are actually pyromaniacs who set the fires themselves. Maybe the "rescuer" image is a boost to the firebug's self-esteem, but it's very difficult for everyone else!

HOW LOW CAN YOU GO?

Some people try to get by doing as little as possible. They seem to view the terms of employment like this: I'll do just enough to keep from getting fired, because I'm getting paid just enough to keep from quitting.

Technically, they are within the limits of their minimal job description, but just barely. So is this game really an ethical dilemma? I think so. Technical compliance isn't the point of setting minimal performance standards—these standards are meant to provide simple guidance that must be supported by a "can do, will do" spirit. The How-Low-Can-You-Go performance problem is an indirect message that the person does not like her job, and an invitation for someone else to take control of the situation by terminating her.

I'VE GOT A SECRET

Here's another attempt to grab or hold onto power. This happens at all levels of the company over the oddest bits of information. This game could also be called Information Upmanship. This is the corporate, adult version of that game we played when we were kids: "I'll show you mine if you show me yours."

How to play: Visualize information in a physical form, say, as chocolate cookies. Prospective players test your availability to play with innocent challenge statements like, "I was surprised to learn that Johnson is going to start the campaign in Dallas." If you're receptive and want to play, you return the challenge with something like, "If you think that's crazy, did you know that he's going to use radio instead of TV?" The game has now begun. You each have put one "cookie" worth of information on the table. He takes the next turn and tosses in another cookie: "I know he doesn't like the cable network down there." Can you top this? You try with: "Yeah, he said in the proposal that it was too expensive." Too obvious—everyone who has read the report knows that. You lose that round.

His turn, his cookie: "I'll bet he just didn't have his other market plans ready." This is the setup to you, and you raise the ante to win the game (thereby proving that you DO know more than he does). "Nope. I typed up the other market plans, too, so I know they're done. The real reason he's doing radio in Dallas now is because I think he slept with the sales rep when she was in town last Friday." The skunk you're playing with resigns by throwing up his arms to indicate he can't possibly top that secret, but he goes for a freebie anyway. "How do you know that?" he challenges. You have to respond to this direct assault, so you give up the evidence that will be used to embarrass and degrade Johnson later: "He told me he was taking her to lunch on Friday and didn't come back to the office until after 5. She was with him, and she couldn't keep her hands off of him." Bingo. A first-person witness to Johnson's peccadillo. The skunk gladly gives up the rest of his cookies, and the cookie jar. He withdraws gracefully by pretending it doesn't matter, you haven't told him anything of importance. In this way, he avoids owing you any more cookies in the future. He trivializes the game, gladly defers to your better cookies, and slinks back under his rock. He's lost the small-stakes game with you, but he's going to win the next high-stakes game of Sabotage with Johnson's boss.

Victim

The final game features chronic whining and self-pity. The "poor me" worker has confused sympathy with love, and he seems to believe the more miserable he is, the more "love" he can attract. This person can become quite powerful. People will go to great lengths to avoid launching another complaining jag. The players of Victim posture themselves as people who cannot control the circumstances around them, yet it is common for their imagined hurts to be self-inflicted and exaggerated. I call Victim a game because it is an unethical dodge of personal accountability.

There are other negative behaviors, too. Some that you'll recognize are not following through on commitments, not recognizing others for their efforts, hogging all the credit for the team's work, and taking credit for someone else's work. I regard all of these as unethical because they tear down an office's motivation, morale, productivity, pride, quality, retention, and customer service.

What can you do?

What do you do when people are trying to play games with you? You know intuitively you cannot "win" these games—nobody really wins. The best you can do is to stop the games.

Recognizing the players and their games is 98 percent of the solution to ending the games. The best strategy is to simply name the game. If you confront her, or challenge her, with the simple observation that, "I think you're trying to play a game here," she will almost always retreat while mumbling something about a misunderstanding. Don't forget that she's tipped her hand. The fact that she is trying to manipulate a situation or obtain some information is valuable to know. It will keep you on guard in the future.

Finally, use your ethical compass to decide how much of this game-playing you are willing to tolerate. As soon as it hurts you, your company's productivity, or your boss's reputation—stop, and say nothing more. If game-playing becomes an ongoing problem in your office, it may require an open discussion about the ethics of such behavior. Of course, everyone will deny they ever participated in anything so tacky. But that's okay. In a discussion like this, the point is not to find someone guilty, but to stimulate their thinking and appeal to their better instincts (Abraham Lincoln called these "the better angels of our nature"). If your concern is genuine, you can lead them to the conclusion that the games hurt the effectiveness of the office, and the games will stop.

"When two play a game,
there must be a winner
and a loser."

—Yiddish proverb

16

Lies and
other traps

Think about it: *At the end of the weekly staff meeting, Karina, a supervisor of a data processing department, asked everyone to read the corporate policy on honesty in the employee handbook. In the next staff meeting, she said, "Would all of you who have read the honesty policy please raise your hands?"*

Everyone's hands went up. "I see you're ready to discuss this problem. There is no such policy in the manual — but I see we need one!"

Karina says she has lately become more aware of the variable degrees of truthfulness in her communications. In one recent week, for example, she learned her boyfriend conceals his dates with other women; her best friend really didn't like the present she got her for her birthday; a colleague has asked her to write a glowing letter of recommendation, apparently expecting her to put a "positive spin" on his mediocre performance; her boss told her to "make something up" as an excuse for his lateness with a client; and the co-worker at the next cubicle admitted she lies to vendors about other bids in order to get more competitive prices. Now, Karina is depressed — she wonders if she can trust what others say to her and, if she can't, what she can do about it.

Do you remember the children's story of Br'er Rabbit and the tarbaby? As it happened, they say, Mr. McGregor built a false creature out of tar and straw, then placed it in his garden to scare away Br'er Rabbit. Br'er Rabbit was curious, not frightened, and attempted to engage the sticky creature in conversation. Who was he? Where did he come from? Of course, the rabbit received no response. He became frustrated and flew into a rage, finally shoving the tarbaby in an attempt to get its attention. Br'er Rabbit's paw stuck fast to the gooey mess, and he struck it again with the other paw. That paw stuck, too. He then attempted to kick it away from him, but each move drew him deeper into the sticky trap. Soon, Br'er Rabbit was covered with tar, completely trapped.

This chapter is about the traps and snares you will encounter as you attempt to solve ethical dilemmas. Like the tarbaby, they at first look like something you can handle, but they end up drawing you in further and further until escape is impossible. Some traps are set by clever people who are indifferent or hostile to your efforts to resolve your ethical dilemmas; other traps are injuries we inflict upon ourselves. Hopefully, you'll be able to avoid these traps if you know in advance what they look like!

Trap #1: Lies, all lies!

All lies are *intentionally deceptive* messages. They are explicitly intended to mislead us. We can be misled by erroneous messages, incomplete information, and misinterpreted data, too — but these are not lies. Lies are deliberate efforts to deceive us.

There are two primary ways to lie: to conceal and to falsify. In concealing, the liar withholds some information without actually saying anything untrue. In falsifying, the liar goes a step further. Not only does the liar withhold true information, but he also presents false information as if it was true.

Concealment is passive, and it is generally easier to do because it does not require any false story to be compiled and entered into the record. Concealment is usually safer, too — if the concealment is later discovered, several excuses come to mind easily ("I didn't know"; "I was going to tell you later"; "I forgot about it"). Concealment is the most common way of lying.

Falsification requires a made-up story, an alternate reality, that is believable and can withstand whatever scrutiny it will receive in the short term. It is often used in conjunction with concealment to mask that which is being concealed.

I've been working on the dilemma of truth-telling for most of my adult life. It's a minefield of contradictions, excuses, vagueness, justifications, and self-deceptions. After discussing what goes on at work with thousands of other office professionals during the past dozen years, I know these are the most common ethical questions:

1. So what if I lie—does it matter?
2. Is it always wrong to lie?
3. Can lies ever be excused?
4. How do I avoid being trapped by lies?

1. So what if I lie—does it matter? I do not believe lies are inherently or automatically evil, but I am strongly biased against them for several reasons:

First, I believe lying almost always produces negative consequences. Furthermore, I believe the truth will almost always serve personal and organizational needs better than a lie. Truth, as I am using it here, is the moral truth that is specific to the context and content of a conversation between two people. The truth I am interested in here is limited to the question: Is someone intentionally misleading someone else with false statements? I am aware that the "whole Truth" or "absolute Truth" is unattainable, so you lawyers relax.

Consider the negative consequences of lies in business communications. The liar must worry about getting caught. If he gets caught, his reputation suffers. If he doesn't get caught, he oftentimes must continue to lie in order to conceal the original deception. Worry and anxiety about being discovered, and subsequent energy to cover up the first lie with supporting lies, takes a horrendous toll out of a person's and organization's productivity. And, of course, the lies themselves cause all sorts of mischief and damage, such as poor decisions based on incorrect information.

Finally, lying is most damaging to the trust that forms the basis of our professional relationships. Trust is essential to any cooperative venture; when lying occurs frequently, it undermines trust. Less trust means less constructive communication, and that means less of everything that is good and productive. In short, there is a direct relationship to lies and a negative impact on the organization's economic health. These negative outcomes make lies very difficult to justify. So does it matter when you lie? You bet it does!

Can we agree that truthfulness is generally preferable to untruthfulness? I like the way this was answered by Aristotle, my favorite philosopher, who also articulated the "doctrine of the golden mean" we discussed in Chapter 7. Recall that Aristotle preached the virtue of moderation in all things, arguing against the application of one-answer-fits-all rules. He gives us the basis for our common-sense ethics test, a.k.a. the test of reasonableness. Aristotle says lying is *"mean and culpable* [deserving of blame]" and that *"truthful statements are preferable to lies in the absence of special considerations."* In a moment, we'll take a closer look at those special considerations in which lies may be justified.

Aristotle's premise gives an initial negative bias to lies and an initial positive bias to truth. Lies are exceptions to the way we ought to conduct ourselves. We can presume them to be bad, not good. Lies require justification, whereas truth ordinarily does not. Truth is its own reward.

2. *Is it always morally wrong to lie?* No. In my opinion, there are at least two situations where a person is morally justified to lie. To justify means to defend as just, right, or proper by providing adequate reasons. If a lie is morally justifiable, a liar can take comfort in the judgment that he did nothing ethically wrong. But this is a very tough standard to meet. The list of justifiable lies is short.

Generally, the only lies deemed justifiable — that is, morally free of blame and guilt — are the very trivial lies and the very serious lies. Everything in between is, strictly speaking, a violation of society's ethical code to "always tell the truth." This was Aristotle's view and many other philosophers. It has not been the view of the theologians, however; historically, the religious tradition has held that Truth is absolute and all lies are morally wrong.

The chart below shows you how I think about different types of lies.

CATEGORIES OF LIES   ©1997 Nan DeMars, CPS

*"little white lies"	lies about trivial matters, like false excuses to spare a person's feelings; flattery; "how are you feeling;" "how's it going;" etc. — these lies must be truly harmless and inconsequential, never intended to be given a second thought
placebos	deceptions to make a person feel better (like sugar pills); euphemisms; some self-help gimmickry; false reassurance
pufferies	inflation and exaggeration to make something sound better than it is; false praise; false encouragement; false support
misdirections	false recommendations; intentional incorrect or incomplete answers
bluffs	fake resumes; false credentials
protections string-alongs	lies to protect a colleague; lies to protect a client lies to liars (to teach them a lesson; to give them a taste of their own medicine)

CATEGORIES OF LIES (CONTINUED)

snow jobs	lies to enemies
terminological inexactitudes	lies to the boss (this term was first used by Winston Churchill!); also known as "soft-soaps"
*"defensive lies"	lies in a crisis when innocent lives, health, or safety are at risk

*may be morally justifiable if the lie can pass the "publicity test" (see p.52)

To be morally justified, a liar must be able to explain his lie in such a way that other reasonable people would agree with him that a lie was the best solution to a particular dilemma. This is the "publicity test" whereby the reason for the lie is judged to be reasonable by reasonable people.

For instance, most reasonable people would find it justifiable to lie to a gunman holding hostages in a bank lobby. "If it saves some lives, tell him whatever he needs to hear," would be a reasonable reaction. The moral absolutists, on the other hand, would argue that the lie is morally wrong, no matter what the circumstances. The absolutists argue that "the absolute truth" will always be a better solution. In the case of the hostages in the bank lobby, the absolutists would, for example, argue that the gunman is mentally unstable, and any attempt to lie, should the gunman detect it, would result in even more people being killed.

Public scrutiny is a reliable and useful way to link personal moral behavior with the community's standards. It is, I think, the best way to identify deceptive practices and separate the justifiable lies from the indefensible lies.

Moral justification *cannot* be a discussion between the liar and his conscience — the liar's perspective is distorted, and his evaluation will be flimsy and self-serving. The liar would quite naturally attempt to trivialize the impact of his lie, or attempt to blow it out of proportion by presenting it as "the only possible way" to save innocent lives from a horrible fate. No, justification must involve other reasonable people who can more accurately mirror the values and morals of the community. That's why the "public disclosure" questions in the Ethics Audits in Chapter 1 (Office Ethics Audit), Chapter 3 (Personal Ethics Audit), and Chapter 10 (Situation Ethics Audit) are so meaningful. I've repeated a few of the questions below:

- Is there any behavior or action taking place in the office that you would be embarrassed to see reported in the media?
- Is there anything going on in your office that you would feel uncomfortable about explaining to your kids? a reporter? your parents?
- Am I doing anything I would not want my children to see? My mother-in-law? My spouse?

Do you see the connection? If you can't justify a lie to these reasonable people (who presumably know you and are sympathetic to you), your lie is morally wrong. That doesn't mean you aren't going to do it, and it doesn't mean you don't have a good reason to do it that satisfies YOU, at least — but you must be aware that your lie is probably unethical according to community standards. Maybe knowing that you are stepping over the boundary of ethical behavior is enough to cause you to change your behavior, maybe not. *But at least you should be fully aware of what you are doing.*

Like the lie to prevent serious harm, I believe the little white lie is morally justifiable, too. My definition of a little white lie is pretty narrow, though — the lie must really be "little," meaning it is about something of little or no consequence, and it must really be a "white" lie, meaning it causes absolutely no harm to anyone. But the harmlessness is almost always open to debate. The liar downplays the harm a lie may cause, sometimes even describing it as beneficial. But the test is this: How does the person being lied to feel about the lie?

A few examples from my own life where I might decide to tell a little white lie are listed below. (A note to my close friends — you know who you are — you KNOW you can still count on me to tell YOU the absolute truth!):

- a request for my opinion about another person's appearance (choice of hat, color of tie, etc.). It has been my experience that this person is almost always seeking positive reassurance about her choice, or affirmation and support that she made the right decision.
- greetings, good-byes, thank-yous, and some compliments (such as, "I'm pleased to meet you," "I had a very nice time," "The pot roast was wonderful," and "Sincerely yours").

- occasions when I receive a gift or listen to someone's joke ("It's a lovely color, thank you," and "That's very funny, honey.").
- occasions when a false excuse will spare the feelings of someone making an invitation or request (I might say I can't attend a function instead saying I don't want to attend).

Little white lies serve a purpose. They help us connect with others with an early and simple agreement on a superficial level. The philosopher Jean-Jacques Rousseau justified his little white lies like this: "Never have I lied in my own interest; but often I have lied through shame in order to draw myself from embarrassment in indifferent matters . . . when, having to sustain discussion, the slowness of my ideas and dryness of my conversation forced me to have recourses to fictions [just] in order to say something."

A lot of us tell these lies—and we probably don't see much need to change our behavior, do we? According to my Office Ethics Survey, 85 percent of the respondents told a little white lie to someone face-to-face, and 86.6 percent observed others doing it. It's the same story on the phone, only more so—89 percent reported they told a little white lie over the telephone, and 86.6 percent said they saw others doing it.

Here's my thinking—it's my apology and defense of little white lies: Consider what life would be like without the social graces made possible by the little white lies. The hostess would know exactly what we thought of the evening's meal, the friend would get the unvarnished truth about her inability to find a lover, the child would hear the so-called truth about him or her looks and abilities—never mind the resulting self-esteem problems. Life would be rougher than it is, and relationships would be more difficult to maintain. Politeness, attempts to smooth things over, private times to sulk and lick one's wounds—all that would be gone. We would wilt waiting for only genuine smiles, honest compliments, and truthful praise. Absolute honest kindnesses would be the only type we'd receive, doled out stingily, making life a lot less fun and interesting. And what about flirting? My stars, our entire courtship rituals would disappear! No siree, that kind of gray and sterile world may be more absolutely, ethically correct, but it's not for me!

3. Can lies ever be excused? This is entirely up to you and your co-workers. You have to work with each other the day after you lied to each other. How well you work together depends upon mutual trust, respect, support, and all the rest. If deception creeps into your working relationships, you have to be ready to deal with all of the negative consequences we discussed earlier.

There are times to excuse each other's lies. Even if the lie cannot be justified in a moral context, it may be understandable within the realm of our practical lives. Aristotle realized people have a breaking point and that when this point is reached, wrongdoers are not held responsible for their actions, e.g. a prisoner of war may break under torture and reveal information that will cause the deaths of his comrades, but he is not generally blamed. The modern equivalent to torture is severe pressure at work. If there is no way to escape the situation by appealing to higher authorities, and if a person believe he is going to lose his job, lose his reputation, etc., that person may well have an excuse for lying. That does not make it right, but that makes it understandable.

Personally, I counsel people to take the high road *and do everything they can possibly do to avoid lying*. I think this is an important part of our professionalism. If people sense they cannot trust us, if they perceive our truthfulness as negotiable, we will never earn the respect our profession deserves.

A few elaborations:

Placebos and Pufferies: Offering false encouragement, false praise, euphemisms, etc. may make you feel better, but they are corrosive to relationships. The falseness is hollow, and usually fools no one. Instead of saying what you think the other person wants to hear, take a moment and think of something truthful to say. You'll have to expose yourself a little more, but it will be a positive, not a negative.

Misdirections: If you can't say something positive or constructive, keep quiet. Do not send someone off in the wrong direction with the wrong idea, just to make them go away. If you can't say what they want to hear, state that in just those words, but don't lie. (My uncle is fond of saying it this way: "He missed another golden opportunity to keep his mouth shut!")

Protections: Lying to protect your boss, a colleague, or a friend is one of the most difficult judgment calls to make. I work hard to avoid this *as soon as I know there is a dilemma* so that I can avoid being put into this position. If I wait too long to say, "We can't lie about this," I tend to get trapped. I've learned to get everyone focused on an honest and honorable solution *early,* before lies compound lies.

I know it happens. In my Office Ethics Survey, 57.6 percent of the respondents admitted they sometimes or often lied about their supervisor's whereabouts, and 66.9 percent—two thirds—said they had observed others doing it. And, 36.4 percent said they lied about their supervisor's activities, and 52.5 percent say they had seen others sometimes or often lying about their supervisor's activities. The pressure to do this is relentless, especially if there is a pattern or practice of doing it. Who wants to be the one to stir things up?

String Alongs and Snow Jobs: I don't even lie to liars or enemies. In fact, I am especially careful with them. Liars and enemies are highly motivated to catch you in a lie, however small. What better way to undermine your credibility and boost their own than to portray YOU as a liar? NO, NO, NO—do not play this game. Don't crawl down to their level. These people should bring out your best, not your worst. Let them hang *themselves* with their line of bull.

Terminological Inexactitudes (lies to the boss): When Prime Minister Winston Churchill was still a member of the Liberal Party in the United Kingdom, he rose in Parliament to defend his party against the charge that they had deliberately misrepresented the Conservative Party. The Liberals had accused the Conservatives of practicing slavery in South Africa. Churchill remarked, "I admit the term 'slavery' might be a terminological inexactitude."

At this, Joseph Chamberlain, father of the late Prime Minister Neville Chamberlain, interrupted: "I prefer the ugly little English three-letter word—l-i-e."

Whatever euphemism you use, a lie to someone you are accountable to is still a lie. Air Force lieutenant Kelly Flynn was forced to give up her career in the military in 1997 because she lied to her superior officers repeatedly about an adulterous affair. Again, it's rarely worth the effort. Because you work so closely together, this is one of the most difficult situations in which to lie successfully.

I know this happens, too. I once had to actually write the script for a friend who was terrified to tell the truth to her boss about the difficulties she was having in her new position. I told her: "Admit you are out of your depth with this thing. You misjudged, you screwed up, you even waited too long before coming forward. But now you're speaking up because you genuinely want to help find the solution. You may be judged to be the wrong person for the job, but maybe that's the fact of the matter—you are a bad match for this job. A bad match does not make you a bad person. More opportunities will come. One thing you are not is a coward—so speak the truth, get it behind you, and get on with the new solution." She *was* demoted, but it was a relief for everyone, including her. It had become a no-win situation, and she just needed a little reminder from me to do the right thing. She did the professional thing and fessed up to the problem *before it became a fatal ethical dilemma,* which it would have become if she had continued to lie to cover up her difficulties. By handling it in a professional way, she got to keep her sanity, her health, her self-respect, and her old job.

Consider this example: Imagine a situation between Karina, the data processing department supervisor we met at the beginning of this chapter, and Brenda, a shift leader with some project planning and personnel responsibilities who reports to Karina. Brenda lied to another manager in the company about a project's schedule. Karina caught the lie and confronted Brenda. Brenda now must attempt to justify the lie. Does she lie again? That would make matters worse. Can she justify it? Nope—it's too important to be a little white lie, and it's not at the level of life-or-death. It's in between—just an ugly little wart she has to deal with. Will her explanation be sufficient for Karina to excuse her? Maybe. But the crack in the trust between them will take time to heal.

Save yourself the stress and trouble of lying to your boss, and find a creative way to build a more positive relationship! Learn to tell the truth to each other!

4. How do I avoid being trapped by lies? Simple: Don't tell 'em, don't listen to 'em, and stop 'em whenever you find them. You should not have to lie for anyone, for any reason. If you think about it, you can find ways to avoid situations where you have to lie for yourself or someone else. As your office becomes more ethical, you should encounter fewer and fewer lies—or reasons for lies.

Think about your professionalism, and note the similarities with other professions. It is generally agreed in our free society that when a client gives information to certain professionals (e.g., doctor, lawyer, or clergyman), or when a source talks to a journalist, the information given to the professional merits certain legal protection. This legal shield recognizes that these unique relationships, like that between husband and wife, require that certain secrets be protected. *But few professionals stretch this privilege to the extent of lying on behalf of the person giving them information.* Most of the time, they can just refuse to give up confidential information, and that's that. We can apply the same standards to our profession. We lack the legal protection, so we have to tell what we know in court but, short of testifying, I am perfectly comfortable saying, "That's confidential information. I'm not saying another word." This takes a little more backbone, especially if some wild man boss or client is pressuring you to tell all; but, it keeps you from getting trapped in a lie.

Lies should be rare exceptions to your standard ethical conduct. Lies may be excused, but they cannot be justified unless they are little white lies or lies to prevent great harm. They are ethically wrong. Period. They are risky. And they don't always work. In my opinion, choosing to use deception to get from here to there is like climbing out on a skinny branch in the false hope that the branch is a shortcut. That skinny branch never gets thicker and more stable, and it doesn't go anywhere you want to be. Choose to lie if you must, but be prepared for the negative consequences.

Some colleagues have asked me for just one simple rule they can apply in every situation. They say, "Why can't I just pledge to never, ever tell a lie, large or small, no matter what situation I find myself in?"

I don't think this is realistic. That's too rigid a position. In the first place, you are a part of a team—this fact alone will force you to compromise some of your standards, some of the time. The only way you'll be able to remain "pure" is to work completely alone.

Also, an absolute position against lying can be cruel in its own way. We have all experienced the self-righteous brutality of the person who prides himself on his 100 percent honesty, regardless of the consequences. This person is absolutely certain that his vision of the truth is correct. Pardon me, but I avoid working with people like this. Their preoccupation with telling me about their truth gets in the way of getting my work done!

The absolutist says all lies are wrong, without exception, even if telling a lie would save lives or spare someone great harm. The absolutists are best represented by the 4th-5th-century theologian and bishop, Saint Augustine who saw Absolute Good as the center of reality. German philosopher Immanuel Kant (1724–1804), was also a supporter of the absolute view that we must never lie, no matter what. Kant believed we were all born with an understanding of what we ought to do, and that if a person's actions spring from a good motive, the action is good and moral, regardless of the consequences. It should be noted that Kant never married, raised children, or had some of the bosses I've heard about!

Amazingly, some liars persuade themselves they are not even lying in order to avoid the ethical dilemma caused by the I-will-never-lie position. They subscribe to a theory called the doctrine of mental reservations, and it's a response to the rigidity of the absolutists. (If you have young children who believe they can lie without consequences as long as they have their fingers crossed, you'll recognize this.) In its most extreme form, this doctrine holds that it is not wrong for one person to say something misleading to another, *just so long as the speaker is careful to add a qualifier to the statement in his or her mind so as to make the verbal statement true.* For instance, let's say I am in my boss's office and I pocket a $10 bill I find on the floor. My boss enters his office and asks me if I have seen a $10 bill. According to the doctrine of mental reservations, I would NOT be lying if I said, "I did not see a $10 bill," and then silently completed the statement by saying something to myself like "yesterday" or "on the table."

Lies are just shortcuts to near-term, feel-good benefits. A lie temporarily takes the pressure away from a discussion where the truth may be acutely embarrassing or hurtful, but it is just a delay. Eventually, the conversation will occur and the problem must be confronted. The day of reckoning comes sooner or later. The trap, of course, is getting caught up in multiple lies in the hope that you can rescue the situation before your deception is discovered.

Lying is a habit with virtually no brakes, and this makes it a truly loose cannon on a slippery slope, ethically speaking. The more lies you tell, the easier it becomes to tell more. It is a difficult habit to break away from. Think about some other self-destructive habits like excessive consumption of drugs or alcohol, driving too fast, compulsive shopping, or eating disorders. Society will intervene when these habits appear to be causing a person to become dysfunctional or dangerous to others. There are, quite literally, social brakes that will put a stop to the behavior, one way or another, sooner or later. This doesn't happen when a person habitually lies. There are no thought police or truth squads. This means how often a liar tells lies, and what he is willing to lie about, is a matter between the liar and his own conscience. Once telling lies becomes a habit, it's difficult to stop; it's even more difficult to recover the trust of those you work with.

Sissela Bok's book, *Lying*, is a high-water mark for thinking in this area. She cautions, "Those who begin with white lies can come to resort to more frequent and more serious ones. Where some tell a few white lies, others may tell more. Because lines are so hard to draw, the indiscriminate use of such lies can lead to other deceptive practices. The aggregate harm from a large number of marginally harmful instances may, therefore, be highly undesirable in the end — for liars, those deceived, and honesty and trust more generally."

If you want to read more about the philosophical and theological thinking about lies, I recommend these excellent reference works:

Lying by Sissela Bok
Telling Lies: Clues to Deceit in the Marketplace, Politics, and Marriage by Paul Ekman
James Humber's essay in *Business Ethics* magazine (edited by Milton Snoeyenbos et al.)

Trap #2: Ambition

This is a big, lifelong trap, but it's simple to understand. Ambition can blind you and cause you to lose focus on your priorities. Once tasted, ambition is narcotic. It is not to be confused with assertiveness. Watch out. Manage your appetites so they don't manage you.

Trap #3: Petty theft

This trap has nothing to do with the amount of stuff taken or abused. It has everything to do with the erosion of your integrity and trustworthiness.

Creeping rationalization is the problem here. What level of corruption will we tolerate in ourselves? Or in our office? It starts small, when you steal supplies (60.8 percent say they do it), make personal long distance calls (51.9 percent), make copies for personal use (94.7 percent), or otherwise take advantage of the toys and tools made available to you. The amount is not the issue (is there a dollar amount, or a weight amount, above which your moral standards are stiffer?).

This is an insidious cancer that corrupts the smooth functioning of the office, the integrity of your relationships, the respect of your co-workers, and your self-esteem. You've heard the rationalizations:

- "Nobody cares."
- "Everyone does it."
- "The company can afford it."
- "I deserve this—I can't get paid for the extra work I do at home, so I'll take my fair share here, in this way."
- "Nobody will find out."
- "It's only a pen."   (I love the response from the father who was called to school when his son was caught stealing pens from the school vending machine: "Why on earth would you be stealing pens?" asked his father. "What have you been doing with those pens I bring home from work every day?")

Where do you draw the line against petty theft? What are the long-term consequences of developing a habit of stepping over the line once, twice, regularly? I believe (a) It affects your attitude— if once is OK, once again is OK, too; and (b) It affects your relationships with others. Don't trust the what-you're-doing-doesn't-bother-me attitude of others. Surveys indicate that others judge the petty thief extremely harshly—perhaps because he or she is symbolically showing contempt for the rules that they are trying to live by, or it's a clue to inner character flaws they just don't want to deal with.

Is petty theft a small issue? Don't believe it. It affects you. It chips away at you from the inside. It tears you down. It makes you feel mean and small and ashamed and guilty.

Trap #4: Clichés

I wish there were more pat answers to ethical dilemmas. Platitudes are appealing—sometimes, they make a bitter reality easier to accept and so they help you get through the day. But don't study them too closely, and don't let them be a substitute for your careful thinking. Here are a few I've used when I had to pull the blankets over my head:

"This is my job, not my life." Do you have one set of ethical standards for your business life, and another set of "real" ethics for your "real" life—that personal one? I've met very

few people who can sustain this Jekyll-Hyde dichotomy. It has been my experience that we are what we are—and to pretend otherwise is to trade one dilemma (the one external to us) for another (an internal contradiction).

"What goes around comes around." I hate this one. In fact, very good things happen to very bad people, and vice versa. Some business crooks get rich, and many live long enough to enjoy their ill-gotten gains, too. Good does not necessarily lead to money, success, etc.—so don't get angry or resentful or criminal if you do not get your idea of your just desserts for your good acts.

"Life is not fair." This is a classic cop-out. It is NOT an excuse to stop trying to make life more fair for more people. We all know that bad things DO happen to good people. I take some comfort in the Serenity Prayer from Alcoholics Anonymous: "God, grant me the serenity to accept the things I cannot change—the courage to change the things I can—and the wisdom to know the difference."

"Just follow your conscience." This advice is rarely enough. I think people say this to you only when they think you've already decided to do what they wanted you to do in the first place—so it's their way of giving you an ethical nudge toward what you knew was right all along.

Trap #5: Too many excuses

Do you see yourself as a victim, a martyr, a saint? Do you think your relative position in the office excuses you from speaking up on questions of ethical conduct? I hope you do not see yourself as simply playing a narrow role with a limited script in the discussion about office ethics. If you do, your team will not have to benefit of your best reflective thinking. There are no spectators to this business of building an ethical office. No one person has every ethical dilemma figured out in advance. We all come to these decisions with our own baggage, and you're no different. We owe it to ourselves—and those we work with—to think beyond the easy excuses for not taking an ethical stand. Bottom line: No excuses.

You may be trapped by your own excuses if you're saying any of the following:

"I'm a victim, too."

"It's all my fault."

"It's never my fault."

"We'll never solve this."

"It's none of my concern."

"I'm feeling helpless."

"I'm not capable/competent/smart enough."

"I'm going crazy."

"I'm all alone in this."

"I'm the only one who cares."

"I'm angry, and someone's going to pay."

"I'm ashamed."

"I'm above/below/beyond this—ethics don't concern me, I don't care."

Trap #6: Getting involved in the wrong way and/or at the wrong time

Every time you encounter an ethical dilemma, you have to choose: Do you get involved? If you get involved, how can you do so constructively and not make matters worse? Before you wade into someone else's problem, there are a few rules of engagement you need to keep in mind:

1. Pick your battle carefully.

Can you actually help and make a difference?

2. Be certain you have all the information.

Ask yourself, What's really going on here?

3. Are you the best person to say what needs to be said? Will the parties involved listen to you, or is there someone else better suited to delivering a particular message?

4. Try to not confront or shame those involved in the dilemma. If you make a person feel threatened or belittled, he is going to feel defensive. Would an informal or humorous approach be more effective? Or perhaps a quiet, one-on-one conversation?

5. Remember whom you work for, and who "owns" this

dilemma. If you take sides against your company and/or your boss, you're probably going to find yourself in trouble.

6. Don't underestimate the complexity of the problem. Asking the right questions of your co-workers, for example, may be a more effective way to resolve a dilemma than coming up with The Answer.

7. If you choose to get involved, be prepared to follow through and accept the consequences that accompany the risks.

8. Accept an incremental resolution. People don't change overnight, so if the trend is moving in the right direction, and if people are experimenting with new conduct and trying to do better, be a cheerleader, not a judge or jury.

Summary

You may trap yourself when you pursue resolutions to ethical dilemmas. The traps are like flypaper, and you will find yourself drawn in further as you struggle to resolve the issues. Some of the common traps are lies, ambition, petty theft, hollow clichés, getting stuck in narrow roles, and getting stuck when you try to help other people resolve their dilemmas.

Take heart! The traps can be foreseen, and they can be navigated and negotiated. Your trusty ethical compass (see Chapter 8) will guide you. Just keep in mind that no one answer is going to fit all situations, and your preconceptions about how people will or should conduct themselves may get in the way if you attempt to facilitate a resolution.

Sadly, some dilemmas cannot be resolved. In the next chapter, we'll look at few of the no-win dilemmas and what to do about them.

> *"Oh, what a tangled web we weave when, at first, we try to deceive."*
>
> — William Shakespeare

17

Surviving the no-win dilemmas

Think about it: *I recently received a letter from an administrative assistant in the healthcare industry: "One of the most difficult experiences I ever went through was when a secretary, 'Jane,' at age 40, was being terminated. The way it was handled was just so gross.*

"The company wanted Jane to quit. She was worked nearly to death without overtime pay, often receiving assignments due on Saturday and Sunday on Friday at 5 p.m. (several people witnessed her initial receipt of these assignments). Our normal work hours were from 8 a.m. to 5 p.m. The only help Jane received was from one of the other secretaries who would stay and help her, just out of the goodness of her heart. Management refused to cooperate or find help for her when she was overloaded with work.

"The company said they fired Jane, a secretary with 20 years of experience, because she was 'incompetent.' In fact, Jane was fired because she submitted a legal document from her attorney demanding overtime pay.

"One day, a young, provocative-looking woman came in to see Jane's manager. The receptionist and backup assumed the young lady was there for some unethical, immoral reason. No one had any idea she could be there for a job interview. It was very clear by the way she was greeted by the manager and his associates that they had met on a previous occasion. Although personnel (where I worked) had the resumes of many higher-qualified applicants on file, 'Sonja' was hired to replace Jane.

"Sonja, age 19, dressed like a slut and acted in an immature, unprofessional manner that reminded us all of high school. She could

not possibly have had even two years of experience. She did not even know how to open a WordPerfect file, although job applicants were required to be WordPerfect experts, according to the company's recruitment ads. It was stated that Sonja's resume was from our file resumes. I know it was not.

"Sonja received her assignments early enough to complete them on time, and Sonja did not have to ask for help if she needed it; her manager would go out of his way to make sure she had all the help she needed. The other secretaries were supportive of Sonja; after all, she was new and not responsible for what was happening to Jane.

"Jane decided to sue the company. Unfortunately, we do not have Employment Police to stop unfairness and gross behavior. Many managers and employees were subpoenaed by Jane's counsel. I was one of them. Up until that time, I had kept kind of quiet about how I felt about what happened to Jane, as I did not trust the company management. I had just received a promotion, a big raise, and an excellent review, so I thought I was in pretty good standing with the company, but management knew I would stand up for what I believed to be the truth.

"The day I received my subpoena, everything changed for me. My supervisor began allowing a consultant to write untruths about me without my knowledge. These write-ups were placed in my personnel files. The consultant earned $100 + per hour and would bill the company for 8–10 hours to write each of these stories about me. Since this occurred more than once, I guess it did not bother my supervisor that company money was spent in this way. Once I was on vacation when this happened. My supervisor told another secretary (with questionable ethics) to warn me that if my behavior did not change, I would lose my job. She stated that warning me was not a part of her job description.

"The situation became more bizarre. During this time, I had a worker's comp injury. I missed only a little work due to my injury. I went to therapy in the evening after work. However, right after my work injury occurred, I had a minor automobile injury. The worker's comp adjuster and my company's representative tried to have my no-fault insurance policy pick up the remainder of the costs for my work comp therapy. My supervisor called me into his office and explained the company's position on my claim, and said I could use

the company's attorneys to straighten out the no-fault carrier at company expense. In other words, he wanted me to force my auto insurance carrier to pick up the rest of the tab for my work comp therapy. To make a long story even longer, this is an illegal abuse of the worker's comp system in our state — something they both knew, but they obviously wanted to 'play the system' and take advantage of my situation.

"Then my supervisor told me the company's position regarding Jane and gave me a generous 'discretionary' bonus for all my hard work. Suddenly, I was an exemplary employee again!

"The situation struck me as odd, but I didn't see it for what it was until I 'accidentally-on-purpose' was allowed to see the written warnings about my performance. I had never seen these fabrications before, of course, but the company had manufactured documents that said I had seen the warnings and refused to sign the form that said I saw them. I previously had access to my supervisor's personnel files for his departments, but suddenly my file was locked away somewhere else. I finally got the message — I was going to talk the company talk regarding Jane, or I was going to walk the walk of the unemployed!

"I didn't want to, but I finally retained an attorney to advise me through this process. I had seen other incriminating information on other lawsuits, and it appeared to me that my employer was preparing to make anything I ever said look like 'sour grapes' if or when I was called to testify in Jane's lawsuit. I finally figured it out that if I ever gave my supervisor a hint of a warning about how I really felt, I was finished, one way or another. I instead 'kissed up' to my supervisor until I found another job.

"What sweet justice! He had no idea I was looking for a job. However, his ego was crushed when he realized I could still find happiness without working for him, so he retaliated. Two days before my last day, he twisted a circumstance and fired me for 'willful, wanton, and deliberate misconduct.' Even with the way he twisted the incident, no reasonable person would ever conclude that I misbehaved in such a way. Eventually, when I was subpoenaed by my former employer regarding Jane's lawsuit, the company's attorney insisted that I admit that I was fired and that is why I left the company, even though my letter of resignation clearly spelled out that I gave a two week's notice to take another job.

"The job I found was a higher position with a large salary increase. I now work for two of the nicest gentlemen you would ever want to meet. They would never want me to do anything that I considered unethical or inappropriate. They do business on the right level.

"Jane, however, did not do so well. Her attorney was a screwup and did a really poor job. It appears the judge on the case was related to one of the company's board of directors. Jane now has an $8,000 lien against her home by the company! She doesn't have the resources to fight the company's lawyers.

"This company brought out the worst in me. Looking back on it though, I can't think of anything I could have done differently to change things for Jane or me. The company is, I believe, fundamentally unethical. Appealing to their sense of right and wrong made no difference, ever. What's 'right' is what's profitable, period. Management's philosophy is simple: Do the right thing only when it makes something good happen for the company, or, only when it keeps something bad from happening to the company. In an environment like this, if I chose to be the ethical one, I would be played for a sucker.

"I'm not looking for advice now, Nan. I guess I just wanted to tell you that some ethical dilemmas are bigger than we are. Any comments?"

I'm normally an optimist when I approach an ethical dilemma, but this letter depressed even me. It reminded me how hellish some situations can get. I made some calls, asked a few questions, and got some additional insights into this company.

Jane was not the first to be forced out. Like Jane, Sonja, and the writer of this letter, others at this company worked under clouds of worry and stress and frustration. Trapped in a spider web of ethical dilemmas, they could scarcely remember whatever positive feelings they once had for their employer. Each of the three people I talked to was circulating her resume, looking for her next job.

Some ethical dilemmas seem hopeless. They seem too complex, too far gone, too big, or too something else. These dilemmas make us feel helplessness and despair. I call these situations the "no-win dilemmas." They can drive you crazy. And they can be toxic.

No-win dilemmas are different

When people describe their personal no-win dilemmas, they usually add a comment about being "damned if I do and damned if I don't." Here are some of the most frequently mentioned:

Justice dilemmas are society-wide. They are fairness issues like racism, sexism, and pay equity.

Policy dilemmas are situations in your company you observe, but don't participate in directly.

Job description dilemmas occur when your job requires you to do something you find morally objectionable.

Responsibility dilemmas occur when you must choose between two equally strong "right things to do," e.g., work responsibilities versus family responsibilities.

Abusive boss dilemmas are the dark side of the unique relationship we have with our bosses.

Romantic dilemmas make otherwise good working relationships even more difficult.

Contrast the no-win dilemmas with what we've already discussed about the ethical office. In the ethical office, it's okay to discuss ethical conduct. When someone encounters behavior that makes her feel uncomfortable because it conflicts with her morals or values, it's okay to talk about it in order to define what is the right and wrong way to behave. Without penalty, anyone can raise a question like, "Is this the best way for us to handle this?" and declare, "I'm uncomfortable about this because..." or, "I'm not satisfied that we're doing the right thing—can we talk this through?"

When it is virtually impossible to have a discussion about the ethics of a situation, the situation is a no-win dilemma. Yet we have to learn to live with these dilemmas, even though they may remain unresolved for long periods of time.

What makes a no-win dilemma so daunting? It defies resolution because it is:

- beyond your power to remedy by yourself.
- very personal, and therefore virtually certain to keep you in a constant state of turmoil.
- lacking person-to-person communication, so there is no one person you can talk to about the problem to get it resolved.

- ongoing; it is not an "incident," but a chronic condition or situation.

But — no-win dilemmas CAN be resolved

No-win dilemmas can and must be resolved, one way or another. Just because they are more complex than the garden variety of ethical dilemmas does not excuse you from doing something about them. In fact, I would argue that the most difficult dilemmas are precisely the ones deserving of most of your attention.

As we'll see in a moment, no one's ethical rule book is perfect. Not mine and not yours. None is without problems, or contradictions, or inconsistencies. If there was only one theory that fit every person in every company in every industry in all circumstances, ethical dilemmas would be relatively rare and easy to resolve. But, unfortunately, things aren't so simple in real life.

I have a time-tested approach to no-win dilemmas:

First, I force myself to do something.

I stubbornly believe each of us can make a difference, albeit small. My influence and control over an ethical dilemma may be too small to correct the situation to my liking, but I push myself to do my part.

I also believe we are all biased toward doing something to make the world a better place. Many of us are haunted by the quote from Edmund Burke, "All that is needed for the triumph of evil is that good persons do nothing."

Here's how I think about it: Imagine that a human resource director needs to hear negative feedback about one of her policies 10 times before she'll change it. In this hypothetical example, I'm a placeholder, another person voting, on the way to that magic number. When I express my opinion about the policy I regard as unethical, I may not get the satisfaction of a face-to-face discussion. I might even feel like I just wasted my time, even embarrassed myself, because I thought my puny voice would never make a difference in the large organization. But on the other side of the issue, someone is keeping score. If enough people speak up, or resign in disgust, the organization will respond. The company is, after all, an entity committed to its self-protection and self-preservation. When a policy becomes too costly in terms of public relations, employee turnover, poor productivity (because of poor morale), or costly law-suits, change is inevitable. That's why we are obligated—every one of us—to do something to counteract unethical practices when we see them.

(Haven't we all been tempted to "just bail out" when we've been completely disgusted with a job situation? I know I have. Leave 'em twisting in the wind, I used to think. Now I speak up on my way out the door. I want you to do this, too. Insist on one last conver-sation with a company representative—euphemistically called the "exit interview"—to tell them in terms that cannot be misunder-stood that you are leaving because of such and such ethical dilemma. Also, give them the benefit of your thinking regarding what needs to be done to correct the unethical situation.)

Second, I learn to live with that which I cannot change, OR I walk out the door.

Once I've said my piece, and I'm sure I've pushed my point as far as I can without jeopardizing my other priorities (e.g., my rela-tionships, my advancement potential, my status in the office), I make peace with it. (That's easy to remember—say your piece, then make your peace.) I'll try to set the issue aside until I have another opportunity to speak up about it, or I may come to under-stand the company's position and change my mind about it after a few more discussions (see Chapter 9 again for the ground rules about these discussions). Or, I may not be able to get past it and make peace with the situation, in which case I would have to seri-ously consider resigning. If I did resign, however, I would want to do it on my terms and my timetable.

A few examples will help you see what can be done about the seemingly no-win dilemmas (they only seem like no-win situations because you probably won't be around to enjoy the satisfaction of seeing the changes you helped make):

Justice Dilemmas

Your company is small, so it is not technically required to comply with the quota requirements of the anti-discrimination employment laws, such as the Americans with Disabilities Act (ADA). However, you believe your company is morally bound to comply with the spirit of the law. In fact, your cousin is disabled, needs and wants a job, and would be perfect for a new telemarketing position.

(The ADA mandates that every company with 15 or more employees must make "reasonable accommodations" on behalf of a qualified job candidate. The intent of the law is to neutralize the negative effect a disability may have on an otherwise qualified person. The law does not mean the company must hire a qualified person with a disability just because she has a disability; it only asks the employer to base the hiring decision on what the applicant can do, not what she can't do. Bottom line, the company can continue to hire the best person for the job.)

The company president, who is your boss, however, doesn't want to even consider hiring a person with a disability. Buying even a modest amount of adaptive office equipment and software for your disabled cousin would be just an unnecessary expense, she says. She says she survives in the marketplace by choosing which battles to fight, and this is one she wants to pass on. She's sympathetic, she says, but not rich enough to take on this cause, no matter how worthwhile it may be. "There is no room on our small ship for charity cases," was exactly how she put it.

You have tried to persuade her by explaining that this is not a charity case. Cost should not be a problem, you say — in fact, the total cost of the "reasonable accommodations" would be less than $150 for some blocks of wood to raise the desk high enough to slide the wheelchair underneath, some new software, plus a new headset for the telephone. Your logic has not swayed her, even though you know that she knows this is the right thing to do.

You begin to suspect she may be sexist or racist (your cousin is a Native American woman), or she may be much more judgmental than you are (your cousin has made no secret in your small town about her "alternative life style"). You wonder if she secretly fears a lawsuit or higher medical expenses somewhere down the road. You know she has poured her life savings and years of work into her business to build it up, so you understand her concerns about not wanting to put it all at risk. You argue that the risks she imagines are virtually nonexistent. You tell her you know your cousin from a different perspective, and you believe without reservation that she would be a strong addition to the team.

What should you do? Your persistent advocacy for your cousin is beginning to take a toll on your working relationship with the company president.

Your boss is not a bad person — or the enemy — for sticking up for what she believes is right for her. She simply disagrees with you. Her assessment of the situation is different from yours. She actually may be struggling to reconcile her own internal ethical dilemmas; she may be caught between her desire to accommodate you and your cousin with her wish to keep the company free from financial risk.

If you are satisfied she has listened to you fairly, yet she remains unconvinced, back off for awhile. Think about other ways you can make your point (perhaps arrange a social occasion where your boss can meet your cousin? Or what about trying a risk-free internship for your cousin?).

Racism, sexism, homophobia, and other forms of prejudice are still out there, corroding the communication between people who are different from each other. You have to respect the views of others, and acknowledge they are on their own journey to discover the best way to conduct themselves. You can't rush or force-feed tolerance. But just as you listen to them and respect their right to their opinions, make them listen to you with equal respect. Be very clear about your feelings (e.g., when someone tells a racist joke, tell them what you think: "I don't think that's funny at all.").

Pay equity is a pet discrimination issue of mine. I believe unequal pay scales based on gender, not merit, are unethical. This issue is about fairness and respect — neither of which women get enough of — and money is the best way of keeping score.

When I was president of Professional Secretaries International, I chaired the first-ever Secretarial Speakout. Office professionals from throughout the U.S. gathered at the Fairmont Hotel in San Francisco to talk about the image and salary of the profession. Gloria Steinem was our keynote speaker. She and I had a press conference at which we displayed a stunning origami paper rose made out of dollar bills to stress the theme (and consensus) of the conference: Raises, Not Roses! Speaking to the bosses of America, we said: Recognize us in a *meaningful* way by giving us more money, career development opportunities, etc. Roses are nice, but they are a poor substitute for respect as a professional and they do nothing to sweeten our retirement account. When we get the equal pay that comes with mutual respect, then we'll know you really mean it!

Raising the issue of salaries is our only means of combat. We have to shed our "nice girl" attitude about compensation and get unfair and unequal pay onto the negotiating table. As Gloria put it, "We'll never make progress until the secret conspiracy of silence surrounding female salaries is eliminated."

I'll never forget an evening I spent with several other top executive assistants from my city. After a few glasses of wine and lots of great camaraderie, we decided — for the first time ever — to reveal our current salaries to each other. As we stated our salaries, we each added excuses on behalf of our companies or our boss. Each boss was apparently pleading poverty as he told his version of the same story: "You're worth so much more than this, but . . . ." You guessed it — every company had an excuse for not paying us what they said we were worth. Talk is cheap. When the last of us had spoken, we realized what we had said. We ended up laughing hysterically. We were hopeless — *each of us was actually **apologizing** for our low salaries!*

Women need to continue to fight for fair treatment. In 1990, the median annual earnings for a full-time female employee in the United States was $19,816 per year — only 71.6 percent of the median earnings of a full-time male employee. Three years later, in 1993 (the latest figures available), the percentage actually slipped backward to 71.5 percent. This unfair pay situation persists because we let it persist. We continue to say, "Yes, that will be fine," when we should be saying, "No, thank you! I'm sorry, but that amount is not enough to meet my financial objectives." Our individual situations are unique, so the statistics are just the beginning of the discussion.

This economic discrimination doesn't end when we obtain the traditionally higher paying jobs. When men held the positions we are taking now, the jobs paid more. Bank teller salaries are a good example to make my point because they have been surveyed regularly for more than 40 years. In 1950, most bank tellers were men, and they made 120 percent of the median salary for wage earners nationwide. By 1980, 91 percent of the bank tellers were women — and the median salary had dropped to 79 percent of the median salary nationwide. Of the men remaining in the occupation, they made 20 percent more than their female peers. This is why I welcome more men to our ranks as office professionals — because history has taught us that when the number of women in a job category increases, their average pay decreases; and when the number of men in a job category increases, their average pay increases.

I love what Faith Whittlesey said: "Remember, Ginger Rogers did everything Fred Astaire did, but she did it backwards and in high heels."

Each of us can help to move the cause forward by speaking up in our performance and compensation reviews. The situation is improving for us, one woman at a time. Professional women I have recruited and placed are being paid fairly, for example. They are either viewed as equally important co-contributors to the company's goals, or they don't accept the job. (An added benefit of being paid fairly: They are also spared the sexist words and actions of others that would likely be a part of an unfriendly work environment. Mutual respect is the natural byproduct of equal pay.) Bottom line: We are valuable contributors to the company, and we ought to be paid accordingly! Our message is simple: Pay us what we are really worth, not just 71 percent of what we are worth.

Other society-wide dilemmas should get the same kind of attention from you. When it gets personal, you have a chance to be heard. Speak up every time you can!

Policy Dilemmas

Thin excuses from the Legal Department: "Strictly speaking, we are in compliance with all the laws." "We haven't been caught breaking any laws." "We've never been convicted." And, finally, "We have a policy to cover that."

The road to hell, in my imagination, has directional road signs that look suspiciously like pages from a corporate policy manual. I like corporatespeak policies as well as the next person, but I think they are sometimes used to conceal and justify unethical behaviors as often as they are intended to provide direction. (I group policies together with the practices that result because of them. Keep in mind that policies come in written and unwritten formats, and they can be formal or informal.)

Go back to the beginning of this chapter and the actions at the healthcare company that seemed to victimize Jane. Many of you recognize this kind of office, don't you? This company's code of conduct does not seem to be guided by moral rules, and the "rightness" of an action seems to be solely determined by whether it maximizes the company's short-term self-interest. From this company's perspective, getting rid of Jane was the "right" action to take because it saved the company money. Maybe that's true — but why did the company have to work so hard to handle it so poorly?

There are a lot of organizations like this, and worse. Some measure their conduct by how well they follow the law. These companies say, in effect, "Morality is irrelevant in a business context. We obey the law and that's enough."

Other organizations are run on the belief that the rightness or wrongness of an act is ultimately determined by the act's consequences. For example, if an act produces good consequences, then the act is "morally right." This is the argument that "the end justifies the means." The manager who manipulates, harasses, and browbeats his staff to get them to work harder justifies his actions by showing off his results. "True, my style is a little tacky and hard to take, but that's what it takes to get the good numbers," he says.

Your dilemma arises when you witness these policies. What do you do? By all means, you should speak up, but never do it alone if you can possibly avoid it. Talk it up among your co-workers, then draft a letter or petition that makes your collective position clear. Try to get as many people as possible to "sign on" literally or figuratively to the letter or petition. You're trying to spread the responsibility for this message and, in doing so, demonstrate that this is a consensus position. You need the protection of at least a small group of like-minded people, considering the David-Goliath power relationship between you and the company.

Then, make certain that more than one person above your supervisor receives the letter or petition. This will help keep it from getting "lost" or being ignored. Keep in mind that your effort is likely to be interpreted as a direct challenge by at least some managers. If The Powers are not ready to change their policy, it is probable you will suffer some sort of punishment. But if your cause is just, it's probably worth it to stir things up a little bit. As long as the pain is spread over a group, you can take it. Who knows? Maybe your voice of protest is the last one the company wants to hear. Maybe yours is the 10th, or 50th, or 100th voice, and the message finally got through. (If the company is ready to change the policy, you'll probably get a commendation. The company's progressive managers will appreciate a few rabble-rousers on their side!)

Job Description Dilemmas

You are a legal secretary in a law office, working for a controversial attorney. The attorney's new case is defending an abortion clinic. You, personally, are against the pro-choice position on abortion. You would like to see all abortion clinics closed forever. You are very uncomfortable helping mount a defense for this client and you wish you did not have to work on this case. You know your ethical dilemma is affecting the quality of your work. Should you tell your boss about your feelings? Do your feelings even matter in a case like this? Do you have the right to refuse? What should you do?

When I discuss this case in my seminars, I always have a "split" room. Half the room says they would just do their job; the other half (obviously those opposed to abortion) say they would refuse. Keep in mind that you are not being asked to do anything illegal here. It is currently legal for abortion clinics to operate in the U.S.; and, everyone has the right to a vigorous defense. As a legal secretary, you just are being asked to do your job.

How can you resolve the moral dilemma? One option is to go to your boss, explain how you feel, and ask if someone else can handle your responsibilities for this particular case. If it is a large law office, this isn't a major problem. Your boss will probably appreciate your honesty and take the opportunity to put a neutral or more enthusiastic secretary on the defense team. However, if it is a small law office, it may be difficult to substitute for you.

There's another way to look at this, though. I think you have an obligation to see this problem coming long before you get into it. In the first place, being a legal secretary carries certain expectations. You know this. If you want to pick and choose each case you wish to assist your boss on, you're not going to be useful or effective. Ask your prospective attorney/boss: What kinds of cases come through the office? Who are the regular clients? If your attorney defends child molesters, driving-under-the-influence offenders, corporate polluters, or guys who con widows and orphans, get comfortable with that fact or get out. You can expect to do certain types of work for certain types of attorneys. If you anticipate dilemmas with particular types of cases, skip this job offer and take the next one.

The same logic applies to other fields — marketing, medicine, sales, technical support, securities, banking, insurance, etc. All of these have potential dilemmas unique to the business that can be predicted. Be professional, anticipate the potential problems, and plan your response.

It's a big election year, and a secretary in the southwestern U.S. is told to prepare and maintain a report for senior management that details the personal contributions of all managers to political campaigns. She is uncomfortable doing this report because political contributions are supposed to be completely confidential. Her supervisor is sympathetic, but feels similarly bound to comply with upper management's requests. He pulled out her job description and pointed to the "all other duties as requested" phrase. What should she do?

Across the country, another secretary is asked to prepare a database of political campaign contributors and to send them letters. Problem is, this secretary works for the leader of the state legislature. Using state employees (like her) and state equipment (like the computer, phone, mailroom, etc.) for partisan re-election campaigns is strictly forbidden, although the practice is tolerated because it is so widespread. What should she do?

Did you hear the REAL Golden Rule? It goes like this: The person with the gold makes the rules! That's another way of saying the boss does the boss'n, and you do the do'n.

There are limits to what you can and should be doing. When the boss makes a request for a task arguably within your job description, how much choice do you really have? Do you do "it," or don't you? Are you going to say something or keep quiet? Is this a dilemma for you, or are you really just okay with letting the issue slide by?

Tough call, this one. This is a classic case of "it depends." No two people are going to see situations like these the same way. Imagine yourself in one of these secretary's positions. On the one hand, you are supposed to be loyal and respectful. You'd also like to keep your job, which means keeping everyone above you on the corporate food chain liking you. On the other hand, you are very uncomfortable performing this task. Technically, you are being asked to do something illegal, or at least unethical, and you haven't a prayer of blaming the boss if you are subpoenaed to testify in some future hearing after the dust from the election settles. Making a big deal out of this will undermine your credibility and chill what has otherwise been a great job.

It may be time to compromise. I'm NOT suggesting you change your ethics to suit the boss. Do not confuse an ethical principle with a compromise. As long as you make your principle known precisely, it is then possible to compromise. It would sound something like this: "I personally believe it is wrong for us to do this. It is unethical and it is against the law. But I like my job, and I owe you my loyalty, so I'll do it. But I'm on record as opposed to this action. Now you know how I feel."

Going on the record may be as much as you can do right now— but if it is done with tact and professionalism, it may be enough to persuade someone to remove the dilemma, or redirect future dilemmas before they get to you. Again, this presumes you feel more strongly about keeping your job and career intact than fighting for this one issue. If this is a battle you choose to fight, you need only raise the ante by refusing to do the work or by declining to comply. This will force the issue back into the laps of upper management, and they will have to choose another way to get their dirty work done. (They probably will, too—whether you are on the team or not is of little concern to them.) You may suffer some negative consequences, but if it's worth it to you to make your point, you'll have no trouble sleeping.

From the Food for Thought Department: *Industries differ widely in expectations for tolerance and adaptability on the part of employees. Once when I gave a seminar in Las Vegas, most of the attendees were "back-room" employees in casinos (many were clerks and cashiers). They immediately responded to the various case studies we looked at in class with the reply, "Well, Nan, it depends on who the pit boss [the floor manager of a game] is!" This is an interesting problem—how do you hold fast to a set of ethical standards when you literally have a new boss every 30 minutes?*

Responsibility Dilemmas
Imagine a co-worker steals a $100 bill from the cash register. She confides that this money will make the difference between paying her rent this month or slipping back into an abusive relationship with her ex-boyfriend. What would you do?

What do you do when you are confronted by two "rights" that are equally strong? Do you choose to do what is right for the company or what is right for a colleague? What do you do when facing a choice between mutually exclusive alternatives that are equally "responsible"?

For example, we have a moral requirement to keep our promises. We also have a moral requirement to tell the truth. What do you do when these are in conflict?

What about work and family issues? The Job versus The Family is a common source for these kinds of dilemmas. Here are two "rights" that regularly compete for time. Both are predictable only part of the time, and both involve other people we care about. Too often, saying "yes" to one means disappointing the other. Guilt and stress are inevitable.

My advice is to be sure you make *some* sort of a decision. The dilemmas that rotate around conflicting responsibilities have compelling arguments on both sides of the question, so the best solution is rarely obvious. It's easy to do nothing, hoping the scales will tip one way or another to make the decision for you. Don't let indecision paralyze you. In the end, this will probably be a difficult, painful choice. *You must make a decision,* though, based on your best judgment.

I've found that it helps to establish guidelines whenever and wherever you can. This reduces uncertainty, and that's always a positive (even if your boss or your family doesn't like the guidelines), such as: "I'll work late every Tuesday, but that's all."

It also helps to lower everyone's expectations, including your own. You are not Superwoman or Superman every day. Tell your boss and your family the truth about how difficult it is to juggle your competing priorities. They can become a part of the solution if you let them help. At least they'll understand when you say things like, "I can't come to every game and every school program anymore"; and, "When my kids are sick, my priorities change fast. I'm sorry, but that's just the way it is."

Finally, these dilemmas are often dynamic over a period of time. Make that work for you by shifting your focus whenever you can. It's a lot easier for others to accept that they aren't #1 all the time IF they are #1 SOME of the time. Look for opportunities to give extra when you can: "My ex has the kids this week, so I'm staying late to get a head start on the new program"; and, "I can come home from work early today, so let's use the time to do something special you want to do."

Abusive Boss Dilemmas

Dear Nan: "My boss has an explosive personality, and he's especially fond of four-letter words. Although he doesn't swear directly at me, he often says things to me in ways that are demeaning and condescending. Sometimes I feel like a kid who can't do anything right anymore. I think I'm a good assistant, but he makes me think I'm never good enough. Am I just being overly sensitive? I like my job, but I can't take his intimidating ways much longer."

Abusive bosses are harassing their staffs much more often than we know. When I first reported this case in one of my magazine columns, I opened a floodgate of responses from readers who have had similar experiences. Apparently, many bosses have not yet learned how to treat others with respect and common courtesy. The dynamics of harassment frequently make these dilemmas no-win situations for the participants, so I want to give it some extra attention.

What are these abusive bosses thinking? This is one of the few things that really blows the cork of my husband, Lou. When I come home and tell him about a situation where a boss is being verbally abusive to his or her assistant, he is always astonished to hear what so-called "professional" managers try to get away with. Do they actually think they can operate their business better by yelling, screaming, and using abusive language? I don't know about you, but I do *not* respond in a positive way when someone yells at me, criticizes me, and generally assaults my self-esteem! If I am made to believe I am stupid or foolish, my performance will decline to reflect those low expectations.

The results of all of these forms of harassment are the same: Lost productivity, absenteeism, and turnover. In addition, those who rule by intimidation and bullying cheat their organization of creativity and innovative thinking on the part of other employees. When abusive behavior dominates an office, fresh ideas are eliminated and employees become "yes people." NO ONE WINS!

Verbal and emotional harassment are among the few dilemmas that do not respond well to logic, appeals to fairness, or even stiff opposition. After many years of watching many people try different approaches, I've concluded that this type of behavior is too far beyond the influence of another person to change. Harassers almost always have bigger problems, making it virtually impossible for another person to "fix" them.

Typically, the only certain way of resolving this dilemma is to get out of the situation. You have to resign. To stay is to invite infecting yourself with your boss's problems. Hoping to "cure" him, or searching for the "silver bullet" solution that will transform him into a professional manager who deserves your respect, is usually futile. An abusive boss is an angry person with deep-seated anxieties and insecurities that just plain make him "mad at the world." You cannot change this person. Only a professionally trained therapist would have a chance of doing so. Take some comfort in the fact that his or her anger at the world has very little to do with you.

You need to take care of yourself. Give the abusive boss the benefit of the doubt and a fair chance to change his behavior, but then, lacking any improvement, make the tough decision to leave. Just go. Today. This is the only real power you have in this situation, and you should not hesitate to exercise it.

Another case: Sarah's boss was an old-fashioned chauvinist in the auto manufacturing business who co-opted her into helping him steal from the company in several ways. He used a combination of bullying and emotional manipulation to get her to "cross the line" for him. Was she harassed? She believes she was. Finally, her fear of being discovered and prosecuted was so great that she had to resign.

A quick recap of the harassment discussion in Chapter 14: Harassment is frequent, deliberate, and abusive behavior or action that is disrespectful, discourteous, insulting, hurtful, mean-spirited, and otherwise damaging to your effectiveness in your job. Verbal harassment usually takes the form of yelling, excessive criticism, personal insults, or profanity. Emotional harassment is any attack on your self-esteem. Verbal and emotional harassment often come together. If it can be proven the harassment contains sexually explicit descriptions or is directed at you solely because of your gender, it may also be sexual harassment. If you are a victim of sexual harassment, you have the added option of pursuing formal disciplinary action via your company's human resources department. Sexual harassment is the only form of harassment found to be illegal under the anti-discrimination provisions of the Civil Rights Act of 1964. For other kinds of harassment—you are on your own.

Most abusive bosses are men, but their gender does not have a lock on this dysfunctional behavior. One executive at a Minneapolis corporation told me he had to talk with a female sales executive whose style included lots of colorful language on the phone with her clients. The administrative staff sitting outside her office (including the woman's assistant), however, objected to hearing this language. My friend said he had to tell the woman to cease and desist because she was leaving the company vulnerable to a sexual harassment lawsuit! He doesn't know if she cleaned up her act on the phone, but she did at least shut her door.

After suffering the verbal and emotional abuse of her supervisor for five months, Rosemary Deitzer in Ohio tried to solve her problem by transferring to another department. It wasn't enough of a change, and she later left the company. She wrote she could not shake herself of the situation, so she wisely sought counseling. The counseling "was very helpful in that I discovered what it was about me that made me vulnerable for such abuse."

Five years ago, Marilyn Tolley, currently a secretary at Cross-Davidson Real Estate, Mt. Vernon, IL, worked out of her home as the assistant to the owner of a company several states away. They communicated via phone calls, faxes, and a monthly visit from him to her home office. His use of obscene words gradually increased, as did his verbal criticism of her. She came to dread his calls and visits. As a result, she developed severe headaches and insomnia. She lost weight, developed digestive trouble and, after his monthly visits, "collapsed for at least two days," refusing to leave the house, putting the phone on hold and not even speaking to her family. She says she became "run down, lethargic, developed severe back and leg pains, and lost all interest in everything around me." After finally quitting the job, it still took her "six months to get over the stress caused by that 'year of living dangerously'," and, "the damage it did to my self-esteem was immeasurable."

With few exceptions, my column readers and seminar attendees report poor results in their attempts to change or endure these harassment dilemmas. Nancy K. Smith, secretary at DATS Group, Chemical Technology Division, Oak Ridge, TN sums it up best: "There is no chance you will change your boss's personality. His problem, whether personal, financial, or emotional, is not yours to worry about. The way you react to his treatment of you, and what you do about it, is what is changeable here."

Sometimes, the boss manages to get his or her act together and stop misbehaving. This is the exception, however, not the rule. But it does happen. An anonymous respondent to my column from Augusta, MI said she calmly walked into her boss's office after one of his screaming and swearing "spells" and told him, "I am a professional and deserved to be treated accordingly. I would never speak or act in such an unprofessional way to you, and I expect the same courtesy from you. Stop abusing me, or I'll quit!"

Kudos to her! Unfortunately, his verbal barrage soon began again. So, true to her word, she left his office and started packing her belongings. He calmed down and asked her to please stay (although he did not apologize). She reports her boss still has a "spell" about once a week, but "it is short-lived" because she immediately responds with something like, "We cannot work together in this kind of an environment. We cannot afford any emotional outbursts — we just have too much work to do today. It's your choice — do we work or not work?" He stops immediately. "Anonymous" says she likes her job and so she chooses to resolve each spell as it comes up. She explained she was "withholding my name for fear of another screaming spell should he read this."

Remember — follow your Ethical Priority Compass! *You have to take care of yourself.* Document what is said and done, including the date and circumstances, and keep this journal long enough to make your point; then, try to talk to your boss. If you think it will do any good, tell him how his behavior makes you feel. But be realistic. You simply cannot force another person to treat you differently.

As a last resort, try going to a representative in your human resources department. Show him your documentation (but don't leave the originals — copies only!) and ask him to intercede on your behalf. However, don't get your hopes up. By talking to someone else in an official capacity, you are making your boss's problem a part of the company's records. He'll probably go ballistic on you, accusing you of disloyalty and a lot worse.

Kit Robinson, CPS, senior staff assistant at Oglethorpe Power Corporation in Tucker, GA reminds those of you in abusive circumstances to "stay focused, remain flexible, trust your intuition, and believe in the good about yourself. Only then will you be able to take control and improve your situation." Smart lady!

Anonymous from Mansfield, OH wrote me: "As I have lived the scenario of the abusive boss, my advice is to get out — run, don't walk, to the nearest employment agency. For the sake of your sanity, get out! If you spend the rest of your life cleaning restrooms or flipping burgers, at least you will have your dignity and will know that you conducted yourself in a highly ethical manner." When I was growing up, my father had some great advice for those situations where you struggled to work something out with someone else, but failed no matter what you tried: "Put your track shoes on, kid!"

Romantic Dilemmas

Can an office romance work? It's doubtful, but not impossible. If the romance is mutual, consensual, and between people who do not report to each other or work too closely together, the chances are better. But successful relationships are the exception.

Just so you know where I'm coming from: Yes, it's true, I'm a hopeless romantic. I'm an old-fashioned gal who likes flowers, candlelight, and men who stick around. Speaking of men who are dependable, I helped writer Robert Frank explore the phenomenon of romance between secretaries and their UPS drivers in a February 1995 *Wall Street Journal* article. (UPS stands for United Parcel Service of America. 93 percent of UPS delivery-persons are men.) I first heard about these potential affairs in my seminars. The women say, "Here's a man I can count on, even when I can't count on any other men in my life. He visits me every day at the same time, he meets my needs, and then he goes away. He's a made-to-order fantasy." My pussycat husband, Lou, is a romantic all-star in his own right, so when the *Wall Street Journal* article showed up with my name in it, he drove over to the local UPS headquarters and talked them out of one of those signature brown uniforms the UPS guys wear. He wore it all day in his office (he's a municipal bond broker) and got lots of fun comments about his enhanced sex appeal. He delivered for me, too! Now that's romance!

Back to the dilemma: Once a person leaves school, the workplace is likely where they will look for and find their dating partners. And we can't, nor do we want to, kill Cupid! We need to be realistic.

Heck, a love affair is tough to manage even under ideal conditions, so there are never any guarantees. But an office affair is much more complicated because it's entangled in the other big commitment in your life—your job. Presuming there is going to be a normal amount of lusty distractions, tearful misunderstandings, long conversations, etc., this is a bumpy road for even the strong and gentle hearts.

If one partner is reporting to the other, there will almost certainly be extra problems because of the imbalance of power. Even in relationships where the parties are "sophisticated" enough to "handle anything," the dynamics are against a successful long-term relationship. The company policies that try in one way or another to cool these romances are based on bitter experiences and should be heeded. But don't take my word for it—consider the following dilemma sent in by a reader, and then read the follow-up responses from others who share their practical experiences:

Dear Nan,

My boss is having an affair. With me. Honestly, I never planned to get romantically involved. True, I moved to this city to find someone, so I guess I was vulnerable. Who knows how these things happen? In my case, our evening work sessions became more frequent, then more intimate until, finally, he was staying for breakfast.

I don't believe this office romance is jeopardizing our careers (though I'm sure he's having as much trouble concentrating on his work as I am when we are near each other during the day!). We are both 33 years old, not married, and very committed to our respective careers. Both of us are also realistic about the casino-like relationship employers have with their employees in the 1990s.

Here's our ethical dilemma: Our relationship technically violates a company personnel policy that forbids "significant others" from working together. If we "come clean" about our relationship, we just know that we would be broken up as a team because of this policy. I don't think this is fair. Still, we consider ourselves professionals with high personal integrity, so we feel badly about continuing to see each other in defiance of the company policy.

We want to keep working, and working together, in our current jobs with this company. Companies' loyalty to their employ-

ees is only skin deep these days, so why should we let some policy maker dictate how much happiness we can have at this time in our lives? Can't we love our jobs AND each other? Do office romances ever have happy endings? Is it realistic to think we are sophisticated enough to let this situation develop, perhaps even for several years? We have to make some tough decisions in the next few months, and we'd appreciate your advice.

Digital Lovers

Wow! The many responses I got to this reader's dilemma suggest that office romances remain among the most sensitive—and all-too-common—situations we encounter.

The office environment is a fertile place for romance, isn't it? "It's tempting," says Anonymous in Des Moines. "The 'other person' in the office always sees you at your best. Your hair is perfect, nails are done, suit fits well, shoes are shined. Your office paramour sees your professionalism, knowledge, business acumen, etc." She says she's had several affairs with co-workers and, when love is new, she says she describes her personal experience as a "dreamlike state."

Can an office romance have a happy ending? Most readers said, "Yes, it's possible—but, it's not likely." Many shared advice with insights gleaned from personal heartaches. Here's a typical response, again from someone who wanted to remain anonymous: "I am fortunate that my romance with a fellow employee blossomed into a serious relationship, but it wasn't without its troubles from fellow employees. I can't begin to count the number of office romances that I have observed that were and are utter—and sometimes devastating—failures. No matter how professional you view your office conduct, such relationships are in full view of everyone. Day by day, little by little, I noticed fewer people were confiding in me, invitations came to a halt, conversations around the vending machines ceased when I rounded the corner. This 'blackballing' was so hard on us..."

Most readers noted that this kind of relationship cannot remain hidden. Many indicated that—no matter what the people involved thought—their relationship was no secret!

Candace Cox, CPS, Santa Rosa, CA, wrote: "As with other things in life, people catch on far more quickly than we want to believe or admit. Your [she says this to the Digital Lovers] actions are probably worrying, as well as offending, your co-workers." And Karen Bianchino, CPS, Downers Grove, IL, wrote: "Everyone knows about your relationship. Unfortunately, this kind of gossip is often the primary topic of communication in many offices."

Office romances seem to inevitably end up affecting the work of the parties involved. For example, if the couple has an argument on the way to the office that morning, will this argument continue throughout the day and show up in their performance as they try to work together? A small event at the office may quickly become a huge event because of the earlier "domestic" situation.

If other employees have to adjust to the couple's mood of the day, then, of course, the huge problem of favoritism rears its ugly head. Co-workers soon suspect that sleeping with the boss may have tangible benefits. They start looking for telltale signs of preferential treatment—a longer lunch hour, a larger salary increase at review time, a smaller work load, and more time off. These things may or may not be true. Unfortunately, other people's perceptions will often blow up into big personnel problems. When the entire office team gets involved, productivity takes a nosedive.

Can the Digital Lovers "come clean" and make the situation work somehow? Probably not, says Jacqueline Scepaniak, CPS in Maryland. "If they do it in a manner of defiance or begging, they will milk a little more time with the status quo; but, the company will be calling the shots. If the company shunts one or both of them into positions they don't want, not only do they lose professionally, but, if they feel resentment, the personal relationship loses as well. They can end the affair and continue to work together, but that is really hard to do. They're tempted to slide back into it, they're still open to the gossip network, and they could still suffer the unkindest cut of all by being called on the carpet after they've made the 'sacrifice' of giving up the relationship."

Let's look at the legal end of this dilemma and examine the reasons companies adopt policies against office romance. Marital-status discrimination is unlawful today in most states. However, even though employers are not allowed to prevent married or significant-other couples from working for the same company or even within the same department/division, they are allowed to forbid such couples from working *for* each other, such as in a "reporting to" situation.

The reason for this kind of policy is not to get involved in employees' personal relationships, but to protect employees and the company from financial risk. The Digital Lovers describe a classic case of boss-secretary romance. Here are the risks:

Risk to the boss: If the relationship fails, the secretary could charge sexual harassment, claiming the boss coerced her into the relationship (e.g., with promises of a salary increase).

Risk to the secretary: The boss is in control of her performance reviews, salary increases, and promotions. He may not disclose advancement opportunities because he does not want to lose her, or he may retaliate if she decides to end the relationship.

Risk to the company: Another employee may have a claim against the company under U.S. federal guidelines for sexual discrimination remedies. If there is a perception that the involved secretary was receiving preferential treatment because of her involvement with the boss, the company is vulnerable.

If the Digital Lovers are going to continue their relationship, they should seriously consider making some hard choices now, before circumstances — and someone else — makes the choices for them. For instance, one of them could request a transfer or find a new position he or she genuinely wants elsewhere in the company. As another anonymous reader stated: "If the relationship is truly solid, then no matter what the company policy may be, the couple should be able to weather it and find an agreeable solution to all involved."

Margaret H. Caddell, CPS, president of the Alabama Division of Professional Secretaries International, sums it up: "You should respect your company's policies because you will not be able to have a positive and productive relationship with your boss and company if you have problems or if the relationship should end."

Summary

As we go about the process of living and working together, we discover competing ethical frameworks and moral theories. Some of these are bound to be in conflict with your own. The strongest office teams are those that can recognize these conflicts, discuss them in detail, and make peace with them.

Call me Pollyanna, but I fiercely believe that most ethical dilemmas can be resolved to everyone's benefit with the right kind of communication at the right times. For example, discussions about values, expectations, hypothetical situations, and so forth can do much to build an ethical office.

Not everyone shares your desire to resolve ethical dilemmas, though. Some situations look hopeless, and we are tempted to throw up our hands and quit on these seemingly "no-win" dilemmas.

The no-win dilemmas only SEEM impossible to resolve. You may feel you have few or no choices in the situation and consequently lack any power. But just because the company isn't going to change on your say-so, and you can't change the company's culture single-handedly, doesn't mean you have an excuse to keep quiet. You have a moral obligation to contribute your voice to the chorus asking for change. Resigning your job to escape a dilemma is always available as the option of last resort. Even if you can't stay long enough to see the change take place, you can take some satisfaction from the knowledge that you helped improve a situation.

"Respect is mutual."

— African (Zulu)

18

Misdeeds and second chances

Think about it: *Dear Nan—I think I've screwed up my career, but good. My boss caught me in a lie about my work. I'm so ashamed! I'm just sure he's told his assistant, which means everyone else in the office knows, too. It feels like everyone is treating me differently now. I feel like I let down myself and everyone else. I wouldn't blame my co-workers if they never really trusted me again. Is there anything I can do to redeem myself, short of taking another job in a different city?*

Whoa, whoa, whoa! Everyone falls off the ethics wagon sometime. (Wait—that might not be true. I have known only one woman who, as best as I can recall, never compromised her ethics. Ever. She was my mother. She probably knew your mother. And they both talked about us and our horrid ways when we weren't around!)

In the battles between character versus convenience, we will occasionally make an error in our ethical judgment. This is unfortunate, but predictable. It's a simple fact of life in the busy office: Not every decision will afford us the luxury of sufficient time or information needed for a reflective, best-possible ethical choice. Even using the ethical compass and a history of ethical discussions does not assure us of resolving every dilemma satisfactorily.

Yet, because we are professionals, we are accountable for our choices and we must accept personal responsibility for the consequences of our decisions. (Far better this than never being taken seriously!) Rather than making excuses for ourselves, or copping out with a throw-away excuse like, "We've always done it like that," or "I was just doing what the boss told me to do," we must be prepared to stand behind and stand up for our ethical decisions.

Can we recover from an ethical dilemma unhappily resolved? Is there life after an ethical conflict with no good answer? Do we ever get a second chance, or are we doomed to migrating to another job and starting over with a clean record? How do we recover our peace of mind, our self-respect, our productivity, our reputation?

We have all pushed beyond our moral boundaries occasionally. They are a bit fuzzy sometimes, aren't they? And ethical limits are notoriously elastic during times of stress. It seems you aren't even certain where they are until you actually bump into one. In my case, I didn't realize I'd stepped over the line until I was on the other side, looking back.

The good news is this: There is a road that leads back to the place you want to be. Stick with me for the next few pages, and I'll help get you back on the right pathway.

No saints or angels working here

My survey results reveal that office professionals are not all angels all the time. Some of us have lied, stolen, and slept with the boss. Some of us have admitted to destroying information, fabricating data, and telling secrets to those we shouldn't. A few of us even have been convicted of embezzlement and fraud. These are ethical dilemmas of our own making.

If we've fallen off the straight and narrow path, is there any way we can redeem ourselves? Can we somehow recover, regroup, and restart our careers?

Yes. You *can* have another chance.

But it isn't easy.

What follows is a process intended to help you heal, focus on your ethical behaviors, and regain your career momentum. It is a *process of reconciliation* that reconnects you to the community that is your office.

I've discerned this view of the reconciliation process from many, many one-on-one interviews and group discussions with office professionals who have struggled with the issues inherent in the process of starting over. This process is my observation of what has been effective for many others. It doesn't come with a quick-fix or money-back guarantee—but it does come from the experiences of real

people who successfully found ways to recover from their embarrassment, guilt, shame, and loss of credibility. If you are looking for
a second chance, a way to get back into the good graces of your
co-workers, I hope this view of the reconciliation process offers you
a starting point or reference point.

I'll describe the process as a series of steps. Keep in mind that
the objective of this process is to heal and restore. The benefit of
going through the process is personal growth leading to a happier,
healthier, and more productive professional career. You may not be
able to complete every step, or you may have to do them in a rush
during one or two conversations. This is life. If you always had all
the time you need, you'd never make a mistake!

Step #1: Accept reality.

This point was made over and over again by the women I talked
with. When we have done something wrong, and we are suffering
the consequences for that action, we must accept the fact that it
has occurred. We must see things as they are, not the way we want
them to be. This may require us to get angry and grieve when we
have to accept the fact that things aren't going to work out the way
we'd hoped. Don't get stuck in the trap of expending energy to
deny that the incident occurred. Don't waste a minute denying that
the incident has affected you. Denial is a mental illusion, and it is
an obstacle to reconciliation.

(For the purposes of discussion, let's call the "thing" we've done
wrong an "unethical incident." I'm uncomfortable calling it a "sin"
because that presumes too much about a religious context. "Unethical choice" is too narrow, because it excludes the consequences
of a decision. And "mistake" seems too trivial for something so serious that it merits a reconciliation process.)

To accept reality is to take responsibility for the unethical incident. This is the adult and professional response. It is to view a
past event objectively and truthfully. This is very difficult. We have
done something wrong, and we know it. We would do ANYTHING
to undo the incident, relive that decision, and make a different
choice.

Because it is so painful to recall and admit, we naturally tend to
distance ourselves from it, conceal it from others, and put it into
a mental box never to be opened and examined. When we do this,

we are attempting to hide from our reality. But we can't change the past, can we? We need to learn to live with the past so we can turn our attention toward the future.

Some office professionals told me their imaginations got the better of them when they tried to deny their "dirty little secrets." Don't we all do this? Our denial of one of our self-made ethical dilemmas is frequently illogical, self-defeating, and unrealistic. While in denial, we may dwell on our mistake and make it enormously important. Sometimes the imagined problem grows so large it takes on a larger-than-life proportion, and then it begins to have a larger-than-life affect on other decisions, our health, our relationships, etc. In other words, the effort of denial, with its accompanying avoidance, concealment, and other mental gymnastics, has the potential to effect us worse than the problem we're trying to deny.

Incidentally, it doesn't seem to make much difference whether the ethical incident becomes known by others or not. We manage to mentally beat ourselves up in any case!

Step #2: Answer the question:
What did I learn from this experience?

Experience is our best teacher. After suffering as much as we do for a negative incident, it would be a waste to compound the problem by not carrying away the lesson we had the opportunity to learn. If we fail to learn the lesson, don't we run the risk of repeating the incident? We're smart people, so if we can manage to see things as they really are (Step #1), we ought to be able to draw some very important and useful lessons from the experience. Note that I'm asking that we learn our lesson before we forgive ourselves (Step #3). Most people say they feel a positive sense of closure once they analyze the unethical incident and draw some lessons out of it, and this makes it easier to forgive themselves.

Step #3: Forgive yourself.

To forgive ourselves is to let go of the negative feelings associated with an unethical decision. These negative feelings are a combination of guilt, shame, and remorse. They are important as indicators of how far we've strayed from our moral code. However, once the feelings have served their purpose of getting our attention about our behavior, we need to set them aside.

There is no benefit to carrying guilt, shame, or remorse a moment longer than we need to. They are burdensome emotional weights that hold us down, constrict our thinking, and cause us to draw in on ourselves. They can be toxic, just like the kindred emotions of self-pity and worry. All these negative emotions are "indicator emotions" only, not ends unto themselves. Emotions like joy, happiness, and contentment are emotions worthy of pursuit, but none of the negative emotions we've mentioned here are useful except as emotional road signs, pointing the direction toward healthier behaviors. If we feel guilty about something, that's a clue we need to do something about that it — so let's take the message to heart, and then take action!

Forgiving ourselves allows us to let go of the feeling that we must punish ourselves, or be punished by someone else. It allows us to give up our feelings of self-hatred and self-loathing. Unless and until we forgive ourselves, we will be unable to ask for or accept the forgiveness of others in our community; and, without forgiveness, there will be no reconciliation.

Bottom line: Forgiveness allows us to trust ourselves to not repeat the unethical behavior. If we forgive ourselves, we can tell ourselves that we have learned our lesson, and we'll believe it. This mental self-talk frees us to take action and function again, free of negative emotional baggage and confident our future actions will be more ethical.

Step #4: Boost your self-esteem.

Imagine you are working your way back from mental unhealth and dysfunction following an incident where you behaved unethically. You used to be gripped with guilt, and you were paralyzed with remorse. Now you've accepted reality, learned from your experience, and forgiven yourself. Now you would like to rejoin the world and resume your old status on the job. You would like to put this incident behind you as if it never happened.

What you'd REALLY like to do is erase everyone's memory of the incident! One question haunts you, keeping you fearful and anxious: "What if my co-workers do not accept me back?" Fair question. If you forgive yourself, but others don't, you'll be working in disgrace for a long time to come, possibly until you are forced to quit.

A dose of self-esteem is the tonic you'll need to get through this step of the reconciliation process.

Self-esteem, also referred to as self-worth or self-image, is generally regarded by mental health professionals as a critically important dimension of adjustment and well-being. Self-esteem is a complex predictor and motivator of behavior. If a person goes through an ethical crisis that leaves her feeling guilty and ashamed, her self-esteem is one of the chief casualties. "I'm not worthy of anyone else's respect," and, "I'm a fraud, a phony," are two common responses. The challenge, then, is to reconcile your damaged self-image with a more realistic self-image. The reconciliation, at this stage in the process, is almost entirely an internal dialogue with yourself. Others can help you, but external resources will help only if you strongly desire to heal yourself.

I think of this stage in the process of reconciliation as an incubation period, a quiet time of gestation. You're not ready for a lot of close questioning. Your "newly reformed" self is wiser, but not yet stronger. Too much scrutiny and requests for explanations from co-workers are hurtful and embarrassing. Your ego, your self-image of your self-worth, needs to get stronger.

There are at least four ways to recover and rebuild your self-esteem, according to many who have tackled this tough question. With a little help from your friends, you can probably help yourself boost your self-esteem by doing the following:

Reflect about your self-image.
Think about it thoroughly. Which aspects of your life are most important to your feelings of self-confidence and self-worth — social? intellectual? physical? If you know you need to feel competent in an intellectual domain, for example, it's reasonable to do activities that you know will reinforce your "smart-person" image of yourself. If you draw confidence from how you look, put in some extra time at the gym, or buy yourself a new outfit.

Get some emotional support and social approval.
Others can reinforce our internal images of self-worth. They can remind us that no, we are not crazy. Pick someone you can count on for some *unconditional* support.

Solve whatever problems you can.
Facing a problem and coping with it, even if it's a small problem, gives us some practice and confidence in our problem-solving skills. This is an exercise with lots of benefits. It reconnects you to other parts of your life not associated with the unethical incident. Problems with the house, car, checkbook, kitchen, etc., can be hum-

bling, but comforting, too. Problem-solving is also a good way to remind yourself how gol'dang *good* it feels to solve problems like you used to do. It won't hurt you to catch up on some of the things you've been ignoring, too.

Learn a new skill, then use it to achieve something.

Like problem solving, this exercise is rich with benefits. The simple act of learning skills enhances self-esteem because it prepares you to accomplish important tasks and new work. Like solving problems, learning new skills is proof positive that you can still act in a competent and useful way. Pick something you can succeed at in a reasonably short time—this will be a real boost. Community education programs are great therapy for wounded self-esteem, I think—they are usually short, focused, fun, and inexpensive ways to learn something new. (If you're like me, you'll get hooked on them and become a "life-long learner." There's always something new to learn, and it is certain to enrich your life.)

I want to take this opportunity to tip my hat to one of my very favorite books, my friend Gloria Steinem's *Revolution from Within.* I think it's a must-read! Gloria is one of the bona fide founders of contemporary feminism. She speaks to the Big Picture, declaring we must heal and nurture our self-esteem if we are to be prepared to take advantage of the hard-won, and still incomplete, opportunities in society. She believes we start each day with a societal bias against our self-esteem, even before we encounter any ethical dilemmas or other problems. The bias against our self-esteem comes in the forms of totalitarian gender roles, obsession with romantic love, devaluation of feminine qualities, emotional damage caused by IQ testing, stereotypes of race and sex, estrangement from nature, and male-imposed standards of feminine beauty, among others. She admits she continues to struggle with her self-esteem issues, too.

Step #5: Reconnect with your community.

Now it is time to restore the bond of trust with your community of co-workers. Up until now, you may have managed to work side-by-side, despite a lack of trust. (Have you ever heard comments like these?: "Really? Can I just see the paperwork on that to be sure?" or, "We'll have someone else do that for a while."). Or your relationships with co-workers have changed to accommodate their harsher view of you ("Don't tell *her* anything you don't want the boss to hear," etc.). Maybe you haven't been able to work together at all. In a lot of little ways, you know your relationships have been changed as a consequence of the unethical incident. Even if *only you* know about the lie, betrayal, deception, or whatever, you also know in lots of little ways that something has changed between you and your co-workers—and the relationship is the poorer for it.

Now you are ready to reach out to those around you, clear the air of negative feelings, and restore yourself to favor by making amends.

It's impossible to prescribe a formula that will work without knowing the details of your dilemma and your office mates, but consider applying the following. If you think the approach will work, use it!

1. *Acknowledge the problem:* "I sense we have some issue between us. I'm uncomfortable with how we are relating to each other, and I want to clear the air if we can."

2. *Acknowledge and/or admit your responsibility:* "I feel like this is my fault because _____." Or, "I haven't told you everything."

3. *Apologize if it is deserved and if you mean it:* "I'm sorry."

4. *Offer whatever explanations or excuses you think would help:* "I was afraid, and I was a coward." Or, "I thought I was doing the right thing." Or, "I felt I had to do it." Or, "I didn't want to cause you pain, or deal with your pain, so I took the easy way out."

5. *Ask for another chance:* "I want us to go back to the way we were." Or, "I want to clear the air." Or, "I want to work toward a new level of trust."

Step #6: Get on with your life.

Now you've done as much as you can. You've suffered the consequences of your unethical choice, you've learned your lessons, you've rehabilitated yourself, and you've said all you can to meet your co-workers halfway. Now it's time to get on with your life.

Your co-workers may welcome you "back" into their good graces right away with hugs and supportive comments. Or, they may be wary, testing you in small ways. Be gracious, whatever their response. They will usually mirror your attitude, so if you have made peace with the incident, they can, too. If it takes time for these relationships with each other to heal so be it as long as you don't mind waiting.

You'll soon know if your efforts are going to yield a positive result. Time is supposed to heal all things—but this maxim presumes that people are fair and rational in their dealings with each other. This is not true. Some people are going to hold a grudge forever, and enjoy the power and sense of superiority it gives them. (Remember the words of the narrator in the movie, *Babe*, about the pig who learned to herd sheep: "Most cats are nice animals—but, beware of the cat who carries a grudge!" Poor Babe naively trusted the cat to forgive and forget, and then suffered the consequences.)

As soon as you have a sense of whether the relationship has been or will be saved, you can relax and get back to being your normal, productive self—or you can begin looking for your next job. Virtually everyone who has shared their story with me says you can't work happily under a cloud of suspicion or disrespect. If you try to change people's opinion of you, but can't, it's time to move on.

There is life after…

When our choices get us into ethical dilemmas and we step, drift, or wander off the path of the straight and narrow, we need to find our way back into the good graces of our bosses and our co-workers. The good news is that this is possible, presuming that those we are trying to win back are reasonably fair-minded. More good news is that we do get another chance to make the right decision *if we ask for it,* so we can once again be an accepted, well-liked, and fully functioning member of the office team.

All we have to do is our part: We have to accept reality, learn our lessons from the experience, forgive ourselves, boost our self-esteem, reach out and reconnect to our community and, finally, get on with our lives.

I am not overanalyzing the process, merely reporting the idealized process for reconciliation with ourselves and our community based on many, many conversations with office professionals who have gone through this experience. It probably will not always be possible to take all of these separate steps, or to always do them in a way that brings them to closure. Some steps may have to be raced over in a single conversation, and some steps may have to be skipped completely. But if we can do any of the steps, it will help us find our way back.

The most important points I want to make are these: You can have a second chance after you have behaved in a way that is contrary to your ethical beliefs, if you are willing to make the effort to redeem yourself. The rewards for this effort are rich, including the long-term integrity of your relationships, your peace of mind, your self-respect, and your productivity. This kind of self-management is difficult, but it is the mark of a professional.

I am a great proponent of self-talk, that potentially powerful internal dialogue with yourself. When you find yourself stuck in an ethical mess of your own making, tape this poem to your bathroom mirror and say it to yourself every morning.

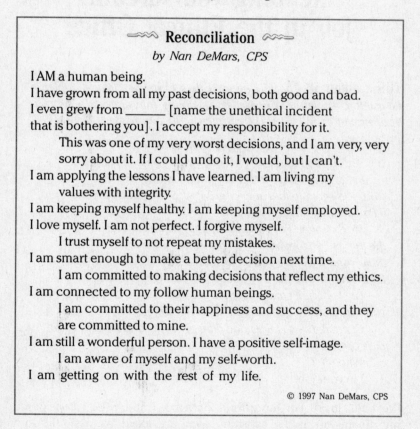

～～ Reconciliation ～～
by Nan DeMars, CPS

I AM a human being.
I have grown from all my past decisions, both good and bad.
I even grew from _____ [name the unethical incident
that is bothering you]. I accept my responsibility for it.
>   This was one of my very worst decisions, and I am very, very
>   sorry about it. If I could undo it, I would, but I can't.
I am applying the lessons I have learned. I am living my
    values with integrity.
I am keeping myself healthy. I am keeping myself employed.
I love myself. I am not perfect. I forgive myself.
    I trust myself to not repeat my mistakes.
I am smart enough to make a better decision next time.
    I am committed to making decisions that reflect my ethics.
I am connected to my follow human beings.
    I am committed to their happiness and success, and they
    are committed to mine.
I am still a wonderful person. I have a positive self-image.
    I am aware of myself and my self-worth.
I am getting on with the rest of my life.

© 1997 Nan DeMars, CPS

*"Whatever disgrace we may have deserved,
it is almost always in our power
to re-establish our character."*

— Plautus

19

Keeping your dream job in the Ethical Office

Think about it: *The following comes from the "Inside Appleton" newsletter, Appleton Wire Division, Albany International Corporation, Appleton, WI 54911 (reprinted with permission).*

A Special Love Letter
You say you love me, but sometimes you don't show it.
In the beginning, you could not do enough for me.
Now you seem to take me for granted. Some days I wonder
if I mean anything to you at all.

Maybe when I'm gone you'll appreciate me and all
the things I do for you. I'm responsible for the food on your
table, for the clothes you wear, for the welfare of your home,
for the thousand-and-one things you want and need . . .

I've kept quiet and waited to see how long it would take for
you to realize how much you really need me.

Cherish me . . . take good care of me . . . and I'll take good
care of you.

Who am I?
I'm your job.

I've been lucky. For more than 20 years, I had what I considered my dream job as the assistant, secretary, executive assistant, and corporate secretary for Judd Ringer, founder and president of Ringer Corporation in Minneapolis. Mr. Ringer was a great boss who believed in empowerment before it was a buzzword. He let me push my ideas on him, and he gave me the freedom I wanted to develop professionally.

Still, I had to pay my dues. I've had to work with and for lots of people who were, shall we say, ethically challenged?

Have I compromised? Yes, when the reasons were right and everyone knew why. Have I *been* compromised? Not since I was young and foolish. Why don't I lower my standards, get down to that lower level? Because it becomes a bad habit, real fast. The cowboy in Larry McMurtry's *Lonesome Dove* said it best: "If you hang long enough, you get used to hanging." I think it's true. Taking the low road when it comes to ethics isn't something you want to get used to.

Remember the wonderful, powerful words of German writer Johann Goethe: "You become what you tolerate." Isn't that true? Haven't we all fallen into situations that we didn't recognize at first for the trouble they would bring us? Haven't we all been tempted to just shut up and "adjust" to the dilemma instead of confronting it? We know, however, that those "adjustments" get easier and easier when we start making them routinely. If we quit fighting back to regain the moral high ground, we'd be quitting on ourselves.

Because I love my job—and all the people associated with it—I refuse to lower my standards. If I didn't, my job would become something I resent and hate. *I don't want that to happen to something I love.* That's why I fight to keep my ethical standards high and clearly visible to all who care to look.

Do you love or hate your job right now? Would you love it more if your office was more ethical? In this chapter, I'll encourage you to rethink your job description and renegotiate those tasks you find most objectionable. I'll finish the book with a list of 22 Golden Keys to Open the Door of the Ethical Office—a collection of suggestions from my clients that will help *your* ethical office to continue to grow and prosper. Then, you can love your job as much as I love mine!

Crossing the "Little White Line"

In the search and recruitment end of my business, I match executive-level assistants with new career opportunities. One candidate reported the following experience she had in a job interview I arranged for her. The position she was applying for was administrative assistant to the CEO of a large manufacturing company.

The current assistant (who was retiring) gave the candidate a tour of the executive offices, including the CEO's beautiful private

*bathroom. Upon leaving the bathroom, the assistant pointed to
the toilet water and said, "That's the color blue he likes in his toilet water!" My candidate laughed. But the assistant insisted, "No,
I'm serious. Part of your job will be to keep the toilet water in his
toilet that color blue!" My candidate declined the position because, "I don't want a job where I have to worry about the color
of my boss's toilet water!"*

This candidate knew where her "little white line" was, and she
knew she could not cross that line and remain happy. Everyone
has a little white line. It's the boundary of personal ethics surrounding your activities. The little white line is your personal list of
do's and don'ts; and, if you are wise enough to know where it goes,
you'll avoid all kinds of trouble. When someone steps over your
ethical line, you have a right — even an obligation — to push back
and insist upon maintaining your standards.

I've heard many other stories about personal requests like this. I
have the strong opinion that bosses generally will keep asking you
to do more and more until they hear "No more!" from you, thereby
indicating where your little white line is. Once you've identified
your limits, they will be respected. But no one will know where
your boundaries are until you tell them. You may not be able to
list everything that is on your "do" or "don't" list off the top of your
head. You may not discover them for what they are until pressed
to do something you find objectionable, at which time you must
speak up clearly and immediately.

Now, you can imagine there are many assistants who regularly
check the color of the toilet water in their boss's private bathrooms.
They don't mind — for them, it's not an issue. For them, what's objectionable is something else. We each have our personal limits regarding what we'll do or not do. What's too objectionable for one of us
will not be a problem for someone else, and vice versa.

The handling of personal tasks for a supervisor has always been
an issue in our profession. The results from my Office Ethics Survey were interesting: When asked the question, "Do you run personal errands for your supervisor?", 55.8 percent of respondents said
they do, and 68.5 percent said they have observed others doing so.
When asked if they handle some of their supervisor's other personal
affairs (e.g. purchasing gifts, picking up dry cleaning, obtaining tick-

ets, etc.), 14.1 percent said they did. *However, less than two per-cent of this group said these duties were specified in their job descrip-tion!* This suggests a dire need for more clarification about what is — and what is not — expected from today's office professional.

The trials of the "office wife"

I must admit I burn my biscuits every time I hear another tale of the "office wife." You know to whom I am referring. This person does an excessive amount of personal chores for the boss, such as fetch-ing dry cleaning, purchasing personal gifts and toiletries, picking up the kids, planning vacations, selecting home furnishings, collecting prescriptions, making personal reservations, wrapping gifts, paying bills, feeding pets, and generally anything else the boss delegates (whew!).

Wouldn't it be great if we all had access to this kind of help? Life would certainly be simpler. Considering the ever-increasing stress associated with reconciling the demands of work and family today, it's easy to understand why your boss may be tempted to lean on you for a little bit of extra help from time to time. But watch out for excessive, undocumented personal service requests.

The "office wife" trap is a byproduct of too little communication with the boss about specific duties. The penalties for not clearly defining the little white line between professional duties and per-sonal favors range from bruised self-esteem to getting fired to being held liable for your boss's misdeeds.

Again, ALL of the personal responsibilities listed above are cer-tainly acceptable — *IF agreed upon at the time of hiring AND IF doc-umented in the job description.* When expectations for help with personal tasks are clearly understood from the get-go, there are no surprises and few problems. But this degree of clarity is unusual. Most assistants' responsibilities are described in vague terms, capped by a catch-all phrase like, "...and all other duties deemed neces-sary by the supervisor."

You are Mr. Benson's secretary. He is a vice president of mar-keting and regularly travels all over the world.
He is unmarried.
You have become increasingly uncomfortable with his pre-sumption that you can, and are willing to, help him manage

*his personal social calendar. Due to his busy travel schedule,
the differences in time zones, and the unavailability of reliable phone service, he cannot play "phone tag" with his
women friends around the world. Consequently, he is asking
you more and more often to arrange personal dates for him.*

*For example, he will often call from some remote part of
the world and give you his itinerary for the following weekend. Then, he will give you the name(s) of one or more
women he would like to see while he is in town and asks
you to set one or more dates.*

*To his credit, he always makes a point of confirming the
dates personally as soon as he is able. From his perspective,
this process is both practical and considerate, because most
of the women he wants to see are busy professionals themselves (which complicates the game of "phone tag") and
they need some lead time to rearrange their schedule. You,
however, are not happy about coordinating the logistics of
his romances. It's a lot of work for something that seems
beyond the company's real interests and, frankly, you find it
a bit awkward to be asking these women for dates, inter-
preting their responses for him, listening to the women's
scheduling problems, and sometimes breaking the date at
the last minute because of a change in travel plans.*

*Your husband has made the observation that no sane man
would ever try to maintain this kind of complicated lifestyle
if he had to do all the work himself! Mr. Benson is generous
in his appreciation of your assistance and he is otherwise an
excellent manager. Still, being a social secretary is not a part
of your job description. What would you do to resolve this
situation?*

Some of you are probably saying, "Now, wait a minute—secretaries have always been expected to take on a variety of tasks for
their bosses." I know, I know. And as long as you and your boss
have a clear understanding about these expectations—something
that is written into your job description, hopefully—you will not
be put in the position of Mr. Benson's secretary.

The higher your boss is in the organization, the more accepted
the practice will be to have you perform personal services. This

may be a perk or an ego trip (who wouldn't appreciate a personal servant?). It may also be a legitimate attempt on the part of the company to optimize this executive's time. Would it be a good use of this executive's time to leave the meeting early so she can pick up her dry cleaning for a business trip tomorrow morning? Would it be fair to expect her spouse to rearrange his schedule to accommodate her? Life can be tough at the top, so practical assistance that saves the executive's time is usually a good value. As the secretary, you should be doing your part to lighten the executive's burden, but be sure to do it on the company's time, not your own.

How much personal service is too much? The "office wife" role becomes an ethical dilemma when your boss uses you too much for the wrong kinds of personal tasks. This an amazingly easy dilemma to drift into. Say the company is willing to pay you to be available for that crisis rush to the dry cleaners, and it has plainly stated that in your job description. But what about the routine trip to the dry cleaner? Now that you know the way, so to speak, do the crisis trips become convenience trips? And what about those other errands and tasks? There is at least SOME benefit to your boss when you do these things (saving her time lowers her stress, etc.), so it could be argued (by your boss) that you are only fulfilling the requirements of the job description. But you know better. Are you really doing what you think the company wants you to do? If your boss expects you to perform personal tasks on company time, but these tasks would be judged excessive by the company, you have a problem.

Keep in mind that you, your time, and your talents are a valuable company resource. If your boss uses your time for personal purposes and you participate, you are co-conspirators in pilfering from the company. If the tasks are expected to be accomplished on your personal time, and you agree to do them even though you don't want to, you are compromising your own principles by continuing to do them.

So — the question remains, how much personal service is too much? Let's use the guidelines I've gathered from my seminar participants and readers of my column about office ethics:

You're doing too many of your boss's personal chores when:
He or she asks too often. Daily or even weekly requests to run per-

sonal errands are generally regarded as inappropriate. But if the requests are infrequent and easy to comply with, what's to be gained by raising a strong objection? Keep your priorities in order—don't upset an otherwise fine job over a trivial matter.

Compliance costs the company too much. A boss who ties up a secretary's time with personal tasks is literally stealing a valuable resource from the company. If you go along with it, you are an accomplice. Considering the cumulative effect of some of the abusive practices that have evolved in some boss-secretary relationships, this is *not* too strongly stated. If you have to work extra hours to make up for time spent on the boss's personal errands, you and the company are indirectly paying extra time and money to support the boss's bad habit of having you take care of him.

Compliance costs you too much. Let's say your boss wants you to perform his or her personal errands on your own time, without financial compensation or compensatory time off. This is a clear abuse of your services as an employee. Allowing yourself to be taken advantage of like this (a) cheats you of your personal time, and (b) diminishes your professional relationship with your boss. In the end, your boss won't respect you, and you won't respect yourself.

Your boss is too secretive. Does your boss want you to hide from other employees the fact that you are typing his or her son's school paper? If so, find a way to decline. This is a certain warning sign that you are doing too much of a personal nature. By asking you to keep quiet, your boss is signaling that he knows this is a misuse of your time and talents; and now you do, too.

What do you do to get off this slippery slope of personal service requests? Again, a summary of the best suggestions from those of you "on the front lines":

You can stop the requests for personal service if you:
Decide how you really feel about the requests. Are you a passive-aggressive people-pleaser, eager to comply, but torturing yourself later for your inability or unwillingness to stand up to your boss and say "No!"? Or, are you really okay with the nature and frequency of these requests? An anonymous CPS from Dayton, OH writes: "I enjoy getting out of the office every now and then to run errands for my boss. It adds variety to my job. It gives me the opportunity

to run a quick errand for myself, too." Susan Jones of Cupertino, CA makes the excellent point that *how* your boss asks you may be more bothersome than doing the tasks themselves: "I would gladly handle all the personal tasks my boss often asks of me if he would treat me with respect and appreciate what I do accordingly. I *do* resent all of these requests when he demands them and acts as though it is expected of me."

If you decide to make an issue of personal service requests, get prepared. Document a few weeks of abuses and keep this "memo to yourself" in your personal files. Write down what you were asked to do and how much time it took. At the very least, this is proof of your concern for the problem. This way, if your boss is ever discharged or disciplined, such a file can protect your job and your professional credibility.

Examine your job description. A fair question for a secretary to ask in a job interview is: "What kinds of personal service responsibilities are required in this job, if any?" This is a good way to get everyone's expectations discussed before the position is accepted, but it's not foolproof. Requests for personal chores have a way of creeping into a boss-secretary relationship. To deal with a situation that is gradually getting excessive, Carol Rhodes, CPS of Carol Rhodes Business Services in Houston, TX suggests that the boss and the secretary independently write their own versions of the secretary's job description. The secretary will, undoubtedly, list personal tasks among her duties. If the boss does not mention them, the secretary has another excellent opportunity to say that she prefers not to do these tasks, yet they are becoming more frequent.

Discuss your concerns with your boss. Give him or her a chance to reform. Perhaps your boss has chosen to forget how many times you are being imposed upon; perhaps there are temporary circumstances that will soon render the problem moot. Both of you need to be specific, so the expectations are clear. You need to say things like, "I don't mind stopping by at the library on my way home, but I dread having to go shopping for your wife." One secretary told me she told her boss she would be happy to handle all the personal services outlined in the job description (and there were many) with one exception: She refused to pick up his dry cleaning. She told him she hated to pick up her own dry cleaning, and she didn't want to add his to the list. Apparently, dry cleaning was on the other side of her little white line. Her boss's response? "Fine," he said, and he deleted it from the list.

Learn to say "No" politely, but firmly. Following a discussion of your respective expectations, the line between professional duties and personal favors should be clear for all to see. Carol Rhodes says: "...Thereafter, each time you are asked to do something of a personal nature, you can politely refuse, reminding your boss about your job description, your preferences, and your previous discussions. If you are consistent, eventually the boss will stop asking."

Finally, keep the "big picture" in focus. Keep in mind the broad goals of your office. An executive once said to me: "The main goal of my 'team of two' is to effectively and efficiently accomplish my job description. To do this, if my secretary has to serve coffee occasionally and run personal errands for me to ease my pressures, and she thereby helps me perform my job better, then she should understand that these responsibilities are part of the job. They all help accomplish OUR ultimate goal."

(The secretary who objects to serving coffee to anyone in the office, anytime, probably misses the important point of getting the job done. I was discussing this aspect of the who-gets-coffee-for-whom question with a good friend of mine, Marilyn Jamison, a secretary at Honeywell, and she echoed the "team" message: "Honeywell is a global organization, so we often have international visitors. If we do not offer them coffee, it would be considered rude. This kind of hospitality is simply considered being gracious; and, I think graciousness on the part of any assistant is always in order.")

If you have cultivated an environment in the office where you are comfortable discussing the dilemmas that concern you, you'll be fine. Communicate, communicate, communicate. I hear all kinds of stories from assistants who suddenly find themselves mired down in a mundane personal task for their bosses and it remains a point of continuous irritation between them. Example: A secretary to a major ball club owner said every time her boss was in town (which was quite often, because the team played at "home" a lot), she was expected to bring him a bag lunch that she had prepared herself for him to eat at his desk. She said SHE never "brown bagged" lunch herself—she liked to go out at noon—but, he preferred her homemade lunches. She told me that, after eight years of doing this, it was finally beginning to bother her! She went into his office one day, sat down, and said: "Could we please have a tunafish sandwich discussion?" When she had explained why she did not wish to continue this practice, his simple reply was: "Good—I was beginning to get tired of your sandwiches anyhow." Now, who says the great gaps in our communication between us cannot be mediated?

The craziest request I ever heard in the personal services category was from an apparently stressed-out boss who called his secretary and said, "Sally, I'm running late for my therapy session. Can you go and cover for me?" True story! And he was serious!

Open communication is going to serve you well with your boss and even your potential boss. In addition to asking in the job interview: "What kinds of personal tasks am I expected to perform on the job?" also ask, "May I see the job description?" It's rare when the two match. Try talking about the differences without jeopardizing your chances to get the job offer. You can be 100 percent certain other personal service duties will seem to somehow "creep in" when expectations are allowed to drift. So go into the job with your eyes open. Be wary of situations where the boss seems particularly needy. And don't set yourself up for a nasty confrontation later on because one small aspect of the job (like picking up dry cleaning) turns out to be a surprise. The lack of good communication upfront could spoil an otherwise wonderful position.

There are many keys to the Ethical Office

This book is about how to build an ethical office. If I could wish just one wish, I would get every person in every office thinking and talking about ethics in general—and then, when they felt safe enough to raise the ethical dilemmas that were bothering them, I would want them to talk about the ethics in their offices with their bosses and co-workers.

Creating the ethical office does not require a lot of money, but it does take time. It also requires a corporate conscience, a commitment to do the right thing, and the desire and skills to communicate with each other. The people who work together must learn to talk to each other in a different way that allows for the tough questions to be discussed. If we can all begin communicating about the ethical dilemmas that worry and frustrate us, people will begin making different choices. What a world that will be!

The case for the ethical office is a moral and economic imperative. Office ethics are the hinge upon which so many other productivity-building programs swing. It's just that simple: ***Improve office ethics and you improve office productivity.***

When people working together share a common understanding of office ethics, they work smarter, with more enthusiasm, and get more of the important work done. Lies, second-guessing, deceptions, fabrications, harassments, favoritism, lack of trust, lack of confidence, cover-your-behind activities—these are the aspects of office work that drag people down, draining them of their potential contributions. Think about it. Imagine an office team working together without all of the "ethical static" confusing the communication. A single ethical office can have a profound effect throughout an organization.

Bottom line: A well-defined set of ethical practices and expectations, when practiced consistently, makes it easier to do business because people trust each other. An ethical office results in more enjoyable and productive activity. When you think about it, the pride, satisfaction, and financial rewards we get from our work depend almost entirely upon the integrity of our relationships. *Why not improve those relationships in whatever ways we can? Would the quality of our relationships be a worthwhile investment of time and effort? Would our co-workers appreciate and respond positively if we called on them to be their very best?* Absolutely!

Building an ethical office comes down to managing the practical aspects of everyday tasks and relationships. That's what this book has been about. In the remaining pages, I want to leave you with some of the best reminders I've collected from some of my clients' ethics programs:

The 22 Golden Keys
to Open the Door of the Ethical Office

1. ***See things as they are, not as you want them to be.*** The lies we tell ourselves can be the most hurtful. Poet Robert Burns put it this way: "I would some power that the giftie gie us to see ourselves as others see us."

2. ***Lead by setting an example of good ethical conduct and good***

ethical problem-solving skills. A good example has a power-ful effect on the work environment. Your sense of what's right and what's wrong is important to share, and you owe it to yourself and your company to reconcile the important differences between you and your boss as they arise. Main-tain consistent ethical standards. Ethical standards are not relative; they do not ebb and flow, changing from circum-stance to circumstance. Feelings, profits, and the thermome-ter go up and down, but ethical standards do not. Just like you can't be "a little bit pregnant," you can't be ethical "on occasion." Either you are — or you aren't!

3. ***Never give the impression that you don't care that improper actions are taking place.*** Never look the other way, or pre-tend to look the other way. I believe our lives are not shaped by the circumstances we encounter; instead, it's what we DO about the circumstances that really matters. We can't control what other people do, but we CAN control how we react to their conduct.

4. ***Commit to being involved in the process.*** Office ethics are about what gets done and how something gets done. You are a central player in these proceedings, so you are entitled to have a voice.

5. ***Anticipate ethical conflicts.*** Look ahead and pre-empt the need for complicated responses. For example:

If you have a boss who wants you to sign correspondence without initialing (actually, he's asking you to forge or fake his signature to create a specific impression), type up a letter on his stationery, date it, and say, "To whom it may concern, I give my assistant, [your name], authorization to sign my correspondence." Have your boss sign it, tuck it away in your personal file, and hope never in your lifetime do you have to take it out. This is just one more small case of how times have changed — you have to do this because you must expect to be treated like a professional. If you tried to explain in court why you blithely faked your boss's signature as a standard operating procedure, you'd be portrayed as anything but professional.

Here's another example: "Sue, you observed that Carmine was harassed in your office. Carmine has sued the company.

You didn't report this incident, so the first we heard about it was when it was too late. Carmine has named you in her lawsuit against the company. She can't charge you with anything, but you have to testify about what you saw."

Now, the tricky part here is that when the incident you observed occurred, Carmine might not have thought it was sexual harassment. That doesn't make any difference. If you think it's harassment, you should report it to someone in the human resources department and document your observations. Maybe nothing will ever happen. But, if something does come up later, you'll have an accurate record of what you saw already on record — and that's going to definitely help the company and Carmine get to the truth of a situation.

Some states (Minnesota is one of them) are working on legislation that requires a person to report when spousal abuse is observed. In other words, if you observe someone physically abusing their spouse, you would be required to report it to the proper authorities or you will be charged (not just named as a witness). This is a trend to make everyone more accountable for misbehavior, even their neighbor's. Someday, we may even see laws like this reach into the office.

6. **Communicate well.** Tell the truth. Be open. Be concise. Provide your boss with the complete facts.

7. **Establish the language of ethics with those in your office.** Ask for feedback, and give it to others, about specific conduct and dilemmas. If someone does a great job handling a tough dilemma, make sure she gets some recognition, at least informally, so she feels like the hero she is instead of the Lone Avenger or a chump. You can do a lot by shifting negative self-talk (like, "I can't do anything about it") to positive self-talk (e.g., "How about if we try it this way instead?").

8. **Expect different people to have different standards.** They are not better, not worse — simply different.

9. **Remember that people are normally not as ethical as they think they are.** We tend to judge ourselves by our best actions and best intentions, and we judge others by their worst.

10. *Define ethical expectations early in the relationship.*
11. *Support your boss's efforts to uphold high standards for ethical conduct, communicate about ethics, and solve ethical dilemmas.* Communicate your respect and trust in her ethical judgment, and let her know you have high expectations for her. People tend to live up — or down — to others' expectations as they perceive them. Good managers strive to create a work environment that is most conducive to productivity. If she's careful about communicating honestly, you know it's important to her that you do likewise. Does she know you support these efforts of hers?
12. *Be patient with each other.* Don't expect perfection in yourself or your boss. When performance ebbs and flows, review the good and bad news as soon as you can, be candid, and look for ways to set meet more reasonable goals in the future. Your boss will not always have the right answers. You have an obligation to speak up and make recommendations. Passive compliance is destructive. Be proactive and assume responsibility. One person observed, "One good way to make your supervisor fail is to always do exactly what you are told, no more and no less."
13. *Be consistent. Be predictable.* Build a track record of dependability. Fulfill your promises, exceed expectations. The best surprise is no surprise.
14. *Pay attention to details.* Sweat the small stuff. Do your work thoroughly. Give your manager confidence that you are looking after the details. Mutual trust and candor will grow. New technology, more complicated business relationships, a faster pace of work — all of this pressure requires you to do your best. Not one of these tasks compares with rocket science or brain surgery, but balancing all of them rivals conducting an orchestra!
15. *Nurture the communication process with your boss.* You will not keep your job if this is ignored. Never mind your wonderful qualifications, or the generous and forgiving nature of the boss — if you don't have a positive "chemistry" when working together, you will be looking for a new job soon.

   Never was this brought home to me better than when I

helped a new CEO for a manufacturing company find a new executive assistant.

"Mr. M" and I worked together on this project by telephone as he was preparing to relocate. We had narrowed our search down to five excellent candidates. He called to say he was traveling to London the following Monday; could I arrange back-to-back interviews with these candidates if he had a brief stopover in Minneapolis? I did, and he did. I met him at the airport. He threw his briefcase in the back seat of my car, and, without any notes, proceeded to talk to me about the candidates on our ride downtown. I was impressed that he had studied each one's qualifications so thoroughly that he knew them as well as I did.

He knew I was worried about our handling five interviews and making such an important decision in just the few hours we had scheduled. So, when we pulled into the parking garage, he turned to me and said, "Nan — I know you are concerned about our accomplishing all of this in so short a period of time. But I've studied all the candidates' resumes. I know all of them are qualified to handle the job. All I will be assessing in these interviews is 'chemistry' — whether or not I think we can work together. And, I'll ascertain that within the first few minutes of the interview."

With that, we trotted upstairs to the interviews. All Mr. M had in his hands was a notebook for his notes and a 3 x 5 card on which I had listed the names of the candidates in the order we would see them. I sat in on those interviews with Mr. M, and I realized I was "working the chemistry" also — watching how well they interacted with each other. We accomplished all five interviews in our allotted time frame. All five candidates interviewed beautifully. Mr. M and I hopped on the elevator in record time, proud of the fact we had accomplished our task with ample time to get him back to the airport. Then, he whispered to me, "Who is your choice?" I told him — and held my breath. He showed me his 3 x 5 card. He had circled my choice also! Mr. M and his assistant have made a wonderful team ever since.

16. Ask lots of questions. Questions promote communication, transfer information, encourage candor, and furnish feedback. When in doubt about what is going on, or if you wonder how you should handle something, ASK.

17. **Be organized. Stay focused.** If you are, you will help your boss be the same way. At the same time, we must be flexible and responsive to changes in goals and methods. Being organized and flexible, and also staying focused and responsive, are not mutually exclusive.

18. **Learn to dodge the ethical traps of overthinking and cynicism,** both of which lead to inaction and ineffectiveness.

19. **Remember that virtue is its own reward.** You live a richer, more satisfying life whenever you choose to take the high road.

20. **Protect your key assets:** Good health (for this, you need a daily routine, regular affirmation, and healthy eating and exercise habits), a strong self-esteem (learn something, accomplish something), a desire to improve a situation (follow your moral code), good communication skills, and your reputation as a person of integrity.

21. **Speak up whenever you feel more unethical behaviors are slipping in, or when you sense your collective ethics are getting sloppy, or when you think convenience is becoming more important than character.** You must be very clear in your response to this: Don't participate in the unethical behavior. Express your objections and concerns. Suggest alternatives. Help others understand how unethical conduct in the office detracts from the company and everyone who works there.

22. **Challenge yourself. Keep learning.**

Ethics is the set of ground rules that determine how we relate and conduct ourselves with others. Ethics are like a lighthouse beacon with which we can check our course. When we wander off our ethical course, or exceed our ethical boundaries, we may commit misdeeds and errors of judgment that hurt others and ourselves. Now we have this book to help us. It's the collected wisdom of your peers, guiding us back to our true, straight, and narrow course.

I know you are no stranger to ethical challenges. Every day we learn more about the ethical failings of company leaders and company policies. The response requiring the least effort would be to become cynical about trying to make the workplace more ethical. We're tempted to ask, What can one person do, especially if that one person is *me*? We're tempted to dismiss the exhortations of company leaders to "do better" and "be better" because we suspect it's only a matter of time before he or she is caught with his or her hand in the proverbial cookie jar. *Why bother?* is an understandable response.

Throughout this book, I've asked you to rethink your way of handling the ethical dilemmas you encounter. I want you to start talking about ethics among your co-workers, and discuss how ethics affect your office decisions. I want you to commit to doing a little "remodeling" in your office to make it more fair, more honest, less stressful—in short, more ethical. Perhaps you want to stop a wrongful practice, correct an injustice, cut down on the petty bickering and infighting—or just give your manager a wake-up call that the rules of conduct are a bit too loosey-goosey for the good of the business.

A consistently ethical office features a climate that promotes fairness, mutual respect, and decisions that are extensions of personal beliefs and values. When most of the people in the office are making decisions based on their values, the ethical climate is reinforced and rewarded. As a consequence for sticking to the ethical high road, even when the going gets tough, your office (or department or company) gains a reputation for ethical behavior and thus enjoys the trust and benefits of customers and other employees.

Our leaders will not be able to build a more ethical workplace alone. They need our help. If they are to be strong, ethical leaders, we must be equally strong, ethical followers. We have a responsibility to speak up, make ourselves heard, and let our bosses know that we support their efforts to build a more ethical business. Their priorities relative to ethics must be external, focused on what results can be accomplished for the customer and shareholders. We focus on the process by which those results are achieved—who does what, and how do they do it. If our leaders do not lead us toward increasingly more ethical practices, we have to initiate those actions ourselves.

And we can. When you take responsibility to be true to your personal value system, no organization or person within an organization can force you to act against your will or conscience. We may look like followers on the organizational chart, but we can each be a leader by example!

Clearly, it is my sincere hope that your new thinking about ethics will lead to some positive changes in your relationships with your supervisor, co-workers, and everyone else inside and outside the company with whom you do business!

To build a more ethical office is not a quick or easy assignment to give yourself. You will encounter resistance because change makes people uncomfortable. But the productivity, profitability, and ultimately the well-being of your organization depends upon you consistently deciding to do the right thing for the right reasons.

I wish you courage. Barbara Ley Toffler wrote in a recent *New York Times* article, "For many employees, being ethical is getting to be too risky—something they can't afford anymore. With rampant layoffs and no improvement in sight, it's too dangerous to say no." She continues, ". . . now that job hunting has become the occupation of so many who until recently had good jobs and promising careers, only the morally courageous—or the foolhardy—risk telling the boss no."

I urge you to persevere. Your co-workers long to believe they work for an ethical and honorable enterprise. They will support you if you overcome their cynicism with your example. While the hounds of the media bay for sensational exposés and corporate failings, we must work in the quiet, where people still care about doing the right thing.

You have an important role to play in this, even though you may feel your contributions and efforts are so small as to be inconsequential. That's just not true. The small decisions we make are small steps leading in the right direction—toward more ethical workplaces. We are each important, because none of us can do this alone. Take heart, and be optimistic. *You are in control, and you can make a real difference.*

> *"You see things and you say 'Why?'*
> *But I dream things that never were,*
> *and I say 'Why not?'"*
>
> — George Bernard Shaw

Index